Including Whistler & the Gulf Islands

Vancouver

The Ultimate Guide

Completely Revised and Updated • 6th Edition

Judi Lees & Terri Wershler

GREYSTONE BOOKS

Douglas & McIntyre

Vancouver/Toronto

99 00 01 02 5 4 3 2 1

Sixth edition 1999

Greystone Books
A division of Douglas & McIntyre Ltd.
1615 Venables Street
Vancouver, British Columbia
V5L 2H1

Originated by Greystone Books and published simultaneously in the United States by Chronicle Books, San Francisco.

Canadian Cataloguing in Publication Data

Main entry under title:
Vancouver, the ultimate guide

ISSN 1194-3033

   1. Vancouver (B.C.)—Guidebooks.   I. Wershler, Terri, 1950–
II. Lees, Judi, 1944–
   FC 3847.18.W47   917.11'33044'05   C93-030872-7
F1089.5.V22W47

Editing by Catherine Bennett
Cover design by Jill Jacobson
Cover photo by Brian Sprout, Image Network
Text design by George Vaitkunas
Maps by David Gay, Barbara Hodgson, Brenda Code and Fiona MacGregor
Typeset by Susanna Gilbert, *Descriptions Design*
Printed and bound in Canada by Friesens
Printed on acid-free paper

The publisher gratefully acknowledges the support of the Canada Council for the Arts and of the British Columbia Ministry of Tourism, Small Business and Culture. The publisher also acknowledges the financial support of the gov-ernment of Canada through the Book Publishing Industry Development Program.

Contents

List of Maps

About Vancouver

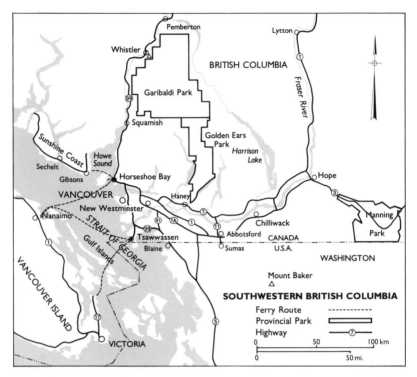

Map labels: Pemberton, Lytton, Whistler, BRITISH COLUMBIA, Garibaldi Park, Fraser River, Squamish, Golden Ears Park, Harrison Lake, Sunshine Coast, Howe Sound, Sechelt, Gibsons, Horseshoe Bay, Hope, VANCOUVER, Haney, Manning Park, New Westminster, Nanaimo, STRAIT OF GEORGIA, Chilliwack, Tsawwassen, Abbotsford, CANADA, Park, Gulf Islands, Blaine, Sumas, U.S.A., VANCOUVER ISLAND, WASHINGTON, Mount Baker, SOUTHWESTERN BRITISH COLUMBIA, VICTORIA

Ferry Route · Provincial Park · Highway
0   50   100 km
0   50 mi.

The Look and Feel of the City

The quintessential handshake with Vancouver, rain or shine, is to walk the Stanley Park seawall. Go ahead; don your walking shoes and meet this city where the ocean laps below you, the mountains provide a magnificent backdrop and thickets of trees border the walkway. Sometimes, as you pause to ponder a passing seal or listen to spirited birdsong, it is difficult to believe that you are in the centre of a bustling metropolis. At other times, viewing the passing traffic—joggers, mothers pushing strollers, couples holding hands—you feel Vancouver's special kinetic energy.

This West Coast city is lively. Its centre is close to some of the best neighbourhoods as well as to wilderness. Those living in the densely populated West End, popular Kitsilano or trendy Yaletown can walk or cycle to work in the city's skyscrapers. They can also stroll a wooded path or in-line skate a seawall over lunch, be on their skis within an hour of leaving work, kayak to view the cityscape from the ocean or sail away from a marina just outside their office door.

The cliché that you can ski and sail on the same day is true, thanks to our high mountains and temperate climate. The southern West Coast has Canada's mildest weather, and while locals may laugh at the description of "Lotus Land," truth is, Vancouver does resemble California's cities more than Eastern Canada's, both in architecture and in its laid-back lifestyle.

The look of the city has changed drastically over the last few decades with both the Coal Harbour and False Creek waterfronts adding everything from high-tech towers to green spaces. Unique façades such as "The Sails" of Canada Place, the Vancouver Public Library and the acclaimed Chan Centre for the Performing Arts have put this city on the architectural map. The next major development will be Portside. The massive construction site that we see today on the harbour east of Canada Place will increase convention space as well as add hotel rooms and public space. Accessible by foot, car, SeaBus and SkyTrain, Portside will feature a vast waterfront plaza.

Once criticized for being more an outdoor mecca than a cultural one, Vancouver now offers the best of the entertainment world. Audiences can choose between a large-stage production or a hot jazz cellar, a world-class ballet or a lounge crooner, a renowned pianist performing in an acoustical wonder or folk singers on the beach.

Vancouver has come of age when it comes to dining out, too. In this city, more than in any other in North America, you should take an Asian culinary tour—though to do it justice, it would take months of eating out. You can also dine in a restaurant lauded by *Gourmet Magazine* as being among "America's Top Tables" or survey a multipage wine list that has been acclaimed by *The Wine Spectator*. Awards and plaudits aside, there are fish and chips sold on a wharf; native dishes served in a long house; succulent salmon savoured along with incredible city views, and Greek treats, Spanish *tapas* or other ethnic dishes served by the family that made them.

Ranked as the second-best city in the world in which to live by the Corporate Resources Group of Geneva in 1996, Vancouver invites exploration. From an introductory walk on Stanley Park's seawall to whatever is your pleasure, this West Coast city won't let you down.

Getting Oriented

Because the city centre is encompassed by water on three sides, newcomers should become familiar with the many bridges that connect the city to its environs. Burrard Inlet, which separates the North Shore communities of North and West Vancouver from the city proper, is spanned by two bridges. The Lions Gate Bridge links downtown with the North Shore; one end is in Stanley Park and the other between West and North Vancouver. The Second Narrows Bridge runs between the East End of Vancouver and North Vancouver.

False Creek juts into the heart of the city and is crossed by three bridges connecting the West End and downtown to the rest of Vancouver. From east to west, these are the Cambie St Bridge by the stadium at B.C. Place, the Granville St Bridge and the Burrard St Bridge. The Fraser River, which marks the southern limit of the city, is spanned (from west to east) by the Arthur Laing Bridge, the Oak St Bridge, the Knight St Bridge, the Alex Fraser Bridge, the Pattullo Bridge and the Port Mann Bridge. South of the city is Vancouver International Airport, located on Sea Island at the mouth of the Fraser River.

Most of Vancouver's streets form a grid, laid out by surveyors who had utility in mind, and this makes simple work of finding your way around. The area south of False Creek is especially easy, since east-west roads are numbered avenues.

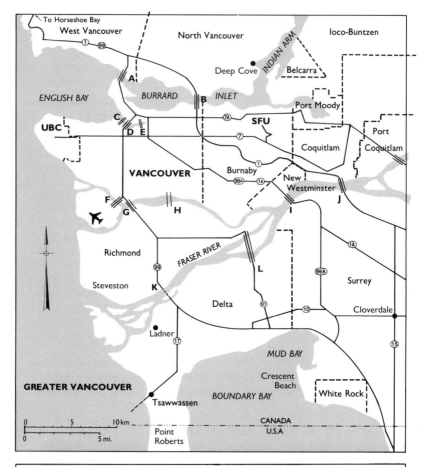

A	Lions Gate Bridge	**I**	Pattullo Bridge
B	Second Narrows Bridge	**J**	Port Mann Bridge
C	Burrard St. Bridge	**K**	George Massey Tunnel
D	Granville St. Bridge	**L**	Alex Fraser Bridge
E	Cambie St. Bridge	**UBC**	University of British Columbia
F	Arthur Laing Bridge	**SFU**	Simon Fraser University
G	Oak St. Bridge	**✗**	Vancouver International Airport
H	Knight St. Bridge	**—⑨①—**	Highway

The dividing line between east and west is roughly Main St. To avoid confusion, be sure to check whether avenues are preceded by a "W" for West or "E" for East.

Hwy 1, the Trans-Canada, goes through east Vancouver, crosses the Second Narrows Bridge to the North Shore and ends at Horseshoe Bay. At Horseshoe Bay, it becomes the Sea to Sky Hwy, which runs to Whistler. From Horseshoe Bay, ferries run to Nanaimo on Vancouver Island,

Towering Douglas firs on Granville St in the 1880s. (Vancouver Public Library, Historical Photos)

Langdale on the Sechelt Peninsula and Bowen Island.

Hwy 99 runs south and goes under the south arm of the Fraser River via the George Massey Tunnel. Past the tunnel, Hwy 17 branches off for Tsawwassen and the terminal for ferries sailing to Victoria, Nanaimo and the Gulf Islands. Hwy 99 itself continues on to the U.S. border, about an hour's drive from downtown.

Hwy 99 also runs northward to the ferry terminal at Horseshoe Bay, then on to Whistler and points beyond.

Hwy 91 runs from the border to the eastern municipalities of Burnaby, New Westminster and Port Coquitlam.

Greater Vancouver consists of the city of Vancouver and a number of communities. Across Burrard Inlet are Lions Bay, West Vancouver and North Vancouver. South of the city, across the Fraser River, are Richmond, Delta, Surrey and White Rock. To the east are Burnaby, New Westminster, Port Moody, Port Coquitlam, Coquitlam, Ioco-Buntzen and Belcarra. In many of these communities, avenues run east-west and streets run north-south. Often the names of both avenues and streets are numbers, so take careful note of addresses.

History

Native People

The Coast Salish have had villages on the shores of Burrard Inlet and the Fraser River delta for more than 5000 years. The three principal villages in the late 1700s were at Locarno Beach, at Stanley Park and on the North Shore east of the Capilano River. Their ancient culture was highly developed, and they were master carpenters and canoemakers and exquisite craftsmen.

After the Great Fire of 1886, the first City Hall was in a tent. (Vancouver Public Library, Historical Photos)

Exploration

1791 A Spanish navigator, José María Narváez, was the first European to arrive in the immediate area. He sailed into Burrard Inlet but did not explore the inner harbour.

1792 Capt George Vancouver arrived and claimed the land for Britain while searching for a northwest passage to Asia. He spent only one day on the site of the city named after him 100 years later. After charting Burrard Inlet, he had an amicable meeting with a Spanish explorer, Dionisio Alcalá Galiano.

Although the Spanish did not play a large part in the history of this area, they left their mark with place names: Alberni, Galiano, Cordova, Langara, San Juan, Saturna and Juan de Fuca.

1808 Explorer and fur trader Simon Fraser of the North West Company reached Georgia Strait overland by a river he thought was the Columbia. It was not, and the river was later named after him. He did not reach Burrard Inlet.

Settlement

"By all accounts, from the present Granville Street to the tip of Point Grey grew one of the most magnificent stands of virgin timber the world has ever seen." Alan Morley, *Vancouver: From Milltown to Metropolis*

1827 The Hudson's Bay Company set up a fur-trading post, Fort Langley,

48 km (30 miles) east of Vancouver on the Fraser River. It was the first settlement in the Lower Mainland, but homesteaders were not encouraged since land clearing would drive away fur-bearing animals.

1858 Gold was discovered up the Fraser River, and the valley was flooded with 30,000 prospectors, mostly from the depleted gold mines of California. To provide law and order among the gold seekers and to secure the land from encroachment by the United States, the area was declared the Crown colony of British Columbia.

1859 New Westminster, a town on the Fraser River, was named the capital of British Columbia.

A British survey ship discovered coal on the shores of Burrard Inlet. (This bay at the entrance to Stanley Park is still called Coal Harbour.)

1862 Unable to find gold, three British prospectors acquired 200 ha (500 acres) of land on the south shore of Burrard Inlet to start a brickworks. It failed—who wanted bricks with all that wood? (This land, now the entire West End, is one of the most expensive pieces of real estate in Canada, but it was then valued at $1.01 per acre.)

1867 John Deighton, called "Gassy Jack" because he was so talkative, opened a saloon near Hastings Mill on Burrard Inlet. Since liquor was prohibited on company land, business boomed for Jack; he was so successful that a community known as Gastown grew around his saloon.

1869 Gastown was officially incorporated as the town of Granville.

1884 The Canadian Pacific Railway (CPR) decided on Coal Harbour, at the mouth of Burrard Inlet, as its transcontinental terminus. This deci-

sion was pivotal to the subsequent rapid development of Vancouver.

For a time the CPR controlled the town. It was, in fact, the general manager of the CPR who chose the name Vancouver.

Vancouver As a City

1886 The town of Granville, population 1000, became the City of Vancouver. On 13 June the entire city was wiped out in less than an hour by a clearing fire gone wild. Fewer than half a dozen buildings remained.

Despite the chaos of rebuilding, the inaugural city council showed remarkable foresight by turning the First Narrows Military Reserve into a park. It was named Stanley Park after Governor General Lord Stanley. (The Stanley Cup is also named after him.) After the fire, the city grew at a rapid rate. By the end of the year there were 800 buildings.

Later Landmark Years

1887 The first CPR train chugged into Vancouver. The transcontinental railway was complete!

1889 The original Granville St Bridge was built, the first to span False Creek.

1893 The Hudson's Bay Company opened its first department store at Granville and Georgia, the same site as the present store.

1908 The University of British Columbia was founded.

1925 The original Second Narrows Bridge opened, connecting Vancouver with the North Shore.

1936 Vancouver's city hall was built in the art deco style.

1938 The Lions Gate Bridge opened.

1939 The Hotel Vancouver (the third and existing one) was completed. Construction was suspended during the depression, so the hotel was 11 years in the making.

1964 The B.C. Lions football team won the Grey Cup.

1965 Simon Fraser University, designed by architect Arthur Erickson, opened for classes.

1970 The Vancouver Canucks hockey team made its NHL debut.

1977 The SeaBus began a regular commuter ferry service between North Vancouver and downtown.

1979 The Vancouver Whitecaps won the North American Soccer League championship.

1983 B.C. Place Stadium, the state of the art in inflated domes, opened.

1986 Vancouver's centennial. The city hosted Expo 86, a world transportation exhibition. Canada Place, Vancouver's cruise ship terminal and trade and convention centre, officially opened. A rapid transit service called SkyTrain began operation.

1992 The 200th anniversary of Capt George Vancouver's voyage into Burrard Inlet was celebrated.

1993 Vancouver hosted the Peace Summit between U.S. president Bill Clinton and Russian president Boris Yeltsin.

1994 Vancouver was awarded an NBA franchise and the Vancouver Grizzlies were formed.

The B.C. Lions football team defeated Baltimore in the last few minutes of the game to win the Grey Cup. This was the first time a U.S. team participated in Grey Cup playoffs.

1995 The Vancouver Public Library moved into a new, distinctively de-

signed building; General Motors Place opened to host Vancouver Canucks and Vancouver Grizzlies games; and the Ford Centre for the Performing Arts opened.

1997 Vancouver hosted the Asia Pacific Economic Co-operation (APEC) forum. The largest event held since Expo 1986 saw 5,000 delegates (including 18 heads of state) and 3,500 journalists swarm into the city for the week-long forum.

The Chan Centre for the Performing Arts opened on the University of British Columbia campus and instantly garnered high praise from international critics and performers.

Population

In just over 100 years, Vancouver has grown to be the third-largest city in Canada, after Toronto and Montreal. According to the most recent Statistics Canada estimates, the population of the City of Vancouver is 514,000, and Greater Vancouver is home to 1.9 million. Next to the descendants of British immigrants, the largest ethnic group are the Chinese, and other Asian races such as Japanese, south and west Asian and Filipino add to the area's diverse cultural scene. In Vancouver proper more than 44 per cent of the population is made up of visible minorities.

Chinese. There have been three major waves of immigration: from San Francisco in 1858 for the Fraser Valley gold rush, from southern Guangdong province in the 1880s to construct the Canadian Pacific Railway and, most recently, from Hong Kong.

German, Dutch, Jewish, Scandinavian and Ukrainian. Although these are sizable groups, they have integrated into Vancouver life and are not highly visible ethnic communities.

Indo-Pakistani. Many of the early immigrants came from the Punjab because of their logging skills. The Indo-Canadian shopping area is concentrated on Main between 49th and 51st Ave.

French. The French in Vancouver have their own church, newspaper, and radio and television stations. There is a French community called Maillardville in Coquitlam.

Italian. The Italians also publish their own newspaper, available in "Little Italy" on Commercial north of Broadway. Many Italians arrived at the turn of the century, and a second wave arrived after World War II.

Filipino. Many Filipinos are women who came to Vancouver in the 1960s because of a severe shortage of nurses. More recently many women immigrated because of a demand for nannies.

Japanese. Many immigrated at the turn of the century to fish, farm, work in sawmills or build the railway. Japantown, along Powell east of Main, was much larger before World War II. Steveston, south of Richmond, still shows evidence of its heritage as a Japanese fishing village.

Native Indian. The Coast Salish originally inhabited this area.

Three Salish bands (Burrard, Squamish and Musqueam) now live on two large reserves in Greater Vancouver.

Greek. Most Greeks arrived after World War II, opening restaurants and shops or working in construction. Their community is centred on Broadway west of Macdonald.

Weather

When people talk about Vancouver, the subject of weather invariably arises. Vancouverites are either pitied because of the rain or envied because of the balmy climate. A myth abounds that Vancouver is the wettest city in Canada. It's just not true. In fact, every major city east of Montreal gets more precipitation than this western one. So there.

Summers in Vancouver are warm

Weather Chart

	Average minimum temperature		Average maximum temperature		Days with precipitation	Total precipitation		Hours of sunshine
	°C	°F	°C	°F		cm	in.	
Jan	2	36	5	41	20	21.8	8.6	55
Feb	4	40	7	44	15	14.7	5.8	93
Mar	6	43	10	50	16	12.7	5	129
Apr	9	48	14	58	13	8.4	3.3	180
May	12	54	18	64	10	7.1	2.8	253
June	15	59	21	69	10	6.4	2.5	243
July	17	63	23	74	6	3.1	1.2	305
Aug	17	63	23	73	8	4.3	1.7	255
Sept	14	58	18	65	9	9.1	3.6	188
Oct	10	50	14	57	16	14.7	5.8	116
Nov	6	43	9	48	18	21.1	8.3	70
Dec	4	39	6	43	20	22.4	8.8	44

and winters are mild with little snow, which can result in flowers blooming in February and an almost guaranteed warm, sunny July and Aug. An "Indian Summer" occasionally sees pleasant days extending well into Oct. One reason for the balmy climate is that weather systems move from west to east. So when the rest of Canada is submerged in cold air from the mountains and the prairies, Vancouver basks in warm Pacific airstreams.

Although Vancouver is blessed with mild temperatures, the many microclimates of the region mean that the weather varies drastically from one area to the other. While it can be pouring on the North Shore—the mountains protect the city from wind but also latch onto rain clouds—it will be sunny to the south in Tsawwassen. The closer people live to the mountains, the more they get rained on. For example, the annual level of precipitation on Grouse Mountain is 3500 mm (140 inches), whereas downtown Vancouver receives 1400 mm (55 inches) and sunny Richmond only 1000 mm (40 inches). Rain does have its advantages: the grass stays green, and the air is usually fresh and clear.

If you visit between May and Sept, bring a sweater, a light raincoat and an umbrella. In winter months, you'll need a warm raincoat, an umbrella and waterproof boots.

For a recorded weather forecast, phone 664-9010. For an air-quality report, call 436-6767.

Major Industries

Industry has developed in Vancouver largely because of two factors: the province's wealth of natural resources and the city's great natural harbour.

Throughout the province, industry is based on mining, fishing and forestry, and Vancouver is active in the processing and shipping of raw materials. Mills, canneries and oil refineries are common on the outskirts of the city, and commercial fish boats dock along city waterways, unloading their catches of salmon, shrimp, herring, sole and halibut.

Burrard Inlet is one of the world's largest natural harbours; it is deep, sheltered and ice-free all year. Vancouver is a major North American port because of its harbour and because it is the Canadian gateway for all cargo coming from and going to Asia. Constantly increasing ship traffic saw the refurbishment of the old Ballantyne Terminal, which had been closed for years, as a dual-use port for cruise and cargo ships. Along with the nearby coal superport of Roberts Bank, the Port of Vancouver handles more tonnage than any other port on the West Coast and is among the top five ports in the Western Hemisphere. Outgoing cargoes include grain, forest products, coal, potash, sulphur, fish, asbestos, iron ore and copper.

Freighters anchored in English Bay are as much a part of the city's panorama as the North Shore mountains. In the summer they are joined by an ever-increasing fleet of sleek Alaska-bound cruise ships gliding under Lions Gate Bridge. These elegant liners symbolize the newest star on the city's economic scene: tourism. Growth has been steady in this industry since Expo 86, when Vancouver was "discovered" by the world. Tourism, the world's fastest-growing industry, is alive and well in this city, where it generates $2.5 billion in visitors' spending annually. And there is little doubt that tourism will continue its upward spiral.

Essential Information

Emergency Phone Numbers

Police, Fire, Ambulance
Call 911 in Greater Vancouver.

Doctors and Dentists
A drop-in medical clinic is on the lower level of the Bentall Centre at Dunsmuir and Burrard (683-8138). Open Mon to Fri. Emergency dental services are available from Dr. Jerome Griffiths (872-8201). His office is located at Ste 700-777 W Broadway. Open Tue to Thurs.

Rape Relief and Women's Shelter
Call 872-8212.

Alcoholics Anonymous
Call 434-3933.

Veterinarian
The Animal Emergency Clinic (734-5104) at 4th and Fir is open 24 hours daily.

Legal Services
For a referral, phone 687-3221; for free recorded general legal information, phone 687-4680. These services are offered by the B.C. branch of the Canadian Bar Association.

Marine and Aircraft Emergencies
Call the Canadian Coast Guard at 1-800-567-5111, or cellular call *311.

RCMP Tourist Alert
The RCMP attempts to contact travellers with urgent messages via radio, TV, newspapers, B.C. Travel Infocentres and provincial campgrounds. Call the local police and your information will be forwarded to the RCMP.

Major Hospitals

Vancouver General Hospital
855 W 12th near Oak
875-4111

Area Codes in B.C.

British Columbia has two area codes. The area code in Vancouver and east to Hope and north to D'Arcy, as well as all of the Sunshine Coast, is 604. The area code for the rest of the province, including the Gulf Islands and Vancouver Island, is 250.

St Paul's Hospital
1081 Burrard near Davie
682-2344

B.C. Women's Hospital (Obstetrics)
4500 Oak at 29th
875-2424

B.C.'s Children's Hospital
4480 Oak at 29th
875-2345

University Hospital: UBC
2211 Wesbrook Mall, off University Blvd
822-7121

Lions Gate Hospital
231 E 15th at St Georges, North Van
988-3131

Burnaby Hospital
3935 Kincaid at Sunset
434-4211

Motor Vehicles

Seatbelts are compulsory in B.C.; motorcyclists must wear helmets. Children under 5 must be secured in infant restraint systems.

Right turns on red lights are allowed after you have come to a complete stop. Speed limits and road distances are posted in kilometres, and gas is sold in litres.

Emergency Road Service
The BCAA offers 24-hour emergency road service to its members and

members of other auto clubs. Call 293-2222. (Be patient, since it is often difficult to get through.)

Towing

If you've been towed from the street, call Unitow at 688-5484. The Unitow lot at 1410 Granville at Pacific is open 24 hours. Pay the towing charge ($23.49) with cash, Visa or MasterCard.

If you were towed from a private parking lot your car may be at one of three lots: the Unitow lot at 1717 Vernon at E 2nd (picture identification is necessary at this police impounding lot); the Busters lot (685-8181) at 104 E 1st near Quebec; or the Drake Towing lot (251-3344) at 1553 Powell at Woodland. These lots are open 24 hours. Charges, which may be about $70, can be paid with cash, Visa or MasterCard.

Road Conditions

Call the Ministry of Transportation and Highways at 1-900-451-4997 for a recorded announcement.

Travel Information

In Vancouver

Vancouver TouristInfo Centre
Waterfront Centre, Plaza Level
200 Burrard at Cordova
683-2000
Will book accommodation, tour reservations, car rentals and restaurant reservations. Maps, brochures, long distance phone cards, and B.C. Transit tickets, schedules and passes are available here. Hours: June to Aug, 8–6 daily; Sept to May, Mon to Fri, 8:30–5; Sat, 9–5.

Super, Natural British Columbia is an information and reservation service; call 663-6000. From out of the city, including the U.S., call 1-800-663-6000.

TouristInfo Centre kiosks operated by the Downtown Vancouver Business Improvements Association are in the plaza outside the main entrance to Pacific Centre at Granville and Georgia and in front of Vancouver Trade & Convention Centre. Open daily in summer, hours are 10–6; in Dec, Thurs to Sat, 11–3. These centres are fine for general directions or quick information, but for brochures and details visit the one at Waterfront Centre. During summer, tourism ambassadors wearing navy shorts and jackets are in the downtown sector. They speak a variety of languages and are happy to assist with information and directions.

Information about Vancouver can be accessed through the tourism website: <http://tourism-vancouver.org> or the City of Vancouver website: <http://www.city.vancouver.bc.ca>.

City Hall

The City of Vancouver
453 W 12th Ave at Cambie
873-7011
For questions or complaints, call city hall and you will be directed to the correct department.

Travel Infocentres

Burnaby Travel Infocentre
Metrotown on Kingsway (in the pedestrian concourse between Metrotown and Eaton Centre)
431-8046 (May 1–Sept 30)
294-7944 (year-round)
Open weekdays 11–5; Sat 10–5; Sun 12–5.

New Westminster Travel Infocentre
New Westminster Quay Public Market
810 Quayside at 8th St
526-1905
Open daily.

North Vancouver Travel Infocentre
Capilano at Marine
980-5332 (during summer)
Open daily from Victoria Day to
Labour Day.

White Rock Travel Infocentre
15150 Russell at Johnston
536-6844
Open Mon to Fri, 8:30–4:30 year-
round.

June to Sept there are Infocentres
at West Beach, Marine Dr by the pier
and at Campbell River Store, Pacific
Hwy at 8th; open daily.

**Peace Arch Provincial Visitor
Infocentre**
Hwy 99, Blaine/White Rock crossing;
just inside the Canadian border.
Travel information on all areas of
B.C. Open Jan 2 to May 5, 9–5; May
16 to Sept 7, 8–8; Sept 8 to Dec 31,
9–5. (Closed Dec 25, 26 and Jan 1.)

Solo Travellers

Singles may wish to check into the
following organizations:

Connecting Solo Travel Network
PO Box 29088, 1996 W Broadway,
Vancouver, V6J 5C2
737-7791
1-800-557-1757 (North America)
Members communicate through an
excellent bimonthly newsletter that
includes news about single-friendly
trips. Volunteer hosts meet with singles visiting the city to share information and spend time at a mutually
agreed-upon activity. There is a $35
annual fee, payable by cheque,
money order, MasterCard or Visa.

T.G.I.F. Singles
977 Wellington Dr
North Vancouver, V7K 1L1
988-5231
This 700-member singles club hosts
everything from dinner/dance
evenings to river rafting and horse-

Metric Conversion

Unit	Approximate equivalent
Length	
1 kilometre	0.6 mile
1 mile	1.6 kilometres
1 metre	1.1 yards
1 yard	0.9 metre
1 centimetre	0.4 inch
1 inch	2.54 centimetres
Capacity	
1 litre	1.06 U.S. quarts
1 U.S. quart	0.95 litre
Weight	
1 kilogram	2.2 pounds
1 pound	0.45 kilogram
1 ounce	28 grams
1 gram	0.04 ounce
Temperature	
0°C	32°F
10°C	50°F
20°C	68°F
30°C	86°F

back riding. Annual membership fee
is $75, but solo visitors to Vancouver
can attend functions for a nominal
fee. For example, a dinner/dance
would be about $30; an organized
outdoor excursion may be $5.

Public Holidays

New Year's Day, Jan 1
Good Friday, date varies
Easter Monday, date varies
Victoria Day, third Mon in May
Canada Day, July 1
B.C. Day, first Mon in Aug
Labour Day, first Mon in Sept
Thanksgiving, second Mon in Oct
Remembrance Day, Nov 11
Christmas, Dec 25
Boxing Day, Dec 26

Traffic at border crossings and on the
ferries is extremely heavy around a

holiday weekend; avoid both if possible.

Lost and Found

B.C. Transit
682-7887

Police (Property Room)
717-2726

Foreign Visitors

There are about 50 consulates in Vancouver but no embassies. Check the *Yellow Pages*.

After a 48-hour visit, U.S. citizens can take home $400 (U.S.) worth of goods per person every 30 days. This may include one litre of alcohol for each adult, 200 cigarettes and 100 cigars (not Cuban). After a visit of less than 48 hours, $200 worth of goods is allowed. Call 278-1825 for more information.

Banking

There are more than 25 foreign banks in Vancouver. Check the *Yellow Pages*.

Currency Exchanges

American Express
666 Burrard at Dunsmuir
669-2813
Open Mon to Sat.

Thomas Cook Foreign Exchange
701 Granville at Georgia (Pacific Centre Mall)
687-6111
Open Mon to Sat.
999 Canada Place at Howe
641-1229
Mon to Sat. (Summer, open Sun.)
4700 Kingsway, Metrotown Eaton Centre
430-3990
Open Mon to Sun.

Custom House Currency Exchange
375 Water St at Seymour (The Landing)
482-6000
Open Mon to Sun.
1601 W Georgia at Cardero (Westin Bayshore Hotel lobby)
608-1763
Open Mon to Sun.

Royal Bank
Vancouver International Airport
665-0855
Open daily 5:30 AM–10 PM. Also, 24-hour currency-exchange machines, dispensing 15 foreign currencies, are scattered throughout the airport. Each machine has a different selection of currencies.

Many banks in Vancouver are open on Sat but generally not the downtown branches. The main downtown branches all have foreign exchange departments.

Churches and Synagogues

Some centrally located churches are:

Christ Church Cathedral (Anglican)
690 Burrard at Georgia
682-3848

First Baptist Church
969 Burrard at Nelson
683-8441

Holy Rosary Cathedral (Catholic)
646 Richards at Seymour
682-6774

Redeemer Lutheran Church
1499 Laurier at Granville
737-9821

Vancouver Mennonite Brethren Church
5887 Prince Edward near 43rd
325-3313

Pentecostal Assemblies of Canada
2700 E Broadway near Slocan
253-2700

Presbyterian Church in Canada
1155 Thurlow near Davie
683-1913

Unitarian Church of Vancouver
949 W 49th Ave at Oak
261-7204

St Andrew's Wesley United Church
1012 Nelson at Burrard
683-4574

Beth Israel Synagogue
4350 Oak at 49th
731-4161

Sales Taxes

A provincial sales tax of 7 per cent is applied to most purchases, with the exception of groceries, books and magazines. Goods shipped out of the province directly by the vendor are also exempt.

The 7 per cent federal Goods and Services Tax is also added to virtually everything you purchase except groceries. Non-residents can apply for a rebate of the tax on accommodation and consumer goods taken out of the country if the tax totals at least $14 (but not for such items as restaurant meals, gas and tobacco). Rebate application forms, available at most hotels, must be accompanied by original receipts and mailed to Revenue Canada. (Receipts are not returned.)

If you are driving to the U.S., you have the alternative of taking the original receipts and proof of residence (identification with a picture) to a participating duty-free shop at the border for an immediate cash rebate. At the main border crossing, on Hwy 99 south of Vancouver, this is the Heritage Duty-Free Shop. The last exit, Beach Rd, will take you directly there. The shop is open daily, 5 AM–midnight. Phone the shop at 541-1244 if you need more information.

Post Office

The main post office at Georgia and Homer is open Mon to Fri, 8–5:30. Conveniently located substations are as follows: 595 Burrard at Pender (basement of Bentall Centre), open Mon to Fri, 8–5:30; Hallmark Card Shop at 1014 Robson near Burrard, open Mon to Fri, 9–7, Sat, 10–5, and Sun, 11–4; Eaton's (basement), 701 Granville at Georgia, open Mon to Fri, 9:30–5:30, and Sat, 9:30–4:30.

Postal services are available at designated drugstores and convenience stores Mon to Sat or Sun. Look for the Canada Post sign in the front window.

Late-Night Services

Pharmacies

Shopper's Drug Mart
1125 Davie at Thurlow
685-6445
2302 W 4th at Vine, 738-3138
Open 24 hours.
1020 Denman at Nelson, 681-3411
2947 Granville at 13th, 738-3107
4326 Dunbar at 28th, 732-8855
Open until midnight.

Safeway
2733 W Broadway at Trafalgar
732-5030
The pharmacy in the supermarket is open 8 AM–midnight every day.

Restaurants

The Bread Garden
812 Bute at Robson
688-3213
2996 Granville at 14th Ave
736-6465
Healthy soups, sandwiches, salads and muffins, as well as decadent desserts. Open 24 hours daily.

Benny's Bagels
2503 W Broadway at Larch
731-9730

Funky place serving bagels, of course, plus desserts and salads. Several locations, but this is the only one open 24 hours. See Restaurants (Late Night).

The Naam
2724 W 4th near Stephens
738-7151
A 24-hour vegetarian restaurant with beer, wine and espresso. See Restaurants (Vegetarian).

Hamburger Mary's
1202 Davie at Bute
687-1293
A Vancouver institution for late-nighters, open daily until 4 AM except Sunday night, when it is open until 2 AM.

Babysitting

Most major hotels can arrange for babysitters if notified in advance.

Moppet Minders Child and Home Care Services
942-8167
Same-day booking. Adult sitters; charge is $8.50/hour for one or two children for a minimum of four hours. An additional charge of 50¢ an hour for each additional child. Maximum four children. Payments in cash.

Liquor/Beer/Wine

In B.C. you must be at least 19 to purchase or consume alcohol. Spirits are sold only in government liquor stores, which are also the main outlet for beer and wine.

Private beer and wine stores sell their products at slightly higher prices than government stores but are convenient because they are generally open seven days a week and sell chilled wine and beer.

Pubs have "off-licence sales" whereby they are allowed to sell cold beer to be consumed off the premises.

Centrally located government liquor stores are at the following locations:

1120 Alberni near Thurlow
Mon to Sat, 9:30–9. Includes a specialty store.

1716 Robson near Denman
Mon to Sat, 9:30–11.

1155 Bute near Davie
Mon to Sat, 9:30–6; Fri, 9:30–9.

2020 W Broadway at Maple
Mon to Sat, 9 AM–11 PM.

5555 Cambie at 39th
Mon to Sat, 9:30–9. The largest liquor store in the province; wine consultants on staff.

Only private stores sell chilled wines. Some private stores are:

Granville Island Brewing Co
1441 Cartwright, Granville Island
687-2739
Open daily; call for hours. This company brews and sells B.C.'s best beer and offers a selection of premier B.C. wines as well as international wines. See Sightseeing (Special Interest Tours).

Marquis Wine Cellar
1034 Davie off Burrard
685-2446
Open daily; 11–8. Wine and wine products. Carries labels not found in the government stores.

Broadway International Wine Shop
2752 W Broadway near Macdonald
734-8543
11–9 daily. Good selection of wines from around the world.

Newspapers and Periodicals

Vancouver Sun
Published every morning except Sun. Complete entertainment listings on Thurs, weekly *TV Times* on Fri.

Province
Published every morning except Sat. Entertainment and TV listings on Fri.

Georgia Straight
An excellent free weekly that focusses on entertainment and current issues. Published on Thurs, available at newsstands, corner stores and theatres.

Business in Vancouver
Excellent weekly in tabloid format, published on Fri.

Vancouver Magazine
General-interest city magazine published nine times a year. Available at newsstands.

CityFood
A free tabloid published 10 times a year that focusses on food and includes restaurant reviews.

Coast
Free outdoor recreation tabloid published 11 times annually. Available from outdoor stores, community centres, libraries, some coffee shops and outdoor newspaper boxes.

Westcoast Families
Family-oriented articles and an excellent calendar of fun and family activities. Published 12 times a year and available free from community centres, libraries, children's stores, family attractions and all McDonald's outlets in the Lower Mainland. Sister publications are *Fraser Valley Family* and *Okanagan Families*.

Out-of-town Newspapers
There is a good selection at The Great Canadian News Co. (1092 Robson near Thurlow, 688-0609), Mayfair News (1535 W Broadway off Granville, 738-8951) and The News Hound Magazine Gallery (2997 Granville at 14th, 733-8868).

Where to Stay

Like all world-class cities, Vancouver's accommodation scene covers a wide spectrum—from five-diamond AAA/CAA-rated hotels in the heart of the city to unique bed-and-breakfast rooms in pleasant neighbourhoods. This book covers that range and pays attention to details such as an accommodation's distinctive character, surroundings and price. Sometimes our comments may seem overly enthusiastic, but remember, we've chosen discriminately from many. The hotels are grouped by location and then listed by price (most expensive first) in each section. After the hotels are listings for All-Suite Hotels, Alternative Accommodation, Bed and Breakfast, and Trailer Parks/Campgrounds.

Please note that prices quoted are *starting* prices ("rack rates," as the hotels call them) for a standard double in high season. Always ask about special rates: weekend, weekly, seniors', off season, corporate and so on.

If you are planning an extended stay, you may want to book through **Executive Accommodations** (875-6674), which can find you a fully furnished apartment, condominium, townhouse or house. Accommodation includes a fully equipped kitchen and maid service; it may have a fireplace, plants—whatever makes you feel at home. Children are welcome. Accommodation for pets is limited. For a long-term stay, this type of accommodation represents a substantial savings over a hotel stay. Rates are calculated at a daily rate, depending on the property, of $95–$156 per night.

Hotels

Downtown

Pan Pacific Vancouver
999 Canada Place, foot of Howe
662-8111

1-800-663-1515 (Canada)
1-800-937-1515 (U.S.)
Highlighted by the dramatic "five sails" of Canada Place and the cruise-ship pier, this deluxe hotel is a city landmark. This architectural wonder also includes the World Trade Centre. An eight-storey atrium with totem poles draws you into the Pan Pacific's spacious lobby, where the lounge and café have 12 m (40-foot) glass walls and a panorama of the harbour. To impress out-of-towners, have them book here as all rooms have incredible views (so do the bathrooms in rooms 10 and 20 on each floor). Guest rooms start on the eighth floor and all have been recently redecorated—relaxing neutral tones, exquisite Italian fabrics and tasteful art with furniture reminiscent of a luxurious home. All of the suites have sofabeds. As befitting a hotel of this calibre, the Pan Pacific offers guests every convenience; 17 rooms are even equipped with computers, video cameras and supporting software.

There's an extra charge for the health club, but you'll see why immediately; there's state-of-the-art exercise equipment, a low-impact running track, trainers on duty, racquetball and squash courts, a video aerobics room and the Sports Lounge, with a wide-screen TV. A heated outdoor pool is open year-round.

The Pan Pacific has three restaurants: the Five Sails offers one of the city's best waterfront views, the Café Pacifica features a Friday night Opera Buffet that is popular both for the food and the performing opera singers, and Misaki serves fine Japanese cuisine. Located in the business district, the hotel is close to Gastown and about a 10-minute walk to Robson's shops. It is the city's most expensive hotel, and many people think that it's worth the price. Doubles $430.

Four Seasons Hotel
791 W Georgia at Howe
689-9333
1-800-268-6282 toll free (Canada)
1-800-332-3442 toll free (U.S.)
Stay here if you want to be pampered. Some of the niceties are bathrobes, hair dryers, VCRS, free shoeshine (just leave your shoes outside the door overnight), 24-hour valet service, a year-round indoor/outdoor pool and a rooftop garden. The hotel is conveniently connected to Pacific Centre shopping mall; however, this makes the lobby a thoroughfare. But above the lobby level, this five-diamond AAA/CAA-rated property regains that tranquil feeling of a luxurious hotel.

Children and pets are also pampered here. The younger set receives complimentary milk and cookies on arrival, terry robes, movie videos, aerobic videos in the health club, infant equipment, toys and a children's menu. Fido gets the "silver bowl" service—bottled water and dinner served from sterling silver!

Chartwell remains one of the best dining rooms in the city (see Restaurants, Lunch). The Garden Terrace is a great place to meet a lover or a friend (see Nightlife, Quiet Bars) and the lush greenery gives it an outdoor feeling. Location handy to everything. Doubles $350.

Metropolitan Hotel
645 Howe near Georgia
687-1122
1-800-667-2300 toll free
For a stay laced with luxury, check into the Met, where everything is lavish. Take the rooms: all 197 have European down quilts and Italian-designed, Egyptian-cotton sheets on the queen- and king-size beds, and four-piece marble bathrooms. There

are thoughtful touches like light controls beside the bed, personalized voice mail and complimentary robes, coffee and morning paper. Take the lobby: its elegance is quiet but pervasive, and marble is everywhere. Take the service: always friendly and includes extras like complimentary mending and shoeshine. Business clients' needs are satisfied with a state-of-the-art business centre and technologically-enhanced guest rooms that have extras like fax machines and ergonomic chairs.

Guests have the use of the fitness centre (including racquet and squash courts, lap pool, sun deck, exercise room, whirlpool, massage and, believe it or not, saunas with TV).

Originally a Mandarin Hotel, there is a legacy of Asian art throughout. The Metropolitan is a member of Preferred Hotels & Resorts Worldwide. Attention to detail here is de rigueur. Diva, one of the city's premier restaurants is located in the Metropolitan (see Restaurants, Contemporary). Excellent location. Doubles $289.

The Sutton Place Hotel
845 Burrard near Robson
682-5511
1-800-810-6888 toll free
Gracious and elegant are the words that come to mind when you enter The Sutton Place. The lobby exudes a European ambience, with its extravagant floral arrangements, French provincial furniture and air of tranquillity. The exquisite fittings continue in the 397 rooms and suites, which have detailed mouldings, floral bedspreads and marble bathrooms. This is the place for a romantic getaway; you'll feel you've arrived for a stay in a French manor where your every wish is granted. There is 24-hour room service, same-day

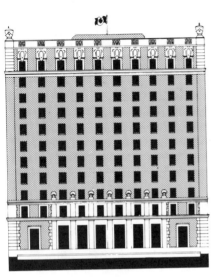

hotel became grand again. The Hotel Georgia is one of those fine, distinguished hotels built in the 1930s. Over the years celebrities such as the Prince of Wales, Elvis and the Beatles have stayed, and over the years the hotel aged, not always gracefully. It was a blessing when Crowne Plaza took it over and slowly, working closely with the Heritage Society, peeled pack the layers of changes that had been made to the hotel. The lobby's carpet was lifted to disclose art deco marble tile, and the grand ballroom's walls and chandelier were restored to their original style and grandeur. Rooms come in many different sizes; all have new furnishings but retain a hint of an earlier era. Many have small bathrooms, but the amenities, such as two phone lines, modem hook-up, express check-out, are all here. There is now a fitness centre, and the Cavalier Grill in the lobby has a bright, fresh look. Vancouver has few historic hotels. The Georgia is the oldest and, once again, among the finest. Doubles $260.

valet service, and complimentary newspaper, shoeshine and umbrella.

Although large, Sutton Place maintains an intimate feeling. Amenities include a business centre, a restaurant and lounge, pool, sun deck and Le Spa Health, Beauty and Fitness Centre.

Fleuri Restaurant guarantees a memorable meal (see Restaurants, Breakfast/Brunch). Afternoon tea (Mon to Sat, 2:30–4:30 PM) is an occasion here with bone china, Devonshire cream—the works. The Gérard Lounge, with its deep-toned wood, fireplace and soft leather seating, is popular with locals and visitors. Movie crews and stars visiting the city hang out here (see Nightlife, Quiet Bars). The hotel is in a good location for business meetings, shopping and restaurants. It has a five-diamond AAA/CAA rating. Doubles $260.

Hotel Georgia
801 W Georgia at Howe
682-5566
1-800-663-1111 toll free
The summer of 1998 a once-grand

Sheraton Wall Centre Garden Hotel
1088 Burrard at Helmcken
331-1000
1-800-325-3535 toll free
The understated elegance of the lobby sets the tone for this luxury hotel—discreet furnishings, fresh flowers and soft lighting. There are 456 rooms in two dark-glass towers. One is an "apartment" tower that provides for long-term as well as short-term stays.

The rooms have a vibrant, welcoming decor, and there are many amenities; each room has several phone lines, voice mail, dataport, a hair dryer, a make-up mirror (in deluxe rooms this is a heated mirror!), an in-room safe, duvets and air conditioning. All the works of art in the hotel are originals by B.C. artists. The Indigo restaurant features West Coast cuisine, and the health club is considered one of the city's best. You can swim laps, enjoy a rejuvenating massage, or work out with weights or cardiovascular equipment. Doubles $250.

Wedgewood Hotel
845 Hornby near Robson
689-7777
1-800-663-0666 toll free

The Wedgewood has a following. Owner Eleni Skalbania runs the 89-room hotel just as she would a gracious home. She is there to greet guests and ensure that they receive first-class service, and she supervises all room renovations. The Wedgewood exudes elegance and charm with its antiques, art and fresh flowers. Extras include flower-adorned balconies, complimentary shoeshine and continental breakfast, a daily sheet of menu specials, 24-hour room service and teleconferencing-capable phones in all rooms. All four penthouse suites have fireplaces. The Bacchus Restaurant (see Restaurants, Lunch) and bar (see Nightlife, Lively Bars and Lounges) are outstanding. This is a favourite with the before- and after-theatre crowd and a great place to relax after a shopping spree. It's a 5-minute walk to the business district. Doubles $220.

Hotel Vancouver
900 W Georgia at Burrard
684-3131
1-800-441-1414 toll free (Canada and U.S.)

Metaphorically as well as geographically, Canadian Pacific's chateau-style Hotel Vancouver is the heart of the city. It's the place to meet friends for drinks or the spot to recommend a stay to really get the feel of Vancouver. Built in 1939, renovations completed in 1996 included the opening of a new restaurant, 900 West (see Restaurants, Before or After the Theatre), and the refurbishing of the lobby. Take a moment to enjoy the gracious arched entranceway, the elaborate buttress and frieze work on the high vaulted ceiling and the ornate Spanish marble floor.

There are 555 rooms; decor is traditional. A standard room is spacious, has either a king-size or two double beds, two robes, coffeemakers, ironing boards, plus such business amenities as a well-stocked desk, data port, voice mail, computer jack and good desk light. For a special treat, stay on the Entree Gold floor, which has premium rooms and exceptional service: deluxe continental breakfast and afternoon canapes served in the private lounge, fresh flowers in the rooms and a concierge for your every need.

Hotel Vancouver has a well-equipped fitness club plus an atrium-style pool complete with Jacuzzi tub and sun deck. On the lower floor, also refurbished, are service businesses such as a GST refund centre, travel agent and the Robert Andrew Salon & Spa. Oh yes, George, the shoeshine man, is still there buffing footwear.

Afternoon tea, once held in the Lobby Lounge, now takes place in Griffins Restaurant from 2:30 to 4:30; as well as the usual scones, there is a decadent dessert buffet. The Lobby Lounge is a happening place at all hours of the day and night.

Staying at a grand old hotel is a special experience and offers a brush with history. The location is excellent for business and shopping. Doubles $200.

Waterfront Centre Hotel
900 Canada Place, foot of Howe
691-1991

1-800-441-1414 (Canada and U.S.)
The Waterfront Centre Hotel pleases everyone. Visitors love the location and locals enjoy some down time in the open-to-the-lobby restaurant and bar. Everything is tasteful, and the service is top notch. The lobby successfully melds the traditional and the contemporary with such touches as fossilized limestone frames around lobby doorways, oxidized iron finishes and weathered wood. All of the 489 rooms were recently refurbished and combine warm shades of gold, butterscotch and terra cotta with relaxing blues and greens. The Waterfront has the unbeatable Entree Gold floor—for a truly pampered stay in a Canadian Pacific Hotel, this is the way to go (see Hotel Vancouver listing).

It's worth strolling the hotel to enjoy the original artwork. Another nice feature is the third-floor terrace herb garden adjacent to the outdoor heated pool. Diners enjoy the bounty from this garden in Herons Restaurant. With floor-to-ceiling windows to show off Coal Harbour and an open kitchen—rare in a hotel—Herons makes you feel that you really will get that three-minute egg or extra-rare steak. Sunday brunches (11:30–3) are a musical treat; entertainment may be courtesy of the Vancouver Symphony Orchestra or a jazz combo. The Waterfront is an award-winner, and you can't go wrong with a stay here. Doubles $195.

Hyatt Regency Vancouver
655 Burrard near Georgia
683-1234
1-800-233-1234
The Hyatt always hums with activity, whether it be in the vast lobby, its large conference facility spread over two floors or the Gallery Bar, a favourite after-work meeting place.

Peacock's Lounge, also off the lobby, is quieter. Like Hyatts everywhere, the service is friendly and everything is up to par. Rooms come with security vaults, voice mail, king-size or two double beds, ironing apparatus, coffeemakers, robes and even umbrellas. Ten executive suites (including two with fancy spiral staircases, balconies and mountain views) are on the 33rd floor. There are 645 rooms, making it one of the city's largest hotels. However, that doesn't necessarily mean that there is room at the inn, as large groups love this facility (probably because the staff is willing to go the extra mile). There is a small business centre, two restaurants plus a lobby coffee bar, a health club that includes an outdoor pool, and you are close to everything. Royal Centre mall is attached. Doubles $190.

Hotel Dakota
654 Nelson at Granville
605-4333
1-888-605-5333
This hotel has been renovated and renamed many times since its birth in 1904, and now has a retro '50s look with brushed chrome banisters, neon sign and photos of the days when this end of Granville was the centre of the city. If you're looking for a well-priced city room you'll be pleasantly surprised here. Features include card-key locks, dataports, duvets on beds, tea and coffee-making supplies. Rooms have either one or two double beds and are bright with upgraded windows and solid wood doors. There's a nightclub in the same building so this is not a quiet area, but care has been given to making rooms as soundproof as possible. A buffet breakfast is served in a bright eating area—$6 in high season; free the rest of the year. Doubles $119.

YWCA Hotel
733 Beatty at Georgia
895-5830
1-800-663-1424 toll free (B.C. and Alberta)

There are 155 rooms on 12 floors; all are bright and cozy. Hardly as basic as "Y" rooms of the past, all have telephones and mini-refrigerators, and there are shared kitchens, TV lounges and laundry facilities. Rooms vary in size; they can accommodate single travellers or families of five. There are both private and shared bathrooms.

Guests have the use of the Health and Wellness Centre at the YWCA co-ed facility at Hornby near Dunsmuir. The indoor pool, steam room, classes in aerobics and aqua fitness, and full exercise facilities are free to Y hotel guests, but massage and other treatments cost extra.

Although this hotel, opened in 1995, is not as close to the business district as the old Y, this location is a short walk to B.C. Place Stadium and General Motors Place and is in the same neighbourhood as Library Square, the Ford Centre for the Performing Arts and the Queen Elizabeth Theatre. It is mere minutes to Stadium SkyTrain Station. No other central location with modern facilities is this cheap. Credit cards accepted. Weekly and monthly rates available. Doubles $65.

Kingston Hotel
757 Richards near Robson
684-9024
Fax 684-9917

The Kingston is a bargain for backpackers and anyone else who wants a cheap, clean, no-frills hotel in the centre of the city. Care has been taken to give this small hotel a warm atmosphere—it's more like a European hotel, complete with continental breakfast. Rooms are small but clean. Prices are reasonable because extras such as room service and TVs have been eliminated, and of the 60 rooms, only 7 have private baths. The Kingston is four storeys high and has no elevator. All rooms have telephones; laundry, sauna and parking are available. Weekly and monthly rates available. Doubles $50.

Robson Street

A stay on Robson St means you are in the heart of the action—close to downtown, Stanley Park and the beaches. It is always lively—some of the city's classiest shops are here, and there are many choices when it comes to restaurants.

See also All-Suite Hotels (Pacific Palisades).

Listel Vancouver
1300 Robson at Jervis
684-8461
1-800-663-5491 toll free
Fax 684-7092

What happens when a small hotel joins forces with a small gallery? Stay at Listel Vancouver and see for yourself. Formerly called O'Doul's Hotel (the bar and restaurant are still O'Doul's), the rooms and suites of this 129-room, four-star hotel have refined furnishings and amenities like dataport capabilities, voice mail, hair dryers, ironing supplies and same-day dry cleaning. There are also extras like the inviting chaise lounge beside a wide window and goose-down duvets. But the pièce de résistance is the Listel's wonderful art. Exiting an elevator on one of the Gallery Floors you view a stunning exhibit, and then you find your room adorned with originals and limited editions of renowned artists—perhaps Bernard Cathelin's peaceful landscapes. The 52 Gallery Rooms (including four suites) have been "curated" by Buschlen Mowatt Galleries and have the ambience of a tastefully designed home. The location and security features (like key-activated elevators and a security gate on the parking lot) have always made this boutique hotel popular, and O'Doul's is known for its brunch and great jazz. Now there is another reason to stay, especially if you appreciate art. Doubles $240.

Riviera Hotel
1431 Robson near Broughton
685-1301
1-888-699-5222 (toll free)
Fax 685-1335
The Riviera originated as a 1960s apartment building. Now it has 13 large studios and 27 one-bedrooms that are spotlessly clean. It's easy to overlook drawbacks like the one small elevator and no bellhop when you consider that all rooms have balconies and well-equipped kitchens, complete with coffeemaker and free coffee. The view of the harbour and the North Shore mountains from the back of the building is terrific. There's also free parking and the location is great—it's about a 10-minute walk to the park and the same to shopping and restaurants. Doubles $128.

West End

Although the West End is a little removed from city centre, it wraps around English Bay and borders Stanley Park. A walk to downtown is about 15 minutes.

The Westin Bayshore Hotel
1601 W Georgia at Cardero
682-3377
1-800-228-3000 toll free
Fax 687-3102
Overlooking the scenic harbour and sitting next door to Stanley Park, the Bayshore is a city hotel with the feel of a resort. Its trademark is the

friendly doormen in decorative Beefeater outfits.

Rooms are available in a tower and a low-rise built around a large outdoor pool and garden, with a marina and the ocean at your feet. All 517 rooms have been refurnished and have a bright, fresh look; the tower rooms are larger and have views and balconies. The best views are on the north or west side of the tower.

Stay at the Bayshore if you want the advantage of a short walk to the Stanley Park seawall; it's definitely more relaxing than staying downtown. A shuttle bus takes you to the heart of downtown in 5 minutes. Doubles $224.

English Bay Inn
1968 Comox at Chilco
683-8002
This beautifully renovated, 1930s five-room inn is a Vancouver treasure. Exquisitely furnished—all rooms but one have a sleigh bed or 18th-century four-poster—it is on a quiet street close to English Bay and Stanley Park. All rooms have private baths.

Breakfast is served in a formal dining room complete with Gothic dining suite, fireplace and grandfather clock. The parlour is elegant and comfortable with high wingbacked armchairs, thick British-India rugs and exquisite antiques. Touches like sherry and port in the parlour each afternoon or, if you prefer, tea or coffee served in your room make a stay here memorable. A small private garden can be enjoyed by guests.

In 1998, the owner added two rooms in the Chilco House across the street. This house is from the same era as the inn, has a lovely sitting room and dining space and faces a small park. The bedrooms are larger and the same care has been given to decor. Frankly, you don't often see furnishings like this.

Unless you prefer the anonymity of a large hotel, this is undoubtedly the best place to stay in Vancouver. Doubles $190 at English Bay Inn and $210 at Chilco House.

Rosellen Suites
2030 Barclay at Chilco
689-4807
Fax 684-3327

The plain exterior of this four-storey apartment hotel makes the black, beige and peach designer furniture in some of the suites even more striking. All of the suites are spacious and amenities in the 30 one- and two-bedroom units include microwaves, remote-control TV, tape decks, voice mail, twice-weekly maid service, washers and dryers, and fully equipped kitchens with juice, tea and coffee to get you started. Each unit is individually decorated and some two-bedrooms have fireplaces and dishwashers. Free health club facilities are in the neighbourhood. The Rosellen caters to the film industry, executive travellers and families. Minimum stay is three nights, and prices go down the longer you stay. Limited parking. Located on a pretty, tree-lined street, the Rosellen is only a few minutes walk to Stanley Park, shops and restaurants. In short, a home away from home. Doubles $175.

Sunset Inn
1111 Burnaby (near Davie and Thurlow)
688-2474
1-800-786-1997 toll free
Fax 669-3340

Thanks to constant upgrading, Sunset Inn continues to be one of the best of several West End apartment buildings that have been converted into hotels. All units—studios and one-bedrooms—have kitchens and balconies. The one-bedrooms have sofa beds and sleep four. The hotel is well maintained and has laundry facilities and underground parking. Located close to shops and buses; it's a 10-minute walk from downtown. Particularly recommended for families and/or long stays. Weekly and monthly rates available except in July and Aug. Doubles $158.

West End Guest House
1362 Haro near Jervis
681-2889
Fax 688-8812

Although it is only one block from the action and glitz of Robson St, this carefully restored Victorian house suggests the comforts and pace of another era. Step into the parlour, and you'll find an old gramophone in immaculate condition, cozy overstuffed furniture and sherry. The original owners had a photography business, and so the early years of the West Coast are chronicled throughout the house in dozens of wonderful old photographs. The eight guest rooms are beautifully furnished, and there are extras like the terry bathrobes and knitted slippers. You're guaranteed a good sleep on feather mattress pads. Each room has a private bathroom, telephone and TV. Breakfast is served in an exquisitely appointed dining room or in bed, if you choose!

In the afternoon, guests gather for sherry in the parlour or iced tea under the shade of the canopy on the sun deck. Parking is available. Doubles $110.

Buchan Hotel
1906 Haro (near Robson and Denman)
685-5354
Fax 685-5367

Located on a quiet, tree-lined West End street, the Buchan is a small, inexpensive hotel. All 64 rooms are meticulously clean, though some are small and half have shared

The Sylvia Hotel on English Bay is a landmark heritage building. (Rosamond Norbury)

bathrooms (these feature an in-room sink). A standard double has two double beds. For the budget-conscious, this is a good deal. Rooms on the east side are brighter and overlook a mini-park. There is a large lounge, and throughout the hotel are some great historical photographs of B.C.

The staff is friendly and helpful, but at these prices some of the usual hotel services are missing. There is no elevator or coffee shop, but there is a laundry room, and vending machines provide snacks. Underground

parking is available nearby. Stanley Park is at your doorstep, and so are the shops and restaurants on Robson and Denman. English Bay beach is 5 minutes away, and downtown is a 15-minute walk. Weekly rates available. Doubles (with bathroom) $108; for four this room is $128.

Sylvia Hotel
1154 Gilford at Beach
681-9321

The ivy-covered Sylvia Hotel evolves but it doesn't really change. The friendly manager says that while they constantly upgrade, they are inclined to paint and recover the same furniture simply because this is what people expect when they come to the Sylvia. The 119-room hotel, built in 1912, has one of the most admirable occupancy rates of any Vancouver hotel. Repeat clients come for the English Bay location, excellent prices and cheerful staff. There are seven configurations of rooms; all have a full bath and 23 have kitchens. The decor is plain but the views are among the city's finest—try to get one facing south or south-west.

The Sylvia Restaurant, which also has good prices, has outdoor dining in the summer and is one of the city's best places to people-watch and catch the sunset. Although the decor in the lobby lounge is uninspiring, it also has a view and is a much-frequented bar.

Because of the Sylvia's popularity, it is necessary to book well in advance for a summer stay. Doubles $65.

Kitsilano

Kenya Court Guest House
2230 Cornwall near Yew
738-7085

So named because the original owner had lived in Kenya, this 1920s guest house facing Kitsilano Beach is a great alternative to staying downtown. It has four units: large one- and two-bedroom apartments that sleep up to six, with tasteful period furnishings and gleaming hardwood floors. ("Immaculate" is taken to new heights here.) All units have kitchens and one unit has a back deck. The friendly couple who run Kenya Court serve a complimentary breakfast simply because Dorothy loves to cook. To reach the rooftop solarium you go through their apartment and up a winding staircase. The breathtaking view of English Bay and the North Shore mountains, along with Dorothy's cooking, is a wonderful introduction to a Vancouver day. Your hosts speak Italian, French and German. On-street parking. Book well in advance for the summer. No credit cards. Doubles $125.

Near the Airport

Radisson President Hotel & Suites
8181 Cambie Rd at No. 3 Rd, Richmond
276-8181
1-800-333-3333 (worldwide)
The Radisson, with a four-diamond AAA/CAA rating, has a modernistic sweeping glass exterior and a lobby highlighted by an open staircase and an impressive two-storey-high glass chandelier.

The 184 guest rooms (39 are suites) are smart and sensible rather than elegant in decor but have many amenities. Each room has a coffeemaker, hair dryer, ironing supplies, safe and refrigerator, as well as two telephones, voice mail and dataport. This hotel, with its first-class business centre and close-to-the-the-airport location, is a favourite with the business set.

The Radisson has an international feel to it, and no wonder—there is a Chinese supermarket and Buddhist temple in the adjacent complex, and the President Chinese Restaurant is renowned for its authentic Cantonese delicacies. Gustos Eurobistro specializes in Mediterranean fusion cuisine. There is a fitness centre complete with pool, whirlpool and exercise area. The hotel is 5 minutes from the airport via the free shuttle service. It's also within walking distance of several large shopping malls and a short drive to golf courses. Doubles $210.

Delta Vancouver Airport Hotel & Marina
3500 Cessna, Richmond
278-1241
1-800-268-1133 toll free
Fax 276-1975
Its location beside the Fraser River gives this 418-room hotel a peaceful feel even though it's close to the airport. All rooms have views— the south side is best—and some have balconies. The rooms are well kept and cater to business clientele. There is an outdoor pool, small weight room and a jogging route along the river; guests have full use of the exceptional facilities at the nearby Delta Pacific Resort & Conference Centre. There are charter boat trips available at the marina just outside the door. A shuttle is available to and from the airport and to Lansdowne Shopping Centre. Doubles $155.

Two new prestigious hotels will open close to the airport in late 1999. A Canadian Pacific Hotel (1-800-441-1414)—400 rooms and conference centre—will be attached to the International Terminal. A 237-room Hilton Hotel (1-800-HILTONS) with full business facilities will be a 5-minute drive away at Westminster Hwy and Minoru Blvd.

Kingsway/Metrotown

Holiday Inn
4405 Central Boulevard near McKay
438-1881
1-800-465-4329 toll free

This 100-room highrise, attached to B.C.'s largest shopping and entertainment complex, is a short walk to 450 stores, dozens of theatres, arcades and restaurants, and is only 15 minutes from the centre of Vancouver as a walkway connects it to the SkyTrain. Rooms, redecorated in 1998, have a full range of amenities, including coffeemaker, refrigerator and in-room movies. There is an outdoor pool. To escape the busyness of Metrotown, guests can take a 15-minute walk to Central Park, a large, wooded area with trails as well as pitch and putt, playground, playing fields and Swangard Stadium sports events. Doubles $149.

2400 Motel
2400 Kingsway at Nanaimo
434-2464
Fax 430-1045

The 2400 has an old-fashioned but appealing look with white bungalows that house 60 units. The bungalows are spotless and have full kitchens, good-size rooms and front and back doors. The grounds are landscaped, and pets are allowed. A playground, park, shops and restaurants are nearby. Try to get a unit at the back as Kingsway is busy. Two-diamond AAA/CAA rating. Doubles $85.

North Shore

Although the North Shore, particularly West Vancouver, is a delightful place, it is difficult to recommend staying there because of the horrendous rush-hour traffic around Lions Gate Bridge. If you choose to stay on the North Shore, plan your day to avoid the bridge at rush hours.

Park Royal Hotel
540 Clyde off Taylor, West Van
926-5511
Fax 926-6082

Call months in advance to stay at the Park Royal. The 30-room hotel is tucked back on the bank of the Capilano River. The ivy-covered building is Tudor in style, and the atmosphere is British country inn, with exposed beams, stone fireplaces and a pub. Rooms are small and cozy, and the ones on the garden side are favourites. From the patio and gardens you can enjoy the view of the river and the surrounding woods, or you can go for a stroll along the riverbank. It's hard to believe that Park Royal Shopping Centre is just minutes away. The hotel is tricky to find; go over Lions Gate Bridge, head into West Vancouver and take the first right onto Taylor Way; then turn right immediately at Clyde Ave. Doubles $155.

There is a small string of motels on Capilano Rd just above Marine. The best are:

Holiday Inn Express Vancouver, North Shore
1800 Capilano off Marine
987-4461
1-800-663-4055
Fax 984-4244
Doubles $135.

Lions Gate Travelodge
2060 Marine near Capilano
985-5311
1-800-578-7878 toll free
Fax 985-5311
Doubles $110

Canyon Court Motel
1748 Capilano off Marine
988-3181
Fax 990-1554, local 391
Doubles $105.

All-Suite Hotels

With most of the amenities of a well-equipped home plus the convenience of a hotel, all-suite hotels have become popular, particularly with corporate clients.

La Grande Résidence
855 Burrard at Smithe
682-5511
1-800-961-7555 toll free
Fax 682-5513

La Grand Résidence is a luxury apartment building connected to and run by the Sutton Place Hotel. It has maid service, 24-hour switchboard, front desk, concierge and all of the other services of the five-diamond hotel. A home away from home where staff will change a flat tire, sew on a button, organize a party or buy groceries. This 18-storey building has 162 completely equipped one- and two-bedroom apartments. Typical of Sutton Place, everything is of exceptional quality, and furnishings are tasteful. All units have dishwashers, microwaves and balconies with patio furniture, and there is storage for bicycles or skis. VCRs are available, and there are also free bicycles for guest use. Views are best on the quiet west side. Spa facilities are shared with Sutton Place Hotel, where the indoor pool opens onto a sunny deck. Guests are just a few steps away from the excellent restaurant and bar in the hotel. Minimum stay is 7 nights; rates are $159–$255 per night.

Pacific Palisades Hotel
1277 Robson at Jervis
688-0461
1-800-663-1815 toll free

The only North American property of the prestigious Shangri-La Hotel Group, the Palisades is a remarkable complex of all-suite accommodation that simply keeps getting better.

The original Pacific Palisades consists of twin 21-floor towers with 233 suites. Some are Executive Suites that have balconies, are very large and are worth the extra dollars. The deluxe rooms are above the tenth floor and have excellent views and extras such as fresh flowers, three phones and two TV sets. The Palisades caters to business clients and is also popular with the swarms of movie people who frequent this city. Benefits include the excellent Monterey Lounge & Grill (see Restaurants, Outdoors), and a huge health club complete with a lap pool, exercise machines, a juice bar, tanning rooms, an outdoor patio and mountain bike rentals. (It's a 5-minute ride to Stanley Park.) Weekly and monthly rates available. Doubles $195.

Additions made over the last few years include 300 extended-stay rooms in four new towers. Most recently opened in April 1998 was The Residences on Georgia. These exquisite one-, two- and three-bedroom suites are every long-term traveller's dream accommodation: earth tones, clean lines, comfortable contemporary furnishings, tasteful art, just the right touches of colour to add warmth, and windows that show off the best of Vancouver. Kitchens are small but well equipped and there are in-suite laundry facilities. All suites have offices with fibreoptic fax and computer technology (there's a direct internet line). The extras are impressive: grocery-shopping service, private concierge, a putting green and, would you believe, a Hollywood-style screening room with a super selection of movies. These amenities are also available in two lovely suites in The Abbott House, a restored heritage home on the property. These new, extended-stay suites start at $3,100 a month.

Delta Vancouver Suite Hotel
550 W Hastings near Seymour
689-8188

This 23-floor hotel opened its doors in March 1998 and put out the welcome mat for business people, with amenities tailored to this clientele: ideal location, fully "wired" guest suites offering extra space for work or meetings, good workout facilities, 24-hour room service and a full-service restaurant. The four-storey lobby has a low-key decor, and Delta's elite clients are guaranteed a one-minute check-in. Extras include two phone lines in each suite, speaker phone, ergonomically designed office chair and a desk on rollers that can be easily moved. Computers and printers are available in the well-equipped business centre or can be brought to the rooms. The Manhattan Restaurant could soon become numbered among the city's hot culinary experiences: its chef comes from one of Vancouver's finest dining rooms. Doubles $240.

Rosedale on Robson
838 Hamilton at Robson
689-8033
1-800-661-8870 toll free
Fax: 689-4426

The Rosedale is located a short walk away from Library Square, the Ford Centre, GM Place and Yaletown. There are 275 one- and two-bedroom suites; each has a separate living room, fully equipped kitchenette (coffee and tea included), minibar, TVs in living room and bedrooms (they have Nintendo), hair dryers, ironing supplies and desk with dataport and voice mail. Every odd-numbered floor has laundry facilities, and you can arrange for extra dishes and linens. Parking is complimentary with a long-term stay. Five spacious suites on the top floor have amenities such as robes, newspaper and complimentary local calls. Corner rooms have two bay windows that give sweeping views. There is a business centre as well as a fitness centre with a lap pool and exercise equipment. As soon as the Rosedale opened in spring 1995, Rosie's, the fun deli/restaurant, became a hit. Guests can get deli goodies here or the basics from a convenience store in the hotel. Doubles $225.

See also Sheraton Wall Centre, Sunset Inn and Rosellen Suites, this chapter.

Alternative Accommodation

If you want well-priced accommodation and don't mind being in close quarters with others, consider dormitory-style rooms.

Walter Gage Residence
Student Union Blvd at Wesbrook Mall
University of British Columbia
822-1010
Fax 822-1001

The residence, open to the public May, June, July and Aug, consists of three towers with a total of 1200 rooms. Six single bedrooms are clustered around a kitchen (with limited cooking facilities), bathroom and living room to form self-contained units.

Single accommodation is provided in these rooms for about $33 a person. Self-contained studios and one-bedroom suites are available for single or double accommodation at $59–105 for the room. Larger suites at $100, usually reserved for families, are the only units available all year. Free visitor parking is next to the residence, and meals are available at the Student Union Building across the street (the food is not bad). Dinner is served daily. UBC is a 20-minute drive from downtown.

Hostelling International—Downtown
1114 Burnaby St at Thurlow
684-4565
Fax 684-4540

The newest of Vancouver's two hostels is modern and bright with room for 239 people. There are 7 double rooms here, unusual in a hostel where most are dormitory style. There is a fully equipped kitchen, laundry facilities, large dining room plus activity space—library, garden patio, games and meeting rooms. Bikes can be rented or stored. This is a very secure hostel with key cards. There is a free shuttle between this hostel and the one at Jericho Beach (see below) as well as to the bus station. Both hostels have visitor information and guest activity desks where a wide range of activities can be booked. An adult Canadian Hostelling Association membership is $27 a year. Member rates for a night here are $19; nonmembers $23.

Hostelling International—Jericho Beach
1515 Discovery near 4th
224-3208
Fax 224-4852

Located beside one of the city's finest beaches and adjacent to tennis courts and a sailing club, this hostel is a favourite. Despite its origin as an air force barracks, the renovated building is far from bleak. Its only drawback is that it's a 30-minute bus ride from downtown.

Food at the hostel is good and cheap. Breakfast and dinner are served during the summer, or you can cook meals in the fully equipped kitchen. There is separate sleeping accommodation for men and women. There are also private rooms, and some are suitable for families. (These must be booked ahead.) Sleeping bags, sheets and blankets are available free. No pets. The hostel has a coin-op laundry, storage facilities, satellite TV and mountain-bike rentals. Parking is available. Unlike some, this hostel is open 24 hours. Although the capacity is 285, you may need a reservation (including one night's deposit) from May to Sept. Members stay for $16 a day, and nonmembers for $20. MasterCard or Visa accepted.

Bed and Breakfast

In Vancouver

A bed-and breakfast stay offers a chance to mingle with the locals. Breakfast-table conversation may cover local politics or the best place to take a tranquil walk, and you could find yourself swapping travel tales with other globetrotters from as far afield as Australia or South Africa.

Don't worry about privacy. The hosts are friendly but seem to know just how much interaction guests want. They will make every effort to ensure that your stay is as private and comfortable as you wish.

Bed and breakfast registries represent homes throughout the city (or the province), with accommodation ranging from a basic room to a gorgeous-view suite. Using a registry is convenient as they do the shopping for you and recommend their listed properties. (Should you have a complaint, and it doesn't happen often, the registry wants to hear about it.)

The advantages of B&Bs are price, which may be less than half what downtown hotels charge; variety; and more contact with the locals.

Some B&Bs accept children, some have facilities for people with disabilities, and some take pets. Discounts may be available for long stays or for off season. MasterCard and Visa are generally, but not always, accepted. Book well in advance. The price for a double with a shared bath is about $95; those with a private bath start at about $105.

There are many B&B registries in the city, and we recommend the two listed below.

Town and Country Bed and Breakfast Registry
731-5942

BayView B&B at Green Gables West

If you appreciate astounding views, old English gardens and elegant surroundings, head to the BayView B&B in a quiet cul-de-sac in West Vancouver. Elaborate wall coverings and bedding, exquisite furnishings and a fine selection of Canadian art make this B&B special. There are three suites with private baths and sitting rooms; in each you can lie in bed and see Lion's Gate Bridge backed by Stanley Park and the city. The downstairs suite is large with a kitchen, queen-size sofa-bed and private entrance. A generous deck overlooks the luxuriant garden, the ocean and the city. A four-course breakfast includes fresh baking. Close to West Vancouver beaches, seawalk and shops, and a 15-minute drive to city centre. Doubles $135–$200.

View of the Bay

This is a large blue house in the heart of Kitsilano that has a great view of English Bay. Your hosts, Helen and Tom Kritharis, are from Greece; there is a European graciousness here, and the white walls and large windows give a definite Grecian feel to the house on a sunny day. One room is upstairs with private bathroom and a deck where many guests choose to have lunch on warm days. The 600-square-foot suite at the back, complete with a large sitting room and closed-off loft

bedroom that has a queen-size bed plus a twin bed, is ideal for a family. There is a private entrance, and parking is available.

You can walk to the beach, Kitsilano Pool, Vanier Park or 4th Ave, and there's easy access by bus to downtown or UBC. Doubles $95–$120.

Graeme's House

Through a pretty arbour and along a walk bordered by greenery, you come to Graeme's house, which is rather like a country cottage. French doors open to a patio, sunshine streams through a bedroom bay window, and the two bedrooms in crisp blue and white instantly feel like home. The Iris Room has a queen-sized bed and stained-glass window, and the Cornflower Room has twin beds and opens to the quiet back yard. They share a bath. A stay with Graeme is the way B&B was originally meant to be: you are welcomed into a cozy home just as though you were a long-lost friend. Children are welcome but pets are not as there is a resident cat. Located in Kitsilano, convenient to public transit, beaches, UBC and bustling Broadway and 4th Ave. Doubles $65–$85.

Old English Bed and Breakfast Registry
986-5069
Fax 986-8810

Queen Anne Manor

This new, Victorian-style home is jaw-droppingly beautiful. More like an elegant inn than a B&B, it features exquisite decor and extras like the sound system that can be controlled in each room, the bright atrium breakfast area that backs onto a lush green hillside, high vaulted ceilings, tasteful antiques and private library. There are three guest rooms. The Primrose Room and Mulberry Room share a bathroom. The Chelsea Suite is spacious with an antique brass canopied bed, fireplace, sitting area and large Jacuzzi. Breakfast on the balcony is an option. All the rooms have duvets and handmade quilts.

The Queen Anne is a short walk to the ocean or the charming waterfront village of Deep Cove (about 30 minutes' drive from the city centre). Children over 12 are welcome. Excellent value for your money here. Doubles $95–$175.

Room with a View

Welcome to the early days of Vancouver. This Edwardian character home, circa 1912, has a garden bursting with colour, a cheerful host and a friendly springer spaniel. If you didn't go out the door, you'd swear you were in a family home from another era. Because this was once a boarding house, each of the large upstairs guest rooms has a small kitchen/eating area. The room with the view—the cityscape backed by mountains—has a full kitchen. The other room has a small fridge, toaster, sink and basic dishes. Guests can choose to be served breakfast ("healthy continental," but special requests are taken) or bring in their own breakfast makings. There are lovely touches like lace curtains and old wrought-iron beds. The rooms share a bathroom that has access to a wisteria-draped deck through a large stained-glass window. There is a private outside staircase entrance. Guests can mingle with the family downstairs if they wish. Doubles $90 with breakfast or $80 if you do your own.

Norgate Park House Bed & Breakfast

Tucked into a quiet and very ordinary North Vancouver neighbourhood, this B&B is a find. The cedar-sided rancher has a strong West Coast ambience, because of both the aesthetically pleasing renovations and the private garden. The three downstairs guest rooms are cheerful and comfy, share a bathroom and are in a private wing, open to the outdoors. The upstairs room has a queen-size brass bed, private bath, large closet and sofa-bed couch. There is a charming den with fireplace and lots of books. Be prepared: your host, Vicki Tyndall, will take your picture to include in her guest book. She is happy to cater to specific breakfast needs. The Norgate takes children over 12. It is close to a park, transportation to Vancouver—15 minutes from the city centre—and shopping areas. Doubles $95–$115.

Near Vancouver

If you prefer a quiet country ambience or an island retreat, here are two B&Bs where you can't go wrong and you are still close enough to sightsee in the city.

Ladner
River Run Cottages
4551 River Road W, Ladner
946-7778

You will look long and hard to find a more romantic getaway than River Run Cottages. Located in the sleepy fishing and farming community of Ladner, River Run Cottages are the stuff of picture postcards. Large decks overlook the Fraser River, in summer hanging baskets explode with colour and fresh herbs, and you're in your own private community—just you and the river view, shared with ducks, swans, loons, eagles and seals.

Waterlily, a homey houseboat, is small but is a favourite, with its queen-size loft bed, claw-foot tub, potbelly stove and private deck. The other suites, *The Northwest Room*, *The Keepers Quarters* and *Net Loft,* line the river bank, are more spacious, open to large decks and are beautifully furnished. Each cottage has a wood-

Water Lily, a floating B&B on the Fraser River, puts a new perspective on a home away from home. (River Run)

burning stove, separate telephone line and a CD player.

Kayaks and bicycles are available. You can walk the dyke into Ladner, cycle to the George C. Reifel Migratory Bird Sanctuary (see Parks/Beaches/Gardens) or catch a ferry to one of the Gulf Islands for the day (see Excursions from Vancouver). It's a 30-minute drive to city centre. Doubles $140–$175.

Bowen Island

Seaside Reflections
365 Cardena Dr, Bowen Island
1-604-947-0937
The ultimate escape. Tucked above Snug Cove, the expansive decks and full-length windows give an outdoor feeling to this adult-oriented B&B. The guest room is lovely, with flowered chintz drapes and spread, and the Snuggler's Den is a cozy haven where you can spend hours with a book after walking the nearby wooded trails. A couple on their own can use both rooms, but it also works for two couples since the den has a comfortable, queen-size pull-out bed.

The two rooms and bathroom are on a lower level and are very private. There is a choice of continental or brunch-style breakfast served on the deck or in the dining room. Freshly squeezed juices, artistically designed fruit trays, and specials featuring healthy, organic dishes are a great way to start the day. A perfect end could be candlelight and wine on your private deck overlooking the cove, mountains and Howe Sound. This place is peaceful and made for romance.

There are express West Vancouver buses (#257) from bus stops along Georgia in Vancouver (call 985-7777 for schedule). Ferries depart Horseshoe Bay between 6:05 AM and 9:25 PM daily. It's a 15-minute ride. Bowen has wonderful walks and a delightful small town to be explored. Rates vary depending on breakfast choice. Doubles $79.

Trailer Parks/Campgrounds

Prices listed here are for a medium-size RV or trailer and two people in

Bowen Island's Seaside Reflections is a peaceful retreat a short ferry ride away from Vancouver. (Seaside Reflections)

high season, with a full hookup if available.

In and Near Vancouver

Capilano Mobile RV Park
295 Tomahawk, West Van
987-4722
Underneath the north foot of the Lions Gate Bridge, beside the Capilano River. Trailers, tents and RVs on 208 sites. Newly renovated facilities include showers, Jacuzzi, games room, pool, laundry room and playground. Sani-station, propane. Reservations for June, July and Aug must be accompanied by a deposit. Surprisingly quiet, considering the proximity to the bridge. Adjacent to shopping centre, beach and park. Five minutes from downtown. $32.

Burnaby Cariboo RV Park
8765 Cariboo Place
Cariboo exit from Hwy 1, Burnaby
420-1722
This highly rated RV park offers a heated indoor pool, Jacuzzi, fitness room, store, sani-station, telephone jacks, laundry, free showers, cablevision and RV wash. Trailers, RVs and tents; 217 sites. Adjacent to Burnaby Lake Regional Park and pickup stop for Grayline Tours. $31.

Richmond RV Park
Hollybridge at River Rd, Richmond
270-7878
Open Apr 1 to Oct 31. Free showers, laundry, sani-station, propane, games room and mobile septic service. Tents, trailers, RVs; 200 sites. Close to miles of riverside trails and public transit. Central location. $22.

Near Tsawwassen

ParkCanada Recreational Vehicle Inn
4799 Hwy 17 (exit north on 52nd St), Delta
943-5811
Near the ferry terminal. Tents, RVs

and trailers; 150 sites. Laundry, free
and water park. $23.

White Rock

Sea Crest Motel and RV Park
864–160th St
531-4720
For RVs only; 31 sites. Showers, laundry; close to beach and golf course.
$23.

Parklander Motor and Trailer Court
16311–8th Ave
531-3711
"Adult oriented"; tents, trailers and
RVs; 31 sites in a parklike setting. No
pets. Showers. $20.

Hazelmere RV Park and Campground
18843–8th Ave at 188th St
538-1167
In a forest setting on the Campbell
River. Tents, RVs and trailers; 154
sites. Showers, laundry, propane,
sani-station, store. $22.

Surrey

Dogwood Campgrounds
15151–112th Ave
583-5585
Tents, RVs and trailers; 350 sites.
Showers, laundry, store, propane,
heated outdoor pool, Jacuzzi, playground, salmon bakes and bus tours.
Natural treed setting. Take the 160th
Ave exit from the Trans-Canada
Hwy. $26.

Tynehead RV Camp
16275–102nd Ave
589-1161
Tents, trailers and RVs; 190 sites.
Heated outdoor pool, showers,

laundry, lounge, store, mini-golf.
Adjacent to forest and near shopping
centre. $28.

Fraser River RV Park
11940 Old Yale Rd
580-1841
Beside the Fraser River. Tents, trailers
and RVs; 135 sites. Showers, laundry,
sani-station, dock, boat ramp and
pub. $21.

Peace Arch RV Park
14601–40th Ave
594-7009
Tents, RVs and trailers on 250 sites.
Heated pool, mini-golf, telephone
jacks, satellite TV, horseshoe pitch,
playground, laundry, free showers.
From Hwy 99 north, take the North
Delta exit and follow signs. $25.

Coquitlam/Port Moody

Four Acres Trailer Court
675 Lougheed Hwy, Coquitlam
936-3273
Close to Lougheed Mall. Trailers, RVs
and tents; 85 sites. Showers, laundry,
sani-station. $15.

Anmore Camplands
3230 Sunnyside, Port Moody
469-2311
Located at the entrance to beautifully
forested Buntzen Lake, with its
beaches and hiking trails. Tents, RVs
and trailers; 150 sites. Free showers,
security gate, laundry, sani-station,
store, heated outdoor pool, covered
barbecue area, fire pits, canoe rentals,
playground, sports court. Horse
rentals and guided trips available
next door at Alpine Riding Academy.
This is not an easy place to find, but
if you want a country stay with lots
of outdoor activity, it's worth the effort. Call first for directions. $25.

Restaurants

Chinese, East Indian, French, Greek, Italian, Japanese, Malaysian, Mexican, Spanish, Thai, Vietnamese/Cambodian, West Coast Native

Broadway (between Main and Granville), Chinatown, Downtown, East Side, Granville Island, Kitsilano/West Side, North Shore, South of 33rd Avenue, West End, Hotel Restaurants

Like all great cities, Vancouver has great restaurants—more than 3000. Picking and choosing from among this banquet is tough. We've included those "top restaurants" that everyone knows about, but this guide concentrates on the full dining picture. We detail, for example, where to find the most exotic of Asian dishes and the most unusual fusions of international fare, as well as an incredibly cheap tucked-away sushi spot or a plain-Jane establishment where the vegetarian crowd hangs out. Some restaurants listed here may seem modest but, when it comes to your palate, they are marvellous. We also include a guide to B.C. estate wines, another on healthy eating in Vancouver and one on "Ten Cheap Treats."

Hotel restaurants have emerged as purveyors of haute cuisine. Gone are the days when you automatically avoided them if you were looking for culinary adventure. Some of Vancouver's award-winning restaurants—acclaimed throughout the continent—are in fine hotels. This trend has prompted us to add a hotel listing at the end of the chapter.

Eating Asian has become de rigueur in Vancouver. Chuchow-style noodle soup from southern China, spicy, succulent satays, geoduck drenched in chilied soya, crisp, chubby *dhosas* that you'd swear were made in India—anything and everything you desire.

Vancouver, of course, offers many other ethnic dining choices, including Italian, French, Greek, Mexican, Jewish and others. Don't overlook our West Coast cuisine, whether it be our famous salmon, organically grown greens or just-plucked fruit baked into a flavourful tart. These dishes radiate freshness.

We recommend the restaurants listed. We visit and eat without identifying ourselves; we ask locals, con-

duct surveys and we seek out experts. However, despite our research, chefs move on, doors close, menus change and a dining experience is a very personal one. These are our choices because each one, whatever its price range, reliably gives good value.

Restaurants marked with one $ are inexpensive; dinner for two, excluding a glass of wine and tip, costs less than $40. In a moderate restaurant ($$), expect to pay $40–$80; and in an expensive restaurant ($$$), more than $80.

One way to figure out a standard tip (12 to 20 per cent) is to double the Goods and Services Tax of 7 per cent, which is applied to all restaurant meals.

Breakfast/Brunch

Fleuri Restaurant $$$
The Sutton Place Hotel
845 Burrard near Robson
682-5511
The refined atmosphere of an elegant manor, discreet service and the sound of classical music—everything about the Fleuri guarantees a gentle entry into a morning. The surroundings are so soothing and the food is so good. As well as the usual run of pancakes and eggs, wake up over crêpes, or venture into a Japanese breakfast: miso soup, raw egg, rice and broiled salmon. The Fleuri is known for having the city's best Sunday brunch, which includes all the usual breakfast fare plus chef-prepared omelets while you watch, seafood specials and a mind-boggling array of desserts. You can also bask in Fleuri's relaxed ambience over lunch, when the menu emphasizes fresh West Coast cuisine, or in the evening, when you can choose from classic European dishes, some prepared with an Asian flair. True chocoholics frequent the

heavily laden chocolate buffet table. Brunch Sun and holidays. Breakfast, lunch and dinner daily.

Gladys $
2153 W 4th near Vine
738-0828

Sometimes when visiting a city, it's fun to breakfast with the locals. In Kitsilano, that means going to Gladys or Sophie's (see below).

Fans travel across the city for Gladys's down-home corned beef hash—bacon, mushrooms, onions, potatoes, spices and the best corned beef. For a more refined breakfast, there's smoked salmon Benedict on a bagel or omelets, French toast and hot cakes.

Gladys's dinners are comfort food—beef stew, barbecued ribs, liver and onions, pastas and seasonal greens. Breakfast is served 8 AM–3 PM; arrive early on weekends, since there's often a line-up by 10. Open daily. Closes at 4 on Mon.

Isadora's Co-operative Restaurant $
1540 Old Bridge, Granville Island
681-8816

Isadora's is the best place in Vancouver to take children for a weekend brunch. Windows on one side overlook the Granville Island water park. There's an indoor play area, children's servings and change tables in both washrooms. Isadora's has good cappuccino, a tasty selection of brunch classics and a sunny, glad-to-greet-the-day atmosphere.

The rest of the day's menu is modern eclectic: herbal fish cakes, healthy pizzas, salads and burgers (including a nutburger). There's a Fast Track lunch of soup and half-sandwich—if you aren't out within half an hour, Isadora pays the $5.95. This is popular for family brunch so go before 10 if you don't want to wait in line. Reservations for six or more. Brunch Sat and Sun; lunch

and dinner daily (no dinner Mon, Sept to May).

Sophie's Cosmic Cafe $
2095 W 4th Ave at Arbutus
732-6810

Even on a weekday loyal locals wait for a table so they can dig into a Sophie's breakfast. There's a large selection of Eggs Benedict; spicy Mexican eggs à la sausage, peppers and onions (made even hotter if you wish by using the hot pepper sauce that comes in wine bottles), but there's also a "light and low cholesterol" breakfast option. Even the "light" is generous in size.

Sophie's is diner decor—booths with red plastic seats and walls loaded with '50s and '60s kitsch. Anyone recognize the "Peanuts" lunch kit? Unless you enjoy line-ups, go during the week. Open daily (8 AM), breakfast, lunch and dinner.

The Tomahawk $
1550 Philip near Marine, North Van
988-2612

The Tomahawk, established in 1926, hums with the happy voices of breakfast-lovers on any given morning. Servings here are gigantic. The Yukon breakfast is five slices of back bacon, two eggs, hash browns and toast. Everything is good—muffins are massive, pancakes are fluffy and the Klondike-style French toast is a winner. The staff is young, cheery and efficient. The decor is native museum style, with portraits of First Nations' royalty, baskets and carvings, settlers' tools—notice the hand-painted saw in the entry hall. Kids can colour the placemats. No reservations, no alcohol. Some breakfasts are served all day. Breakfast, lunch, dinner daily; opens at 8.

Also
Bacchus, see Lunch
Beach House at Dundarave Pier, see
  With a View

Ten Healthy Eats In Vancouver

Healthy, fresh dishes specializing in low fat and high fibre grace some of the city's finest restaurant tables. Today's chefs pride themselves on culinary treats that entice the palate, please the eye *and* help keep you healthy. Here's 10 healthy choices; those marked with a check adhere to the Heart and Stroke Foundation of B.C. & Yukon's Heart Smart Program.

✓1. **The Cannery**　　$$$
See Restaurants (Seafood).

2. **Capers**　　$
　1675 Robson near Bidwell
　687-5288
Casual eatery tucked into a lavish produce, health-products store that serves healthy light meals. Also in West Vancouver.

3. **The Dish**　　$
　1068 Davie near Burrard
　689-0208
Healthy, tasty, fast food and juices.

✓4. **Fish House at Stanley Park**　$$$
See Restaurants (Seafood).

✓5. **Griffin's Restaurant**　　$$
　662-1900
One of Hotel Vancouver's three restaurants that offer healthy menu items. Griffin's is bright, cheerful and has à la carte or a full buffet.

✓6. **Joe Fortes Seafood House**　$$
　669-1940
A lively, San Francisco-style restaurant and bar (see also Nightlife, Lively Bars) with fresh West Coast cuisine.

✓7. **Rubina Tandoori**　　$$
See Restaurants (East Indian).

✓8. **Seasons in the Park**　　$$
See Restaurants (With a View).

✓9. **Surat Sweet Restaurant**　　$
　1938 W 4th Avenue near Maple
　733-7363
Gujurati Indian vegetarian food with a flair.

10. **Tomato Fresh Food Cafe**　$
　3305 Cambie near 17th Ave
　874-6020
Fabulous '50s decor and excellent, reasonably-priced dishes. Also take-out and catering.

Benny's Bagels, see Late Night
Monterey Grill, see Outdoors
The Naam, see Vegetarian
Seasons in the Park, see With a View
Teahouse, see Outdoors
　See Bakery Cafés, below.

Bakery Cafés

Ecco Il Pane　　$
238 W 5th near Alberta
873-6888
2563 W Broadway near Trafalgar
739-1314

Ecco Il Pane—"here is the bread"—was originally a Tuscan country-style bakery on quiet W 5th Ave. It gathered a following and expanded into a cozy eatery that also showcased the sumptuous hand-shaped, stone-hearth-baked breads. The second location on W Broadway is much larger and more stylish than casual. A special feature is the Italian-made, wood-burning stove, where you can observe hot loaves coming out of the oven. This location also serves light dinners.

　Both locations specialize in *pane*

(bread), *biscotti* (cookies) and *dolci* (sweet bread). In the morning, there's freshly squeezed orange juice and a breakfast *panino* (frittata on grilled asiago focaccia with roasted tomatoes). Drop by around noon to munch on a thick sandwich like the Mortadella—tomatoes and provolone cheese on rosemary focaccia.

Don't forget to buy your bread—there's a dozen varieties. You may come in with multigrain on your mind but leave with a loaf packed with green and black olives. For a special treat, don't miss the sour cherry chocolate. Open daily.

Savary Island Pie Company $
1533 Marine Dr near 15th, West Van
926-4021
This is a friendly neighbourhood bakery/restaurant. There's a selection of delicious baked goods, including muffins, cinnamon buns, seasonal pies and the best blueberry scones in town. There are also great snacks—like deep-crust pizza. You can stock up on goodies to take home such as a multigrain loaf or even a flaky piecrust. On weekends, in particular, it's busy all day and evening, since wine and beer on tap are served. The staff is friendly and efficient—if you are enjoying pie and coffee, they won't rush you out at closing time (11 PM). Open daily.

Terra Breads $
2380 W 4th near Vine
736-1838
Everything about Terra Breads is warm—the atmosphere, the terra cotta flagstones on the floor, the wide, wooden counters and especially the breads and treats. All Terra's breads are healthy (no fat, eggs, dairy products or preservatives) and crusty, since they're baked directly on the oven's stone hearth (no pans or tins used). Fragrant breads and buns come in 18 imaginative flavours, from multigrain to fig and anise. This makes for a delightfully bewildering choice so it is best to decide over a cappuccino and biscotti, or a sandwich and coffee, or perhaps a tea and scone. Hint: The homemade granola here is *the* best.

Terra Breads has a bakery only at Granville Island Public Market. Both locations are open daily.

Lunch

Bacchus Ristorante $$$
Wedgewood Hotel
845 Hornby near Robson
689-7777
A Vancouver food writer once stated that the Bacchus was perhaps the city's most under-appreciated fine restaurant. It may be true, but many do appreciate this Tuscan-style restaurant tucked into a popular hotel. Save it for days when lunch is the main event, then savour dishes like seafood fettucine with peppercorn sauce bookended by a butter lettuce salad with lemon pine-nut dressing and a chocolate pecan bourbon tart. Or feast on wonderful baked polenta with grilled ratatouille vegetables. Bacchus is a treat any hour of the day. High tea is finger sandwiches plus scones with the trimmings. There are many dinner favourites, but don't miss the minestrone soup. Open daily, breakfast, lunch and dinner. Brunch Sat and Sun.

Chartwell $$$
Four Seasons Hotel
791 W Georgia at Howe
689-9333
If you want to impress a business associate or perhaps get a head start on a new relationship, "do lunch" at Chartwell. Serious power lunchers know this is the right choice. Named for Winston Churchill's country

estate, it has the ambience of a classy British men's club, food that never fails to receive rave reviews and an award-winning wine list. What more do you need? Stilton fans must begin with the seasonal lettuces, walnut dressing, Stilton crumbles and peppered apple chips. There is a mouthwatering salmon dish—Tamari-barbecued salmon, coconut rice, wasabi honey sauce. Some come for the pan-seared veal liver accompanied by pancetta-whipped potatoes. Dessert lovers will revel in the offerings here. À la carte two- and three-course menus are available. A special pre-theatre menu is offered daily, 5:30–6:30. Lunch Mon to Fri; dinner daily.

Gallery Café $
Vancouver Art Gallery
Robson at Howe
688-2233

On a sunny day, meet friends at this upscale cafeteria and munch and mingle on the sunny patio. On a rainy day, meet friends here and afterwards stroll into the Vancouver Art Gallery, which is attached to the café. The fare is light meals, lots of salads, a limited selection of wine and beer, and killer desserts. Located in the heart of the city, it's packed at lunchtime, so somebody has to get there early to get a table. However, the line-up moves quickly. Open daily.

Tony's Neighbourhood Deli $
1046 Commercial at Napier
253-7422

To experience the ambience of "the Drive," as Commercial is known, and to taste the best *panini* sandwiches in town, go to Tony's. Originally a market that was once owned by a Tony, today's deli features rusticca breads and grilled focaccia sandwiches. The counter service offers a super selection of salamis, cheeses and vegetarian specials. Ironically, in Italian, *panini* means "little bread," but the sandwiches are definitely large. There's about a dozen varieties on the menuboard, which changes weekly depending on what's fresh in the markets.

Creaky wooden floors, small round tables—it ain't fancy, but the food is delicious and filling. Breakfast, lunch and dinner, Mon to Sat.

Water St Café $$
300 Water at Cambie, Gastown
689-2832

The homemade focaccia bread arrives warm, the steam clock "plays" just across the street and the service is cheerful and efficient. In Gastown, this is the place for lunch. Regulars love the Fanny Bay oysters sautéed with peppers, creamed sun-dried tomatoes and parmesan gratinee. Shoppers and sightseers fill up on pasta dishes such as potato gnocchi with shrimp and prosciutto in butternut squash and sage sauce. They'll cater to your appetite here: pasta dishes can be ordered in two sizes. Wine by the glass will set you up for many more hours in Gastown.

On a sunny day, reserve early for a table outside or by the windows. Do specify, since there are several tables here where you're in the midst of waiter and customer traffic. Lunch and dinner daily.

Also
Benny's Bagels, see Late Night
Bridges, see Outdoors
Le Crocodile, see French
CinCin, see Italian
Hon's Wun Tun House, see Chinese
Isadora's, see Breakfast/Brunch
Kirin, see Chinese
Pink Pearl, see Chinese
RainCity Grill, see Contemporary
Teahouse, see Outdoors
Topanga, see Mexican

Contemporary

Bishop's $$$
2183 W 4th near Yew
738-2025

Camouflaged by what appears to be a 4th Ave storefront, Bishop's is a haven of hospitality and sumptuous food. For many, it ranks as the city's finest dining experience. John Bishop, the consumate host, greets faithful followers and newcomers as special guests.

Dishes are what Bishop calls contemporary home cooking. That means a mixture of Northern Italian, nouvelle cuisine and East-West crossover. The daily specials are always worth ordering. Lamb receives rave reviews here—Australian ribs with bread crumbs and fresh mint balsamic glaze, served with mashed potatoes and caramelized root vegetables. Halibut is outstanding, as are other offerings such as pan-seared scallops scented with lemon grass and chervil, topped with a crisp potato pancake.

Everything about the restaurant is simple and in excellent taste, the better to focus your attention on the food. A "dessert technician" will visit your table and rhyme off an astonishing list of choices. Bishop's has one flaw: you often have to plan weeks ahead to get a reservation on a weekend. Dinner daily.

Diva at the Met $$$
645 Howe St near Georgia
602-7788

In most cases it is difficult for a hotel dining room to distinguish itself from the hotel. Not so with Diva. Its strong image is defined by a team of award-winning chefs and a decor enhanced with the exquisite glass art of Markian Olynyk, which forms the wall that separates this fine restaurant from the fine Metropolitan Hotel. Diva has won more awards than there is space to name. Suffice to say that *Gourmet Magazine* named it the top restaurant in Vancouver and hordes of diners agree. You can go for brunch (it has far more selection than the average) or pre-theatre to experience a set menu that may include luscious lamb sirloin served with sweet potato gnocchi and balsamic brown butter jus. Or go for

Diva at the Met is one of the city's finest dining rooms. (Diva)

the works on a special evening when you can truly appreciate dinners like roasted venison medallions, caramelized endive, Stilton brioche *panini*, port and sun-dried cranberry jus. Open daily.

RainCity Grill $$
1193 Denman at Morton
685-7337

Just a heartbeat away from English Bay and the seawall, RainCity Grill is known for its unusual menu items and its extraordinary range of wine served by the glass. The menu changes weekly but is always intriguing—breast of free-range chicken with coriander mustard seed, pepper cumin crust, braised carrots and Stilton mash or trout with grilled apple brie, butternut squash, radicchio and brown rice are examples. A wine (or in some cases, ale) is suggested for each meal.

The RainCity is fancy enough for a special occasion, but you won't feel out of place if you've just walked the seawall. The small outdoor patio offers people-watching as well as the panorama of English Bay, although it is on a busy corner. The RainCity gets an incredible amount of drop-in traffic, so reservations are recommended. Brunch Sat and Sun; lunch and dinner daily.

Star Anise $$$
1485 W 12th Ave near Granville
737-1485

Star Anise instantly wraps you in its elegant arms. At a quiet corner table you leave the city's frenetic pace to enjoy fresh, innovative food. An unusual appetizer of sweet breads served between layers of oven-dried tomatoes and crispy wontons can start you off. A pleasing vegetarian entrée may be a whole sweet red onion with eggplant and carrot mousse encapsulated in puff pastry. Star Anise always seems to be full yet

the service is excellent. Despite the fact that it can be crowded, it's still ideal for a romantic dinner. Lunch Mon to Fri; dinner daily.

Seafood

C $$$
2–1600 Howe St near Pacific Blvd
681-1164

Seafood aficionados rejoiced when C opened in May 1997—adventurous offerings by an adventurous chef! Consider the more than a dozen "raw bar" selections, including a tartare trio of scallop, wasabi salmon and smoked chili tuna that comes with pickled ginger, among other nibblies. Revisit dining experiences from another era with an appetizer of crisp frog legs. The entrées that incite praise include catch of the day, Alaskan Arctic char and seabass, all imaginatively served with matchstick-thin vegetables and rice wrap or noodles. The lengthy menu includes wine recommendations for each course; consult the servers—they are excellent sources of information. Plan C for a special event. Settle in to enjoy the minimalist decor and exquisite cuisine, along with one of the city's best views. Lunch Mon to Fri; dinner daily.

The Fish House at Stanley Park $$$
2099 Beach, Stanley Park
681-7275

Approaching this restaurant is like arriving at a gracious country estate: it is set in an oasis of greenery. Thanks to a top chef, the seafood here is among the city's tastiest, plus there is a high-ranking wine list. At the fresh oyster bar you can sample to your heart's delight. Any fish dish you choose can be ordered steamed, grilled, baked or broiled. A starter of the fire-roasted calamari in smoked tomato vinaigrette is an excellent choice. A favourite entrée is the naturally smoked Alaskan black cod served on a bed of spinach, with asiago cheese and new red potatoes. The Pacific sole and tiger prawn satay dishes are also winners. Always check on the chef's daily creation. In warm weather you can dine alfresco on one of two large patios; both have heaters. There is a daily Early Bird Special between 5 and 6 PM—for every two entrées ordered, the bill is reduced by $15. Perfect before or after a seawall walk. Lunch and dinner daily.

The Cannery $$$
2205 Commissioner near north end of Victoria
254-9606

This seafood restaurant has been popular for more than two decades. Part of the appeal, no doubt, is the romantic feel of The Cannery's rich old wood and generous ocean views. As tugs hustle by against a backdrop of the North Shore mountains, the grain elevators and, to the west, Lions Gate Bridge, you ponder a shopping list of fish. Everyone should taste the Vancouver Island oysters coated in Bowen Island ale fritter and served with red and green tomato chutney. The bouillabaisse is hearty, and always ask about the chef's creation. Lunch Mon to Fri; dinner daily.

Also
Accord, see Late Night
Grand King Seafood House, see Chinese
Phnom Phen, see Vietnamese/Cambodian
Pink Pearl, see Chinese
Salmon House on the Hill, see With a View
Szechuan Chongqing, Chinese
Shijo, see Japanese
Tojo's, see Japanese

Pizza

Flying Wedge $
1937 Cornwall near Cypress
732-8840

On some days, pizza by the slice is the perfect hearty snack. For years the Flying Wedge has been a success story with these lusciously laden triangles. The pizzas here have whole-wheat herb crusts and trendy toppings. Tropical Pig is for those who really do like pineapple with ham, plus cheddar and almonds. The Veggie Wedgie is heavily laden, and the Cappocoli with spicy Italian ham, mushrooms, onions, tomatoes and asiago cheese brings tears to your eyes and joy to your tummy. Open daily until 10. Also in Royal Centre.

Lombardo's Pizzeria and Restaurant $
120–1641 Commercial at 1st
251-2240

How much can you say about pizza? Quite a bit these days, when even high-end restaurants have it on their menus. To chow down on what has been ranked the city's best, go to Lombardo's. It's located in the rather ugly salmon-coloured mall that looks out of place on Commercial Dr. The wood-fired oven produces the thinnest of crusts and there's loads of toppings. The favourite is the marcello—fresh tomato with mozzarella cheese, black olives, capers, anchovies and fresh onion. Mon-Sat, 11–11; Sun, 4–10.

Also
CinCin, see Italian
Mangiamo!, see Italian

Vegetarian

Le Veggie $
1096 Denman near Comox
682-3885

If you want vegetarian in the West End go to Le Veggie. Start with the rice vermicelli thick soup and follow with one of the intriguing menu items like chili eggplant Szechuan style or mashed ginger fried rice with diced broccoli. Remember to check the back page that lists the chef's special. Highly recommended is the veggie steak with the house special sauce. This modern little restaurant done in soft greys and greens is quietly developing a reputation for serving the freshest and the finest to nonmeat eaters. No alcohol. Lunch and dinner daily.

The Naam $
2724 W 4th near Stephens
738-7151
Before vegetarian became trendy, before anyone in the city knew (or cared) what a veggie burger or a samosa was, there was The Naam. It has been serving vegetarian food in the same location since the 1970s. Now herbal tea has been joined by cappuccino, and there are some killer chocolate desserts on the menu, but the Naam is still a safe place for people who don't eat animals. Best bets are ethnic specialties. Don't miss the Naam's famous french fries with miso gravy. Although the young staff are always cheerful, the service is no great shakes. Decor is homey, and in the back there is an outdoor courtyard that's a fine, leafy place to be on a warm day. No reservations. Open 24 hours daily.

Planet Veg $
1942 Cornwall near Walnut
734-1001
Planet Veg is a little hole-in-the-wall eatery that garners raves. A favourite are the samosas. The classic—potatoes, peas, spices and tamarind chutney—along with a salad fills you up for less than $6. If you want to get really full, pay a bit more and have a samosa combo or a Katmandu Roll. Or the Basmati Pot with rice, lots of vegetables and "secret" herbs. Probably the reason that everything is always good is that one or two of

the Bansal family, who own Planet Veg, are usually in the kitchen. It's cheap, it's healthy and the location is ideal to pick up a picnic for Kits Beach or settle in with your reading. Open daily, 11 AM–9 PM

Also
Isadora's, see Breakfast/Brunch
Lumière, see French

Before or After the Theatre

Bianco Nero Restaurant $$
475 W Georgia near Richards
682-6376
Ideally located close to theatres, movies and sports venues, this restaurant guarantees that you will be in your seat for the first curtain or drop of the puck. In fact, it specializes in pre-theatre dinners. Italian dishes arrive piping hot, you dine, and then Bianco Nero closes its doors at 8 PM (which can be annoying if you aren't going to the theatre). To make sure you last until the final curtain call, have Pasta 95—a variety of pastas in a rose sauce, topped with hot spicy Italian sausage and grilled prawns. There's an excellent all-Italian, award-winning wine list. Lunch Mon to Fri; dinner Mon to Sat.

900 West $$$
900 W Georgia at Burrard
669-9378
From the decor that boasts Picasso lithographs and funky glass sculptures to the creations extraordinaire that grace your table, 900 West is a winner. Drop into the wine bar before the theatre and enjoy a flight of carefully chosen wines with some chilled oysters or a cheese platter. There are over 300 wines, and 65 are available by the glass. Other menu considerations: smoked, spit-roasted striploin of beef or a rich bouillabaisse served with mahi mahi. Lunch Mon to Fri; dinner daily.

Provence Mediterranean Grill $$
4473 W 10th near Sasamat
222-1980

As we go to press, this delightful
neighbourhood bistro's name is on
the lips of culinary buffs. Although
not in the city centre, its 10th Ave lo-
cation—and marvellous antipasto
bar—makes it an ideal stopover be-
fore a concert at The Chan Centre or
a movie at the Varsity. The beauti-
fully displayed antipasto dishes in-
clude succulent marinated morsels as
well as baked and grilled items. Prices
vary depending upon the number of
items chosen—three choices costs
$7.95. Dinner options include a
seafood-rich dish of linguine that has
earned plaudits.The house chocolate
cake is decadent and delicious.
Lunch and dinner daily.

Also
Chartwell, Lunch
Diva, Contemporary
Monterey Grill, Outdoors
Villa del Lupo, Italian

Late Night

The Accord $$
4298 Main at 28th
876-6110

When it's very late and you are des-
perate for a feast of good Chinese
food, The Accord is as good as it gets.
It's less opulent than the most expensive of the new Cantonese pleasure palaces, but more comfortable
than the old Chinese-Canadian
greasy spoons. Tanks full of live lobster, crab, shrimp and rock cod are
your first hint that the seafood is
ultra fresh. Check out the midnight
snack menu. Try Chinese smoked
pork, tangy beef satay, or prawns
steamed in their shells, to be peeled
and dipped in a brown vinegar, soy
and hot-pepper sauce. Dinner daily
until 3 AM.

Benny's Bagels $
2503 W Broadway at Larch
731-9730

Night owls gather in the comforting
surroundings of Benny's, which
combines a soothing atmosphere
with basic, wholesome food: bagels,
salads, desserts and coffees. It's a
place to people-watch or just sit and
read. Some nights it's difficult to find
a seat. It's a great breakfast spot too,
but we'd sooner drink coffee by candlelight or by moonlight on the
patio. There are other locations. This
is the only one open 24 hours.

Also
Bread Garden, see Essential
   Information (Late-Night Services)
Hamburger Mary's, see Essential
   Information (Late-Night Services)
The Naam, see Vegetarian
Ouzeri, see Greek
Simpatico, see Greek

Outdoors

Bridges Restaurant $
1696 Duranleau, Granville Island
687-4400

Dining outdoors at Bridges bistro is
so Vancouver. You overlook a busy
harbour scene of fishing boats,
kayaks, sailboats and tiny ferries;
seagulls call; the sun glistens off the
cityscape across the water; and you
feel that all is well with the world.
Munch on nachos, nibble on greens,
savour fresh fish, or chow down on
pasta. Bridges also has a lively pub
and a formal dining room upstairs,
but the main floor bistro's huge outdoor deck is the major reason for a
stop here. No reservations. Lunch
and dinner daily.

Monterey Lounge & Grill $$
1277 Robson at Jervis
688-0461

The best way to take in the street cul-
ture of Vancouver is to eat outdoors

at the Monterey. You dine as you watch shoppers stroll, buskers perform, and suit-clad office workers get some exercise on their lunch hour. If you're lucky, a movie star may wander by as the Pacific Palisades, where this restaurant is located, is a home-away-from-home for the film crowd. The Monterey celebrates fresh West Coast cuisine and has excellent evening entertainment. The Thai chicken salad with noodles, sprouts, cilantro and orange in a spicy peanut dressing is popular with the lunch crowd. The crisp-roasted boneless half-duck with red currant ginger glaze is an excellent dinner choice, but then so is everything. The staff is among the city's best. Breakfast, lunch and dinner daily.

The Teahouse Restaurant at Ferguson Point $$
Stanley Park
669-3281

There are Torontonians who come to Vancouver in order to eat at the Teahouse. Little wonder. This Stanley Park restaurant has everything—ocean view, wonderful cuisine and patio dining in warm weather. There's a luscious offering of appetizers (wild mushrooms with escargots, for example), carrot soup to die for, and a sterling selection of seafood and other entrées. Salmon tornado grilled and wrapped in buttered pastry, a dynamite New York steak in peppercorn sauce or a morel stuffed chicken are all possibilities. Giddy desserts, like a choux pastry swan filled with rum-flavoured custard, whipped cream and chocolate sauce are marvellous closers. Here you enjoy all the benefits of eating at a country inn without having to brave a freeway. Brunch Sat and Sun; lunch Mon to Fri; dinner daily.

Also
The Beach House at Dundarave Pier,
  see With a View

Gallery Café, see Lunch
Isadora's, see Breakfast/Brunch
The Naam, see Vegetarian
Seasons in the Park, see With a View
Water St Café, see Lunch

With a View

Anderson's $$
1661 Granville near Beach
684-3777

Anderson's is a perfect place to impress visitors. Floor to ceiling windows frame some of the city's finest scenes. A luxury yacht may drift past, returning from a day at sea, while a haughty heron gulps dinner as it perches on a wharf: all this as you sip a special martini and choose from the daily listing of fresh fish. Menu items are as intriguing as the changing scenery—Ahi tuna served rare with roasted garlic tomato coulis or the grilled Delmonico steak with Cajun spices are only a couple of many. One floor down, The Riley Waterfront Café—same owners, same view—serves more casual fare. Anderson's is open for lunch Mon to Fri; dinner Mon to Sat. The Riley is open for lunch and dinner daily.

The Beach House at Dundarave Pier $$
150–25th St near Marine
West Vancouver
922-1414

You can't beat this waterfront restaurant's view, embracing Lion's Gate Bridge, Stanley Park, and even the mountains of distant Vancouver Island. A lengthy appetizer menu features everything from baked Cambozola in puff pastry to lobster sausage and Sonoma foie gras. Main course offerings are as tempting as the view is wonderful: smoked Alaskan cod with a peppercorn and rum glaze; lobster and potato gnocchi with sweet peppers, cilantro, shrimp and cream; or luscious lamb from either Washington State or Australia. There's also a daily fresh sheet. The Beach House is popular for Sunday brunch—a brisk walk on the seawall followed by champagne and orange juice is a zinger. There are outdoor tables. Catching the sunset here over a port (there is a great wine and port list) makes a fine end to any day. Brunch Sun; lunch and dinner daily.

Salmon House on the Hill $$$
2229 Folkestone Way, West Van
926-3212
Stop to admire the Northwest Coast native artifacts as you enter, then marvel at the panoramic view from this mountainside restaurant. Far below, freighters in the harbour look toy size, and you really get the lay of the land. The salmon here is alder grilled, meaning that it has a distinctive, slightly smoky and succulent flavour. Close to a dozen dishes are alder grilled, including a popular mixed seafood grill. Chef Dan Atkinson is known for his innovative creations; for example, Pacific seabass with crispy potato gallette and orange with purple onion in star anise sauce. There is a daily fresh sheet. A good wine list with an excellent Northwest Coast representation. Brunch Sun; lunch and dinner daily.

Seasons in the Park $$
Queen Elizabeth Park
874-8008
On a warm evening, take out-of-town guests here. Sit on the patio surrounded by the lush, flower-rich Queen Elizabeth Park and take in the view of the city. This park is the highest point within city limits and the view is unparalleled. Menu items are West Coast fresh and flavourful. The chef does wonderful things with grilled salmon, and the lamb garners compliments from even the most picky. Consider Australian ribs mari-

nated in hot mustard, honey, rosemary and garlic then roasted with a martini and rosemary jus, and you'll know why. Pacific Northwest wines are featured, and there is a mouth-watering selection of desserts.

The marriage of lovely surroundings and impeccably prepared menu items is unbeatable. It's good enough for presidents—Clinton and Yeltsin have dined here—and it's a safe bet for any evening you wish to make memorable. Brunch Sat and Sun; lunch Mon to Fri; dinner daily.

Also
Bridges Restaurant, see Outdoors
C, see Seafood
The Cannery, see Seafood
Teahouse at Ferguson Point, see
    Outdoors
Tojo's, see Japanese

Espresso Bars

Vancouver has an ongoing love affair with java. There are hundreds of coffee houses where you can bask in the aroma of freshly brewed coffee and read the daily paper.

Bojangles Café
785 Denman at Robson
687-3622
Sit outside and sip or take it to the beach or Stanley Park.

Caffé Calabria
1745 Commercial near 2nd
253-7017
A winner on the Drive—the area that knows coffee best.

Delany's on Denman Coffee House
1105 Denman near Comox
662-3344
A comfy coffee bar with indoor and outdoor seating; popular with the gay crowd.

Kits Coffee Company
2198 W 4th at Yew

739-0139
Bright and cheerful, in the middle of the action on 4th.

Starbucks
1100 Robson at Thurlow
685-7991
No matter where you are in the city or in the 'burbs, you'll find one nearby.

Also
Ecco Il Pane, see Bakery Cafés
Savary Island Pie Company, see Bakery Cafés
Terra Breads, see Bakery Cafés

By Nationality

Chinese

Grand King Seafood Restaurant $$
705 W Broadway at Heather
876-7855
This award-winning, much-lauded restaurant will never let you or your taste buds down. There's a multipage menu with mouth-watering selections (in the shark's fin section alone there are six choices). The formal *dim sum* is an ideal introduction to Grand King's. Supreme shark's fin soup with dumplings once tasted will not be forgotten. Something even more exotic? Try steamed chicken feet. Or you could simply nibble on honey garlic ribs. These steaming hot offerings are upscale *dim sum* at its best. The chef here is renowned for his creativity: menu items change monthly, and his ingenuity and selection of fresh ingredients have secured this restaurant's popularity, even though it's attached to a Holiday Inn on a busy corner. Lunch and dinner daily.

Hon's Wun Tun House $
108–268 Keefer near Gore
688-0871
Hon's is an institution in Chinatown. It's moved from its original,

long-time location on Main St, but Hon's, now housed in a modern Chinatown building, is still popular. People line up for lunch, and it's probably because Hon's kept its original menu with only slightly higher prices. There are other Hon's in the city and the suburbs, but this one remains a favourite.

The speciality here is noodles—try them with shrimp and meat dumplings or, for a noodle dish with some zing, go for the one with oyster sauce, ginger and green onion. The food is so yummy that you may want to exit through the adjoining take-out shop and purchase Hon's treats for your freezer. Lunch and dinner daily.

Kirin Mandarin Restaurant $$$
1166 Alberni near Bute
682-8833
This restaurant (and Kirin Seafood Restaurant) is far removed from the old-style Chinese drop-in joints. This is an upscale dining room, with trendy postmodern decor—soft greens and black lacquer accented with pink tablecloths—and a professional staff. The Kirin is often full of oriental business people choosing lobster fresh from the large tank and ordering with aplomb from the multipage menu, which is a mix of Szechuan, Shanghai and pan-regional party food, with a few Cantonese favourites, such as scallops in black bean sauce. Peking duck does not have to be ordered in advance here. A memorable Szechuan dish is the hot chili fish. There's quite a selection of shark's fin here but it is expensive. Lunch and dinner daily.

Pink Pearl $$
1132 E Hastings near Glen
253-4316
If you wish to experience Cantonese dining in the same style that has

Dim Sum

Dim sum originated in Canton, so most dishes are subtle and lightly cooked, usually steamed. (Northern restaurants serve their own version of *dim sum*.)

Carts piled with bamboo steamers of hot food are wheeled around the tables. A steamer usually contains a plate with two or three dumplings of some sort. Savoury dishes are on the top of the carts, and sweet ones below; the Chinese intermingle the sweet and the savoury during the meal. Don't sit in a corner or you'll be watching most of the carts pass you by. After eating your fill, signal a waiter, and he will tally your bill by counting the number of dishes on the table. Average cost is $8 per person.

Dim sum is a fun affair. Take your family and friends. It is served from about 10 AM to 2 PM every day.

been popular in this city for decades, head east on Hastings and enter this unpretentious restaurant. Bring the kids. Pink Pearl has a comfortable, family feel, and no one is bothered by a crying baby in the midst of the bustle. Service is efficient but unceremonious. Live seafood tanks near the door hold crab, shrimp, geoduck, oysters, abalone, rock cod, lobsters and scallops—all offered in a dozen or more ways.

Try clams in black bean sauce as a first course and spicy prawns sautéed in chili sauce to follow. There is a super selection of vegetable dishes. Arrive early for *dim sum* if you don't want to wait in line. On a weekend night, you may run into several wedding parties. The Pink Pearl is never quiet but always fun. Lunch and dinner daily.

Szechuan Chongqing $
2802 Commercial at 12th
254-7434
This unassuming restaurant has been on the same corner for years and was among the first to serve excellent cooking from the southwestern Chinese province. It has new owners and now has other outlets. Good news—it's still a darn good place to eat. Two dishes to try: fried green

beans Szechuan style, steamed and tossed with spiced ground pork; and Chongqing chicken, boneless chicken on a bed of fried spinach that has the crispness of dried seaweed and a taste that is salty, rich and nutty all at once. Food here is hearty, with plenty of garlic and red peppers. Order steamed buns to mop up the tangy, hot sauces. Lunch and dinner daily.

East Indian

Del-hi Darbar Restaurant $
2120 Main St near 5th Ave
877-7733
You must dine at this plain, family-run restaurant for both lunch and dinner. Because owner Maynk Toprani's mid-day chef comes from southern Indian, it was decided the restaurant would specialize in *dhosas* for lunch. Traditionally, these crispy, crêpes are served for breakfast in southern India but they have proven a winner for lunch in Vancouver. Try a savoury Rava Masala *dhosa* (spicy semolina crêpe with vegetable filling) served with coconut chutney. There are no dinner *dhosas* but everything is tasty. The *dal* here is as good as it gets outside of India. Dal Maharani (black lentils and red

beans simmered in spices overnight) is one of many reasons to go back. Another is the *naan*. This leavened bread baked in a tandoor oven can be stuffed with onions, chicken, nuts, etc., or can be eaten plain. Any Indian meal is best finished off with the sweet, cheesy Gulab Jamun.

Lunch and dinner Tues to Sun.

Rubina Tandoori $$
1962 Kingsway near Victoria
874-3621

Kingsway is not the most pleasant route to follow heading out of the city but Rubina Tandoori is a good reason to take the plunge.

The Jamal family owned a restaurant in London before coming to Vancouver; son Shaffeen is the maître d' and has a phenomenal memory for faces. His mother, Krishna, does most of the cooking. Walk in past the display cases of desserts and *chevda*, a nuts-and-bolts salty snack you can buy by the pound, and watch them make *naan,* the wonderful flat bread, in the tandoori oven. One regular has tasted everything here and swears it's all good; lamb chops done in yogurt and tomato sauce or any of the 16 vegetarian offerings win raves. The menu covers the range of subcontinental cuisines, from south Indian seafood to Punjabi dishes from the north. Lunch Mon to Fri; dinner Mon to Sat.

Vij's Restaurant $
1480 W 11th near Granville
736-6664

Singlehandedly, Vikram Vij brought East Indian cuisine up a notch in this city. When he opened his own restaurant, his goal was "homey cooking, clean and fresh," and he went to his family for their favourites. The recipes worked, and soon he had to move out of his first, tiny restaurant to keep the masses happy. The menu items are just as wonderful as ever, but he's now lauded as offering true fusion cuisine. Alas, Vij's still does not take reservations, so you may have a bit of a wait to savour some of his offerings, including eggplant, bell peppers and potato curry or a Bengali-style cod on basmati rice. Menus change seasonally. Dinner daily.

French

Café de Paris $$
751 Denman near Robson
687-1418

To experience a Parisian-style bistro, meander into Café de Paris. While the passing crowd may not be quite as interesting as that on the Left Bank, the food, service and decor are as good as the real thing. Subdued wood panelling, mirrored bar, posters and photographs, lace curtains and the table d'hôte menu written on a chalk board are all typically French, and so is the cuisine. Chef-owner, Andre Bernier, makes the classic Le Cassoulet as rich and flavourful as you'd taste in Toulouse. For cholesterol overload, treat yourself to the New York steak served with Café de Paris butter. All main courses come with crispy *frites* (French fries) that are, frankly, the best in the city. Cheerful, efficient service is guaranteed as the chef and two manager-owners are always there. Brunch Sun; lunch Mon to Fri; dinner daily.

Le Crocodile $$$
909 Burrard at Smithe
669-4298

True gourmets beat a path to Le Crocodile. The menu includes Steak Tartare, the room has a Parisian ambience and chef/owner Marcel Jacob's Alsatian origins and fine touch with flavours are a delightful combination. If you don't care for Classique Tartare there is a salmon, wasabi-spiked counterpart among the many tantalizing Les Entrées Froids. For the adventuresome there is boneless rabbit with wild mushroom and spinach stuffing, and for the traditionalists there is a pan-seared beef tenderloin with potatoes Anna, goose liver and Perigordine sauce as well as grilled calf liver with fried onions. There are typically rich, decadent, sent-from-heaven desserts, and the service is commendable. Lunch Mon to Fri; dinner Mon to Sat. Closed Sun.

The Hermitage $$
115–1025 Robson near Thurlow
689-3237

It's a cosy, pretty room tucked into a courtyard and it has a true European feel: rather unpretentious, with a class and charm enhanced by warm brick, elegantly set tables and French-speaking waiters. The Hermitage offers comfort as well as fine cuisine. Some say the French onion soup here is unrivalled, and you can follow this with a medley of poached seafood and shellfish with a delicate fresh lobster sauce. A crêpe dessert is always an excellent choice. A word about the bread: it's a cross between French and Italian, is popped in the oven just before lunch and dinner and is a bread-lover's dream. Lunch Mon to Fri; dinner nightly.

Lumière $$$
2551 W Broadway near Trafalgar
739-8185

Chef Rob Feenie's innovative creations (described as "contemporary French") have catapulted Lumière into the front ranks of Vancouver's best restaurants. Its list of accolades is as long as its wine list. (It was chosen *Vancouver Magazine's* best restaurant two years running.) Go to Lumière (which means "light" *en français*) for the sheer joy of eating. All the menu items are delicately balanced, incred-

ibly fresh, beautifully presented and meticulously prepared. Consider a roasted veal tenderloin with shaved black truffles bathed in bone-marrow truffle jus. Each evening two "tasting" menus are available; they are seven course, fixed price—one vegetarian, and one featuring meat, fish or fowl. Tastefully designed with the utmost simplicity, Lumière seats 50; In summer, enjoy drinks and hors d'oeuvres on the small patio, which catches the early evening sun. Dinner Tues to Sun.

Moustache Cafe $$$
2118 Burrard at 5th Ave
739-1990

Moustache has a solid reputation founded on its North Vancouver location. It opened late in 1997 near 4th Ave, and has served a steady stream of food aficionados ever since. *Vancouver Magazine's* food critics voted it best new restaurant for the year. Little wonder when you consider treats like a duck breast and arugula salad adorned with roasted red peppers, artichokes and polenta croutons and flavoured with a tangy balsamic-based dressing, or a Moroccan-spice lamb shank with saffron mashed potatoes. Moustache is a large, airy café with an open kitchen; patrons can eat at the bar and admire the talents of the chefs. You may encounter one rather pretentious waiter but the rest of the staff is friendly and helpful. Lunch Mon to Fri; dinner daily.

Greek

Kalamata Taverna $
478 W Broadway at Cambie
872-7050

The dolmas served at Kalamata aren't just the best in the city, they are as good as any served in Greece. Little wonder that you may be surrounded by Greeks as you dine.

Kalamata specializes in southern Greek home cooking and, as well as the garlic-laden hummus and tzatsiki, there are also imaginative salads and roasted vegetables and a not-to-be-missed lentil, fresh tomato and garlic soup. Kalamata is uncluttered and cheery. It's on a rather ugly, busy intersection, but that doesn't turn off its faithful following. Dinner daily.

Ouzeri $
3189 W Broadway at Trutch
739-9378
In Greece, you go to the *ouzeri* to drink and nibble before dinner. For many, the best memories of an Ouzeri evening are of sitting outside in summer, savouring Greek appetizers and taking in the Kitsilano street scene. Probably the first Vancouver Greek restaurant to specialize in serving pre-dinner delectables, the Ouzeri is the quintessential neighbourhood bistro where you always have a lively time. The food includes everything Greek you could wish for, as well as some specials like the vegetarian moussaka, and it never lets you down. And should you feel the need for, say, some crispy chicken livers after midnight on the weekend, head for the Ouzeri. Lunch and dinner daily. Open until 1 AM on weekends.

Simpatico Ristorante $
2222 W 4th at Vine
733-6824
Simpatico has been a fixture on 4th Ave since 1969, an enduring source of nourishing meals at low prices. Order one of the whole-wheat-crust pizzas—every table has a black metal pizza stand—or venture into the Greek menu. Cornish game hen with rice, potatoes and Greek salad is a hearty, robust meal. Decor is generically Greek, with pathos plants, white walls, wooden floors and ta-

bles, and blue-and-white checked tablecloths. Students eat here, and young families, and the rest of that vast army of us with more appetite than cash. Lunch and dinner daily.

Italian

Arriva $$
1537 Commercial near Grant
251-1177
If you have a yen for authentic Italian sauces in a friendly, neighbourhood-style restaurant, go to Arriva on the Drive. Even though Commercial is no longer known as "Little Italy," there are still some fine pasta places here. If you must have spaghetti and meatballs, you can, but there's also fusilli with wild game, spicy prawns and linguine in white wine sauce or a large selection of vegetarian pastas.

The antipasto plate is heaped with octopus, shrimp, roasted red peppers, cheese, sausage and fat lima beans in a herby marinade. And the soups are thick, fresh and filling.

Arriva bustles in the early evening (reserve after 8 PM for a quiet dinner), and the waiters greet you like an old friend. And they're more apt to greet you in Italian than English. Lunch Mon to Fri; dinner daily.

CinCin $$
1154 Robson near Bute
688-7338
Climb a wide staircase to leave bustling Robson St and enter Italy. Murals on soft ochre walls, terra cotta tiles, a few statues and an open kitchen from which garlic and olive oil fragrances waft. Crusty, freshly baked bread arrives instantly and, if you wish, piping hot pasta dishes follow. The paella here—with homemade sausage—is for those with a healthy appetite. As well as the full range of Italian, including a polenta dish, there is a wide variety of other

offerings. CinCin has an alderwood-fired grill, which gives special flavour to dishes such as the rotisserie game hen served with oyster, mushroom risotto, honey-glazed root vegetables and thyme demi glace. At CinCin you feel that nothing is too much trouble for the accommodating staff. There is an excellent wine list. Toast the fine food! Lunch Mon to Fri; dinner daily.

Il Giardino di Umberto $$$
1382 Hornby at Pacific
669-2422

Il Giardino was the start of restaurateur extraordinaire Umberto Menghi's success. Now you can partake in his Italian feasts in a number of his restaurants; if you are well-heeled, you can even attend his culinary school in an Italian villa. Il Giardino's warm Mediterranean ambience and fine food attracts the city's stockbrokers, lawyers and social set. It's one of *the* places to be "seen." Il Giardino is known for hot, hearty pastas and game dishes—although this is "raised" game as opposed to "wild." Roasted reindeer loin with port peppercorn sauce or Fraser Valley ostrich in a berry sauce are examples. The service is always good. Despite the soft-toned surroundings, Il Giardino is more lively than quiet. In summer, the sun-dappled patio is delightful. Lunch Mon to Fri; dinner Mon to Sat.

Mangiamo! Restaurant $$$
1116 Mainland near Helmcken
687-1116

Mangiamo! means "let's eat," and you'll be ready to by the time you've considered the well-thought-out offerings. You may get bogged down in the fine array of unusual (and expensive) appetizers, and then you must decide whether to feast on succulent fish such as a mouthwatering Chilean seabass or indulge in the rack of lamb that regular Mangiamo!

patrons swear by. And then there is the seven-page wine list! Those who wish to avoid the dilemma of choice should consider "Ken's Dinner," a surprise three-course ($40) or five-course ($54) meal prepared at the whim of owner/executive chef, Ken Bogas, each day. Lunch Mon to Fri; dinner Mon to Sat.

Piccolo Mondo $$
850 Thurlow near Robson
688-1633

Wine aficionados will revel in the choices (the cellar has over 4000 bottles), be it a '96 Brusco Barbi from Tuscany served by the glass with lunch or an 80-year-old Armagnac befitting a special-occasion dinner. Piccolo Mondo has received many notable wine awards, and has twice made the cut on the *Wine Spectator*'s coveted "Best Award of Excellence," a distinction shared by only 12 restaurants in Canada.

The 75-seat, elegant dining room specializes in mouth-watering Northern Italian cuisine. For starters, savour grilled sweet and sour prawns, vegetable compote and crab vinaigrette, and then move on to the veal loin studded with garlic, roasted mustard seed and tarragon sauce. However, if you are an osso buco fan, you must have it here. Lunch Mon to Fri; dinner Mon to Sat.

Villa del Lupo $$$
869 Hamilton near Smithe
688-7436

For one of the city's most memorable meals go to the "house of wolves." It's perfect for either business or romance. The lovely Victorian house is cozy and tastefully finished and the food is frankly marvellous. Every stock, soup and sauce is made daily from scratch. Starters include a grilled herb polenta with poached asparagus and a duck and pistachio terrine with pear and chilies mar-

For a romantic evening, as well as fantastic Italian fare, you can't beat Villa del Lupo. (Villa del Lupo)

malade. Next, you may wish to treat your tastebuds to the oft-ordered lamb osso buco flavoured with cinnamon, among other spices. There's also seabass wrapped with Parma prosciutto and sage. Pasta reaches new heights here; try the tagliatelle with seafood sausage, tomatoes, sun-dried tomatoes, roasted garlic and tarragon. Dining at Villa del Lupo is a leisurely affair and should be savoured. It is perfect after the theatre as you can pre-order a "Sweet Deal"—a choice of dessert with espresso, cappuccino or latte. Available 9:30–11:30, it costs $8.95 per person. Dinner daily.

Japanese

Bon $$
53 W Broadway near Manitoba
872-0088
Japanese food purists should head to this rather unvisited section of Broadway. The Bon would probably rate a 3 out of 10 in atmosphere (it was formerly a diner and still has some booths) but its food ranks close to 10. The best of Japanese food has a clean, fresh taste that tingles the most naive taste buds. Bon food does just that. Everything is good. Sashay up to the sushi bar and feast on *tekka don* (tuna on sushi rice) or snuggle into one of the old-fashioned booths with friends and dig into a hot pot, udon noodle dish or tempura. The Bon has garnered some high praise and you'll understand why once you dine here. Lunch Mon to Fri; dinner daily.

Tojo's $$$
777 W Broadway at Willow
872-8050
The years pass but some things never change. A recent *Vancouver Magazine* poll of food writers confirmed, once again, that the best Japanese food in the city is prepared by Hidekazu Tojo. Like a composer of a fine piece of music, he orchestrates amazingly delicate dishes. First-time diners here will experience tantalizingly unusual dishes—shrimp dumplings with hot-mustard sauce or the catch of the

Sushi

We can't imagine finding better sushi anywhere in Canada. If you're new to sushi, imagine fish—the freshest you've ever had—with a delicate rather than a fishy taste.

There are three kinds of sushi. One kind is a small patty of rice that is covered with a thin slice of raw tuna, salmon, mackerel or other fish, and is called *nigiri*. Another is *maki*, a roll of rice covered with a paper-thin sheet of crisp seaweed and filled with tuna, salmon, salmon roe or cucumber. The third is crisp seaweed or salmon skin rolled into a cone and filled with rice and fish.

If you are trying sushi for the first time, order just enough for an appetizer—an assorted sushi plate will do for two to four people. If you're more adventurous or experienced, wait for a seat at the sushi bar, where you can be part of the banter and watch the sushi master at work. At the bar you can order particular types of sushi, one or two pieces at a time.

After sitting down you will be presented with a hot towel for your hands, because sushi is eaten with the fingers or chopsticks. Sake, green tea and beer are all appropriate and should be ordered from the waitress, though you order your sushi directly from the sushi chef.

You can also order soup (to be drunk from a bowl) from your waitress, but traditionally nothing but sushi is eaten at the bar.

Pick up a piece of sushi, dip it fish-side down into the little dish of soy sauce, and then pop it into your mouth (still fish-side down). The taste is clean, pure and delicious. The hotness comes from a thin layer of green horseradish called *wasabi* between the rice and the fish. Refresh your palate in between courses of sushi with a piece of shaved pickled ginger.

day splendidly sautéed, perhaps? Don't leave without a taste of Tojo's tuna, one of his hallmark dishes. There are splendid views of False Creek and the North Shore mountains. Take money (the price reflects the quality of the food) and indulge in an evening of blissful eating. Dinner Mon to Sat.

Shijo Japanese Restaurant $$
1926 W 4th at Cypress
732-4676
Shijo is a chic sushi bar. Located up one flight from Kitsilano's main artery, it is a modern, contemporary, light-filled room where a team of sushi and robata chefs crack jokes behind the bar. Jazz plays discreetly in the background. You may be sur-

rounded by Japanese tourists as the sushi leaves little to be desired here. The sunomono salad is an excellent starter. Then check out the grill offerings. Ask for Japanese eggplant cooked on the robata and, if they're available, shiitake mushrooms cooked in foil. Lunch Mon to Fri; dinner daily.

Chiyoda $$
1050 Alberni at Burrard
688-5050
This city-centre robata bar lures the business crowd and shoppers up to its second-floor location with the promise of fresh, grilled-in-front-of-you food. It never disappoints. The Chiyoda was designed in Japan, right down to the shapely little beer

glasses. The bar is a set of concentric circles: a wood counter, a band of ice with the day's offerings displayed in wicker baskets, an inner circle of grills and then the chefs, who hand over your food on long paddles. Snapper, prawns, oysters, eggplant, mushrooms, onions, potatoes: there are about 30 choices to be grilled, seasoned with soy, lemon and *ponzu* sauce and served to eager onlookers. Chiyoda's bar can be hilariously convivial. Lunch Mon to Fri; dinner Mon to Sat.

Malaysian

Banana Leaf $
1016 W Broadway near Oak
731-6333
Word spreads quickly among Asian food lovers and the word is go to the Banana Leaf for a superb meal. It won't hurt your wallet, either. The aroma of curry greets you as you enter this small restaurant with bright tie-dyed tablecloths. There is a lengthy menu, including several pages of seafood alone. A *roti canai*

(Malaysian pancake with vegetarian curry sauce) may start your meal. If you love greens and spices, go for the spinach seafood. A special, seasonal treat is Malaysian curry crab. Feel free to order extra hot or not so hot when it comes to chili-based dishes; the staff is most accommodating. The Banana Leaf is a little restaurant that caters to big tastes. Lunch and dinner daily.

Mexican

Topanga Café $
2904 W 4th near Macdonald
733-3713
The Topanga's heaping plates of Cal-Mex food at low prices have been catering to enchilada feasters for nearly two decades. No nouveau cuisine here; Mexican fare is reliable, if not fancy. Kids can colour blank menu covers while waiting for food; adults can scan the hundreds of framed copies of patrons' coloured menus (done by young and old) on the walls for inspiration. No reservations. There are only 40 seats, so ar-

British Columbia Wines

In recent years B.C. wines have been scooping medals at high-profile competitions out from under the noses of their international counterparts.

Travel the backroads of the Okanagan, Similkameen, Fraser and Cowichan Valleys and you'll find premium wineries that are making the most of B.C.'s northerly latitudes. Like other northern growing areas, this one leans towards whites, both table and dessert wines. Some of B.C.'s grape varieties are familiar: Riesling, Gewürztraminer, Pinot Blanc and Chardonnay.

Newcomers, like Auxerrois (oh-zair-WAH), Ehrenfelser (AIR-en-fel-zer), Bacchus and Ortega, tend to be subtly fragrant and fruity. Reds include Pinot Noir, Merlot and lesser-known varieties such as Chancellor, Marachal Foch and Chelois. The makers of premium wines promote their product through the Vintners' Quality Alliance, whose "VQA" symbol on the neck of a bottle indicates that the wine meets strict standards.

For more information, contact the British Columbia Wine Institute at 664-7744 in Vancouver.
—*Elizabeth Wilson*

rive before 6:30 or after 8 if you don't want to wait in line. Lunch and dinner Mon to Sat.

Spanish

La Bodega   **$$**
1277 Howe near Davie
684-8815
When you drop by the Bodega, you can be assured of two things: the crowd is always interesting and the food is garlicky and good.

The dark, cozy *tapas* bar under the Chateau Madrid fills every night. Endless plates of *patatas bravas*—potatoes fried and doused in a spicy, garlicky tomato dressing—mussels in vinaigrette and *chorizo* sausage are washed down with gallons of beer, tubs of wine and pitchers full of sangria.

Eat as little as you like or as much, come in a big noisy party or with your one best friend, have lunch or stay till midnight—La Bodega is a kind of rolling Spanish theatre that lets you do precisely what you please. The staff here stays forever; consequently, there is always a familiar face to greet you. Flamenco music plays, sangria flows and conversations are animated. Lunch Mon to Fri; dinner Mon to Sat.

Thai

Montri's Thai Restaurant   **$**
3629 W Broadway near Alma
738-9888
This cosy, intimate restaurant has been serving up wonderfully traditional Thai dishes for years—so traditional that essential ingredients are flown in from Bangkok. Tried and true favourites are the stir-fried eggplant with garlic and beef sauce and B.C. salmon à la Thai—simmered in a thick red curry and coconut sauce. Regulars request Pla Lard Prig, a whole fresh fish (cod or snapper),

deep-fried and topped with Montri's special three-flavoured sauce. All dishes can be spiced to suit your taste buds. Remember, Thai food comes hot, very hot and very, very hot. Thai Singha beer soothes the tingling tongue. The decor is not fancy but food is reliably good. Dinner nightly.

Sawasdee Thai Restaurant   **$**
4250 Main near 27th
876-4030
Many Thai restaurants have come and gone, but the Sawasdee, which opened in the spring of 1986, remains a crowd-pleaser. Locals cut their teeth here on chili-rich food, and then return whenever they need a fix.

While you may not be able to pronounce *goong phad med-ma-muang*, you will relish the stirfried prawns accompanied by cashews, sweet peppers, onions and chili. That's only one of many offerings that please palates in this friendly, comfortable eatery. Service is so convivial that you start to believe in the Land of Smiles as something more than a travel cliché. Lunch Tues to Fri; dinner daily.

Vietnamese/Cambodian

Phnom-Penh   **$**
244 E Georgia near Gore
682-5777
955 W Broadway near Oak
734-8898
Same family owners, same menu but no comparison when it comes to atmosphere—we prefer the Chinatown location simply because it has more of an Asian feel. The menu is divided into Cambodian and Vietnamese, and there are Chinese dishes as well. For many, the main draw is the spicy garlic crab, finger-licking good and not something you can order in every Asian restaurant. Another favourite is "Special Prawns," a seasonal dish. It's

the best garlic and pepper prawns in the city. To avoid disappointment, call and order it ahead.

Other offerings include hot and sour soup, stirfried season's greens, *Bank Xeo* (Vietnamese crêpe made from crisp bean pancake wrapped with bean sprouts, shrimp and ground port) or squid with peppery lemon sauce: all great eating. A family restaurant with a genuine feeling of hospitality. Lunch and dinner daily, except Tues.

West Coast Native

Liliget Feast House $$
1724 Davie near Denman
681-7044
If you'd like a pleasant surprise, enter this very ordinary restaurant-front and head downstairs: you'll find yourself in the world of the Coast Salish nation. The Liliget "longhouse" was designed by architect Arthur Erickson several decades ago. It is reminiscent of a clearing in a forest: a narrow path between raised concrete platforms, a dozen or so log columns, low tables and walls and columns hung with Northwest Coast art.

Native cuisine attracts food lovers probably because it is so different as well as so tasty. Some of the game dishes are particularly intriguing; for example, an appetizer of smoked buffalo or main course of wild Arctic caribou, alder grilled with Saskatoon berry sauce. First-timers may want to indulge in the Potlatch Platter for two, which includes everything from salmon and smoked mussels to grilled venison. Be forewarned: it is filling. This is the city's only native restaurant and it is much more than just a novelty. Dinner daily.

By Location

Broadway (between Main and Granville)

Banana Leaf, see Malaysian
Bon, see Japanese
Grand King Seafood Restaurant, see Chinese
Kalamata, see Greek
Phnom-Penh, see Vietnamese/Cambodian
Star Anise, see Contemporary
Szechuan Chongqing, see Chinese
Tojo's, see Japanese
Vij's, see East Indian

Chinatown

Hon's Wun Tun House, see Chinese
Phnom-Penh, see Vietnamese/Cambodian

Downtown

Anderson's, see With a View
Bacchus, see Lunch
Bianco Nero, see Before or After the Theatre
CinCin, see Italian
La Bodega, see Spanish
C, see Seafood
Chartwell, see Lunch
Chiyoda, see Japanese
Le Crocodile, see French

Diva, see Contemporary
Fleuri, see Breakfast/Brunch
Gallery Café, see Lunch
Il Giardino, see Italian
The Hermitage, see French
Kirin, see Chinese
Mangiamo!, see Italian
900 West, see Before or After the Theatre
Piccolo Mondo, see Italian
Starbucks, see Espresso Bars
Water St Café, see Lunch

East Side

Arriva, see Italian
Caffé Calabria, see Espresso Bars
Del-hi Darbar, see East Indian
Cannery, see Seafood
Lombardo's, see Pizza
Pink Pearl, see Chinese
Phnom-Penh, see Vietnamese/Cambodian
Rubina Tandoori, see East Indian
Sawasdee, see Thai
Szechuan Chongqing, see Chinese
Tony's Neighbourhood Deli, see Lunch

Granville Island

Bridges Restaurant, see Outdoors
Isadora's Co-operative Restaurant, see Breakfast/Brunch

Kitsilano/West Side

Benny's Bagels, see Late Night
Bishop's, see Contemporary
Ecco Il Pane, see Bakery Cafés
Flying Wedge, see Pizza
Gladys, see Breakfast/Brunch
Kits Coffee Company, see Espresso Bars
Lumière, see French
Montri's Thai Restaurant, see Thai
Moustache Cafe, see French

Naam, see Vegetarian
Ouzeri, see Greek
Planet Veg, see Vegetarian
Provence Mediterranean Grill, see Before or After the Theatre
Shijo, see Japanese
Sophie's Cosmic Cafe, see Breakfast/Brunch
Terra Breads, see Bakery Cafés
Topanga Café, see Mexican

North Shore

The Beach House at Dundarave Pier, see With a View
Salmon House on the Hill, see With a View
Savary Island Pie Company, see Bakery Cafés
Tomahawk, see Breakfast/Brunch

South of 33rd Avenue

Seasons in the Park, see With a View

West End

Bojangles Café, see Espresso Bars
Café de Paris, see French
Delany's on Denman Coffee House, see Espresso Bars
Liliget Feast House, see West Coast Native
RainCity Grill, see Contemporary
Starbucks, see Espresso Bars
Teahouse at Ferguson Point, see Outdoors
Le Veggie, see Vegetarian

Hotel Restaurants

Bacchus, The Wedgewood
Chartwell, Four Seasons
Diva, The Metropolitan
Fleuri, The Sutton Place
Monterey Grill, Pacific Palisades
900 West, Hotel Vancouver

Ten Cheap Treats In Vancouver

When you want to fill up on the cheap but don't want to skimp on atmosphere, here are some reliable outings.

1. **Anton's**
   4260 E. Hastings, Burnaby
   299-6636
Large servings is an understatement here—buy dinner and you also get lunch for the next day. May have to line up.

2. **Dundarave Concession**
   Dundarave Pier, foot of 25th St, West Vancouver
Although on a pier, its claim to fame is having one of the city's best burgers. Have dinner in a bun, then walk the seawall.

3. **Marineview Coffeeshop**
   611 Alexander at Princess
   253-0616
Possibly the city's best crab or seafood sandwich platters. If you love seafood, it's worth the trip to this eastside locale. Lunch only.

4. **Planet Veg**
See Restaurants (Vegetarian).

5. **Sophie's Cosmic Café**
See Restaurants (Breakfast/Brunch).

6. **Subeez Café**
   891 Homer at Smythe
   687-6107
Casual, California-style food. Enjoy the funky, recycled decor but be prepared for loud music. Interesting clientele.

7. **Sushi Inn**
   1179 Commercial near Charles
   251-1788
Simple decor, great Japanese. Sushi is fine but other dishes, like the Udon (soup with fat noodles) are more memorable. More lively in evenings.

8. **Tony's Neighbourhood Deli**
See Restaurants (Lunch).

9. **Topanga Café**
See Restaurants (Mexican).

10. **Won More Szechuan Cuisine**
    1184 Denman near Comox
    688-8856
Good, gutsy Szechuan made before your eyes. Utterly reliable, garlicky dishes. Also on 4th Ave.

Getting Around

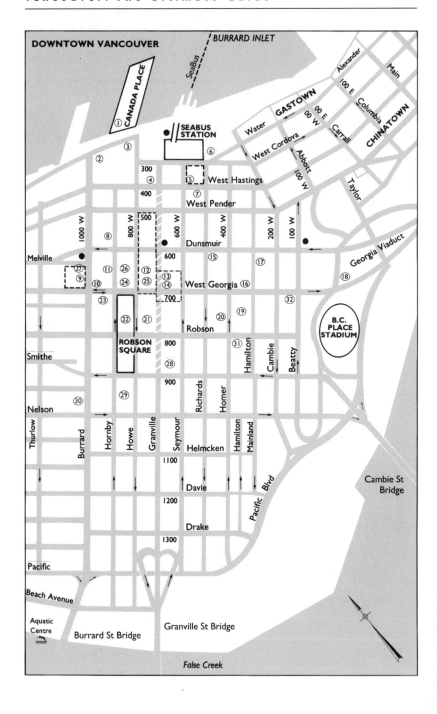

DOWNTOWN VANCOUVER

BURRARD INLET

CANADA PLACE

SeaBus

SEABUS STATION

GASTOWN

Water

West Cordova

West Hastings

West Pender

Dunsmuir

Melville

West Georgia

Georgia Viaduct

Robson

ROBSON SQUARE

Smithe

Nelson

B.C. PLACE STADIUM

Richards

Homer

Hamilton

Mainland

Cambie

Beatty

Helmcken

Davie

Drake

Thurlow

Burrard

Hornby

Howe

Granville

Seymour

Pacific Blvd

Cambie St Bridge

Pacific

Beach Avenue

Aquatic Centre

Burrard St Bridge

Granville St Bridge

False Creek

Alexander

Main

Columbia

Carrall

Abbott

CHINATOWN

Taylor

Public Transit

City Buses

521-0400

B.C. Transit buses accept cash fares (exact change is required), pre-paid

1. Vancouver Trade and Convention Centre/Pan Pacific Hotel
2. TouristInfo Centre
3. Waterfront Hotel
4. Sinclair Centre
5. SFU Downtown Campus
6. The Landing
7. Delta Hotel
8. YWCA
9. Royal Centre Mall
10. Christ Church Cathedral (Anglican)
11. Canadian Craft Museum
12. Pacific Centre Mall
13. The Bay Dept Store
14. Vancouver Centre Mall
15. Holy Rosary Cathedral (Catholic)
16. Main Post Office
17. Queen Elizabeth Theatre/Playhouse
18. GM Place
19. Library Square
20. Ford Theatre
21. Eaton's Dept Store
22. Vancouver Art Gallery
23. Hotel Vancouver
24. Hotel Georgia
25. Four Seasons Hotel
26. Metropolitan Hotel
27. Hyatt Hotel
28. Orpheum Theatre
29. Law Courts
30. YMCA
31. Rosedale on Robson Hotel
32. YWCA Hotel
- ▨▨ Buses/Taxis only
- • SkyTrain station
- ⬚ Underground shopping
- → Traffic direction

"Faresaver" tickets and monthly passes. Regular adult fares are $1.50 for travel in one zone, $2.25 for two zones and $3 for three zones. Concession fares are for seniors (65 plus), children aged 5 to 13, and high school students with valid GoCards; costs are $1 for one zone, $1.50 for two zones and $2 for three zones. After 6:30 PM on weekdays, and all day Saturdays, Sundays and holidays, discount fares are in effect —all three zones may be travelled for $1.50 (adult) and $1(concession). Transfers, issued only when the fare is paid, are valid for 90 minutes for two-way travel and are good on buses, the SeaBus and the SkyTrain. Thus, you can make a stopover and return on the same transfer. Service on most routes ends about 1 AM; a few buses on major routes continue to operate until about 3 AM.

Faresaver tickets are sold in booklets of 10 and start at $13.75 for adults. Monthly passes cost $54 for adults. These are one-zone fares but are valid for travel across several zones as long as it's not rush hour. Faresaver tickets and monthly passes are sold at retail outlets (look for the blue and red "FareDealer" sign in the window) including Safeway and 7-11 stores. They are not available from transit operators. Day passes ($6 for adults, $4 concession) are good for unlimited travel and are available from FareDealers or from ticket vending machines in SkyTrain and SeaBus stations.

Approximately half of Vancouver buses are equipped to accommodate people who use wheelchairs and scooters.

B.C. Transit has a number of publications to assist travellers. A "Transit Route Map & Guide" shows all routes in the region and is available for $1.50 from FareDealer outlets. Route maps are also located at major bus exchanges, transfer points and SkyTrain and SeaBus stations. *Discover Vancouver on Transit*, available free at Travel InfoCentres and most major hotels, tells how to reach major attractions in the Lower Mainland and Victoria.

Transit information is available at 521-0400 seven days a week, 6:30 AM–11:30 PM. Persevere and you will eventually get through to this busy number. Printed timetables are available at municipal halls, public libraries and Travel InfoCentres. Transit information can also be found on the Internet at <www.bctransit.com>.

On the North Shore

To travel to West Van—roughly anywhere west of the Lions Gate Bridge on the North Shore—call West Van transit information at 985-7777. Although the blue West Van buses are part of a separate system, transfers from B.C. Transit are valid; transfers from the West Van buses are also valid on B.C. Transit. Fares start at $1.50.

In North Van—that is, east of Lions Gate Bridge—buses are part of the B.C. Transit system.

Airport Bus

See Coach Lines (Vancouver Airporter) and Vancouver International Airport in this chapter.

Scenic Routes

Some Vancouver bus routes are particularly scenic and offer an easy, cheap way to see the city. As always, it's best to avoid rush hour. Some suggestions are:

• **#250 Horseshoe Bay** bus to West Van and along Marine to Horseshoe Bay. Catch this blue West Van bus downtown on Georgia going west. This is about a 50-minute trip each way. You get to ogle fancy homes, and enjoy forest and ocean views

1. Rosellen Suites
2. Buchan
3. English Bay Inn
4. Sylvia
5. West End Community Centre
6. Robson Street Market
7. Westin Bayshore
8. Riviera
9. West End Guest House
10. Listel Vancouver
11. Pacific Pallisades
12. Aquatic Centre
13. Granville Island Ferries dock
14. Sunset Inn
15. Sheraton Wall Garden Hotel
16. YMCA
17. Sutton Place Hotel
18. Wedgewood Hotel
19. Hotel Vancouver

while someone else drives. **Don't miss** buying fish and chips at one of the several small places on the main drag at Horseshoe Bay. Either eat on a patio or walk across to the small waterfront park where you can watch ferries and pleasure craft. If you think of it, pick up some feed for the park waterfowl.

• **#1 Waterfront Station/Beach** bus through Gastown, downtown and the West End and along Beach Dr from English Bay. This short loop should take only about 45 minutes to get you back where you started. Catch this bus going either direction on Burrard.

• **SeaBus** to North Vancouver (described below).

• **SkyTrain** to the New Westminster Public Market (described below).

SeaBus

Crossing Burrard Inlet every 15 minutes during the day since 1977, the SeaBus (521-0400) connects

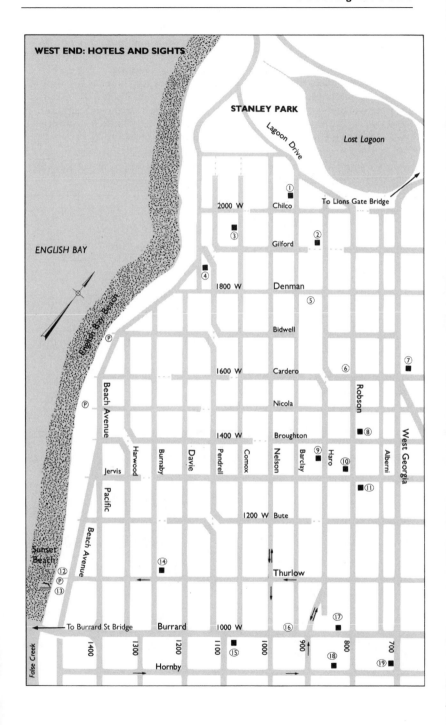

WEST END: HOTELS AND SIGHTS

STANLEY PARK

Lagoon Drive

Lost Lagoon

To Lions Gate Bridge

① Chilco

2000 W

③

② Gilford

ENGLISH BAY

④

1800 W   Denman

⑤

Bidwell

English Bay Beach

Ⓟ

1600 W   Cardero

⑥

⑦

Robson

Nicola

West Georgia

1400 W   Broughton

⑧

Beach Avenue

Harwood

Burnaby

Davie

Pendrell

Comox

Nelson

Barclay

Haro

Alberni

⑨

⑩

Jervis

⑪

Pacific

1200 W   Bute

Beach Avenue

Sunset Beach

⑫

Ⓟ

⑬

⑭

Thurlow

To Burrard St Bridge   Burrard   1000 W

⑯

⑰

False Creek

1400

1300

1200

1100

⑮

1000

900

⑱

800

700

⑲

Hornby

downtown to North Vancouver, reducing the rush-hour snarl on the bridges. Two 400-passenger catamaran ferries, the *Burrard Otter* and the *Burrard Beaver*, make the 12-minute trip. Unfortunately, there is no open-air deck, but the views from inside—of the bridges and busy harbour—are spectacular.

The SeaBus is part of the B.C. Transit system; the same fares and rules regarding transfers apply. It leaves from the SeaBus Terminal located in the lovely old CPR Station on Cordova near Granville and goes to Lonsdale Quay, where there's a lively public market. The market has everything from clothing boutiques and toy stores to vegetable stalls (food downstairs and shops up).

A sunny plaza off the market has a tremendous view of Burrard Inlet and downtown. The restaurants, fast food outlets and pub will come in handy once you've finished exploring.

The SeaBus departs every 15 minutes Mon to Sat during the day, and every 30 minutes on Sun and during the evening until just after midnight. In the summer, late June to early Sept, there are also 15-minute departures on Sun.

Avoid the northbound trip during afternoon rush hour.

Connections with SkyTrain can be made at the downtown SeaBus terminal.

The SeaBus accommodates wheelchairs and scooters. Bicycles are allowed at no extra cost.

SkyTrain

The SkyTrain is Vancouver's rapid transit system. It runs 29 km (18 miles) from Surrey, through Burnaby and New Westminster, to the Canada Place Pier (Waterfront Station) downtown. (For SkyTrain information call 521-0400.)

Except for a few underground stations in the centre of the city, this trip is above ground. So far it follows a single line with 20 stations.

Four-car trains depart every three to five minutes and reach 80 km/h (50 mph). A trip from one end of the

Snowcapped peaks provide a dramatic backdrop to the SkyTrain on its route over the Fraser River. (SkyTrain)

line to the other takes 39 minutes. The driverless trains are run by computers monitored at SkyTrain headquarters. Security and information officers ride the trains and are at stations. The SkyTrain is wheelchair accessible. Tickets are sold by machines at each station; exact change is not necessary. The machines accept $5 and $10 bills, as well as coins. A trip to the New Westminster Quay Public Market is a fine way for visitors to experience the SkyTrain. Take the train to the New Westminster Station; the market is about half a block away on Front, right at the edge of the Fraser River. There's a large indoor market with fresh vegetables, fish and pasta, an excellent bakery and many small kiosks selling arts and crafts. You could plan a full day for this excursion.

Don't miss a walk along the Fraser to watch the river traffic. Some river excursions depart from here. (See Sightseeing, Touring Vancouver). The Paddle Wheeler Neighbourhood

Pub is ideal for lunch. To end a market visit with an elegant dinner, walk four blocks east on Columbia to Restaurant Des Gitanes (524-6122). The Swiss-French cuisine is excellent. (The restaurant guide rating is $$$.)

Coach Lines

The bus depot is located in the Pacific Central Station, 1150 Station St. Formerly a train terminal, it now services motorcoach and train travel. Although it is not in the city centre, it is close to the Main Street/Science World SkyTrain station.

Greyhound
482-8747
Service across Canada and to the Yukon.

Greyhound
1-800-231-2222
For service to all U.S. destinations.

Malaspina Coach Lines
682-6511
Service to the Sunshine Coast,

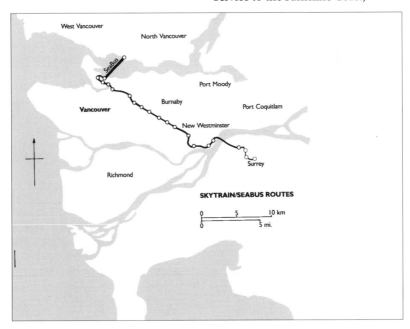

including Gibsons, Sechelt, Madeira Park and Powell River.

Maverick Coach Lines
255-1171
Buses go to Whistler and to Nanaimo on Vancouver Island.

Pacific Coach Lines
662-8074
Buses go to Victoria. See also Ferries (Bus Passengers).

Quick Shuttle
940-4428
Quick bus service to Bellingham Airport, Everett, downtown Seattle and SeaTac Airport. The 3½-hour trip from downtown to downtown costs $31.

Bus service to Vancouver International Airport:

Vancouver Airporter
946-8866
Leaves Level 2 of the airport every 15 minutes, 6 AM to midnight. There are pick-up points from major downtown hotels and the bus depot every 30 minutes. At Hotel Vancouver departures are every 15 minutes. The one-way fare is $10.

Cheam Tours
1-604-823-0196 (Chilliwack)
Pick-up at the Vancouver International Airport, Level 1. Transportation to destinations in the Fraser Valley as far as Hope. As well, pick-up in Chilliwack to Vancouver International.

Cars

Rentals

Avis
757 Hornby near Georgia
606-2847

Budget
501 W Georgia at Richards
668-7000

Hertz
1128 Seymour near Davie
688-2411

Thrifty
1400 Robson near Broughton
(Landmark Hotel)
606-1666

Tilden
1130 W Georgia near Thurlow
685-6111

Rent-a-Wreck
1083 Hornby near Nelson
688-0001
Cheap car rentals.

For something grander—a Porsche, Corvette convertible, Mercedes or Ferrari—call:

Exotic Car Rentals
1820 Burrard at W 2nd
644-9128

Parking

Finding parking may be a challenge. The main parkades are at Pacific Centre (entrance on Howe at Dunsmuir), the Bay (entrance on Richards near Dunsmuir) and Robson Square (entrances on Smithe and Howe). You may get lucky at the lot at Granville Square at the north end of Granville, the multi-level lot on Seymour just after you pass Pender or the lot on Georgia just east of Seymour. Many downtown parking lots, both attended and metered, will take credit cards as well as cash.

Parking meters take $1 and 25¢ coins. Time limits are strictly enforced, and cars are towed (even if you have out-of-province plates) from rush-hour "no parking" areas. Check the parking meter and street signs for times. Parking in commercial alleys is illegal. See also Essential Information (Motor Vehicles).

Taxis

Vancouver has never been an easy city in which to hail a taxi other than in city centre. Service charge is $2.10 and $1.21 per kilometre travelled. To find a cab quickly, head for a downtown hotel (there are cab stands at the Hotel Vancouver and the Hyatt) or call:

Black Top
731-1111, 681-2181
Request a Checker car with "collar-and-tie service," which is a black late-model car, guaranteed spotless, along with a neatly dressed, knowledgeable and friendly driver. All at no extra cost.

MacLure's
731-9211, 683-6666

Vancouver Taxi
255-5111, 669-5555
Has oversized cabs for wheelchairs.

Yellow Cab
681-3311, 681-1111
Yellow will take you for a personal tour of the city on its suggested routes. Prices are the regular meter rate.

HandyDART
430-2692
For those who are physically or mentally unable to use public transportation. Book 24 hours in advance. Fares begin at $1.50 and vary depending on the number of zones travelled.

Limousine Service

There are about 50 limousine companies in the city. For information, call the Talking Yellow Pages at 299-9000 and dial 9717.

The recorded message gives comprehensive information on hiring for specific requirements.

Trains

VIA Rail
1-800-561-8630 toll free (Canada)
Canada's national railway has a transcontinental train that departs and arrives from the Pacific Central Station at Main and Station St on Sun, Tues, and Fri. A popular route from Vancouver on these same days is to Jasper, Alberta. Call the above number for reservations and information.

Call 1-800-835-3037 for arrivals and departures.

Amtrak
585-4848
1-800-USA-RAIL (Canada and U.S.)
The Mount Baker International departs daily from Seattle at 7:45 AM and returns from Vancouver at 6:00 PM from Pacific Central Station. The trip takes about four hours and stops in Bellingham, Mount Vernon, Everett and Edmonds. Cost is as low as $27 one way. Reserve early as prices vary depending on availability.

B.C. Rail
631-3500, 1-800-339-8752 (within B.C.), 1-800-663-8238 (outside B.C. and U.S.A.)
Trains operate out of the station at 1311 W 1st St in North Vancouver. If you have an inclination to see more of British Columbia—the Coast Mountains, forests and some small interior towns—take the B.C. Rail Cariboo Prospector train 253 km (157 miles) northeast to Lillooet. You can get there and back in a day, with a 2½-hour stopover for lunch and exploration. The train leaves every day in summer at 7 AM and travels via Horseshoe Bay, Squamish and Whistler, arriving in Lillooet at 12:30 PM. (There are also trips to 100 Mile House, Quesnel, Williams Lake or Prince George, but these require an overnight stay.) The Cariboo Prospector arrives back in North

The Rocky Mountaineer travels from Vancouver to the Rockies in daylight. (Rocky Mountaineer)

Vancouver at 8:45 PM. The return fare is $128, with discounts for seniors and children, and includes breakfast and dinner. All passenger trains are non-smoking. B.C. Rail also offers packages; for example, golf and ski excursions as well as a circle trip to Jasper. See also Sightseeing (Train Trips).

West Coast Express
683-RAIL
1-800-570-7245 (from Mission)
This commuter rail service operates between the town of Mission, located on the northern bank of the Fraser River, and downtown Vancouver. The 65-kilometre trip takes 73 minutes one way and costs $13.65 for a return ticket. The West Coast Express is a boon to downtown office workers who live in these suburban communities. For visitors, it gives an opportunity to view yet another picturesque route as the train rolls through verdant farmland, occasionally borders

the mighty Fraser River and is overlooked by the towering Coast Mountain range. Trains depart the Vancouver SeaBus terminal in the afternoons so it means either a late-evening return or a stay in one of the seven communities where it stops. Tickets are sold at vending machines (cash and credit cards accepted) at each station. Tickets are not sold on the train.

Rocky Mountaineer Railtours
1-800-665-7245 toll free (Canada and U.S.)

The Rocky Mountaineer is the only train that takes in the rugged beauty of the Rockies by daylight. The two-day trip from Vancouver to Jasper, Banff or Calgary includes a one-night hotel stay in Kamloops. It consistently rates plaudits and has been called "the most spectacular train trip in the world," and this company has improved its product. It now offers dome coaches and luxury service along with its original Signature Service, and there is a mindboggling choice of package tours.

Sightseers and train buffs revel in this leisurely paced, scenic rail trip. Even if you've travelled the highway a dozen times, you'll find that this route, which follows the tracks of Canada's first transcontinental railways, gives the best perspective of the wild, undeveloped backcountry. People from all over the world take this trip, so book early.

Ferries

Travelling from one point to another in B.C. is often a memorable experience, and the reason can be stated in a word—scenery. A trip on any of B.C. Ferries' fleet of 40 modern boats is such an experience. Each year over 22 million people take a ferry ride to delight in what are arguably some of the world's best vistas. Even the locals never tire of watching for whales and taking in the tree-shrouded coastline of lonely islands. To accommodate the increasing traffic between the mainland and Vancouver Island, B.C. Ferries has continually added to and upgraded its fleet. There are some extraordinary vessels. Designed and built in B.C., the *Spirit of British Columbia* and the *Spirit of Vancouver Island* each carries 2100 passengers and 470 vehicles. In 1998 the *PacifiCat* vessel was added to the fleet. The second-largest, high-speed ferry in the world, the catamaran carries 250 vehicles and 1000 passen-

gers and reduces the trip between Horseshoe Bay and Departure Bay in Nanaimo by about 30 minutes.

The larger ferries each have a cafeteria, snack bar (some have cappuccino machines), newsstand/giftshop, video arcade, children's play area and ship-to-shore telephone. Smoking is allowed only on the outside decks. Pets must remain on the car deck.

Schedules

For sailing times call 277-0277 (24 hours) in Vancouver or 1-888-223-3779 (toll free within B.C.) for a recorded announcement, or pick up a schedule at the Vancouver TouristInfo Centre at 200 Burrard St or at major hotels. The website, <www.bcferries.bc.ca>, includes current traffic conditions at major terminals.

Vancouver is near two ferry terminals. Tsawwassen is an hour's drive south of downtown. Sailings from this terminal go to Swartz Bay (a 30-minute drive from Victoria), the Gulf

B.C. Ferries provides an ocean voyage that takes in green-shrouded islands. You may even spot a whale on this journey. (B.C. Ferries)

Islands and to Duke Point, a terminal that opened June 1997, south of Nanaimo.

Horseshoe Bay, the other ferry terminal, is a 30-minute drive north from downtown. Sailings from here go to Nanaimo, to Bowen Island and to Langdale on the Sunshine Coast.

The busiest routes are from the mainland to Vancouver Island.

From June to Labour Day, there are hourly sailings from both Tsawwassen terminal and Swartz Bay 7 AM–10 PM for the 90-minute crossing. The rest of the year, except for holidays, sailings are generally every two hours. From Tsawwassen and Duke Point, as well as from Horseshoe Bay and Nanaimo, there are a minimum of eight round trips daily. It is best to call for information on additional sailings during peak travel times.

Fares

There are 25 routes with a variety of weekday and weekend rates. Check the latest B.C. Ferries schedule. B.C. seniors, but not their vehicles, travel free Mon to Thurs, except holidays. Seniors must show their B.C. Gold Care Card to confirm their age and full-time residency in B.C.

Bus fare from downtown Vancouver to downtown Victoria, including the ferry, is $25 one-way.

Travel Tips

Car Passengers

Car reservations only are accepted on the Tsawwassen/Swartz Bay, Horseshoe Bay/Nanaimo and Tsawwassen/Duke Point routes. Call 1-888-724-5223 for reservations or 604-444-2890 if you are calling from outside B.C.; there is a $15 fee.

Reservations for all vehicle types are accepted on the Tsawwassen/Gulf Islands, Port Hardy/Prince Rupert, Prince Rupert/Queen Charlotte Islands, and Port Hardy/Bella Coola routes. Call 1-888-223-3779 (within B.C.) for reservations.

All other routes are first come, first served. Reservations by phone must be paid for by Visa or MasterCard. Summer and holiday reservations should be made as far in advance as possible.

At any time of the year, it is wise to arrive early if you are taking your car. You can pass the time at the retail stalls at the terminal. The local crafts—from wood carvings to silkwear—are good quality and prices aren't bad. Once you are on the ferry, don't lose your car—it's the quickest way to be spotted as a tourist. Some boats have three vehicle decks—all are numbered.

BC Ferries carries some 26,000 passengers and 6000 vehicles between the mainland and Vancouver Island every day during the summer; avoid peak times like weekends and holidays. Do try to travel before sunset;

Orcinus orca, the Killer Whale

More killer whales are found off the coast of British Columbia than anywhere else in the world. Of the local population of 350 whales, 80 reside in southern waters—the Strait of Georgia, Juan de Fuca Strait and Puget Sound. On a B.C. Ferries trip you will occasionally see a group of dorsal fins 60 to 120 cm (2 to 4 feet) long as the whales cruise the waters near Tsawwassen. Killer whales live and travel in pods of 5 to 50.

Orcinus orca is 6 to 8 m (20 to 26 feet) long and can swim at 20 km/h (12 mph), leaping out of the water when it travels at top speed. Because it is a toothed whale and a successful predator, it has ended up with the unfortunate name of killer whale. It generally feeds on salmon but also preys on porpoises, seals, sea lions, birds and even other kinds of whales.

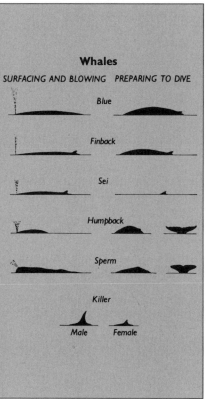

Whales

SURFACING AND BLOWING   PREPARING TO DIVE

Blue

Finback

Sei

Humpback

Sperm

Killer

Male   Female

you'll miss the scenery if you sail in the dark.

Consider leaving your car behind, especially at busy times. But on holiday weekends don't count on leaving it at the Tsawwassen parking lot. Although there is parking for 1100 cars, the lot is frequently full. Parking is not allowed along the lengthy causeway to the terminal, but there is a privately operated, well-signed Park and Ride service at the foot of the causeway.

Foot Passengers

Foot passengers can avoid car line-ups and walk right on board. It's a costly trip by taxi from Vancouver to either ferry terminal—about $55 to Tsawwassen and $35 to Horseshoe Bay. Taking public transportation to Tsawwassen from Vancouver is a long trip and not practical if you have luggage. Take #601 South Delta from city centre (catch it on Howe St beside Pacific Centre Mall) and change at the Ladner Exchange to bus #640 Tsawwassen Ferry. Call B.C. Transit (521-0400) to check schedules.

To reach the Horseshoe Bay terminal, take the blue #250 West Van bus to Horseshoe Bay from downtown (it picks up passengers at bus stops on the north side of Georgia). The bus takes you to within walking distance of the Horseshoe Bay terminal. Call 985-7777.

Foot passengers must purchase tickets at least 10 minutes before sailing time (this is a strict rule; don't be late). If you require bus transportation upon your arrival, listen for announcements giving bus information during the trip. Tickets are purchased on the ferry, and you board the bus before the ferry docks. Buses take you to downtown Victoria, Nanaimo or Powell River or to designated stops in these areas. (Note that some sailings do not have bus service during the winter schedule.) Foot passengers can check luggage at the ferry terminal where tickets are sold. Don't forget to mark the destination on your bag. You can carry your bags onto the ferry, but there are no lockers and space is often at a premium.

Bus Passengers

Buses are the first vehicles on and off the ferries. To get to Victoria, take a Pacific Coach Lines bus that leaves from Pacific Central Station. No reservations are necessary, but arrive at least 30 minutes before the bus is scheduled to depart. The fare (about $25 one-way) includes the cost of the ferry. You can board the bus at the bus depot or at designated stops on the way. To arrange for the bus to stop and pick you up, you must phone Pacific Coach Lines (662-8074) at least an hour before the bus leaves.

If your destination is Nanaimo, catch a Maverick Coach Lines bus (255-1171). Buses to Nanaimo are generally every two hours. To reach the Sunshine Coast call Malaspina Coach Lines (682-6511); there are two trips daily.

Ferry Food

BC Ferries is the largest fast food outlet in the province after McDonald's, and although it is not known for its wonderful fare, on-board dining has improved. Vegetarian dishes are now available, and some vessels, like the *Spirit of British Columbia* and *Spirit of Vancouver Island,* have buffets where

freshness is emphasized. And let's face it, you can't beat the view from a ferry's dining room. If you are departing from Tsawwassen, you can get into the ferry line-up early and grab a snack at Galley West, a large food fair featuring healthy sandwiches, great frozen yogurt and decadent cookies.

Short Ferry Trips

Personally, we're sold on the ferries. Nothing can beat the scenery and salt air as you lounge on the deck on a sunny day. If the weather is good, take binoculars out on deck to watch the marine traffic: fish boats, freighters, sailboats, yachts, tugs and other ferries. You may even catch sight of seals, otters or whales.

Some of the following short ferry trips are perfect if you want to experience the coastal waterways. Save these trips for a sunny day; it makes a big difference.

Horseshoe Bay to Bowen Island

This is one of B.C. Ferries shortest runs, about 20 minutes to go 5 km (3 miles) one-way. It is possible to do this trip from Vancouver in an afternoon with time to browse Bowen—do a historical walk, tour a brewery, perhaps even meet a famous writer. Take the bus to Horseshoe Bay and travel as a foot passenger or take a car. Phone B.C. Ferries for times and prices. See also Where to Stay (Bed and Breakfast).

Sunshine Coast

Another pleasant day trip. The mainland coast north of Vancouver is accessible by a road-and-ferry system for only about 160 km (100 miles) because of the rugged fjord-cut terrain. Phone Malaspina Coach Lines (682-6511) for times and fares to Gibsons. The ferry ride from Horseshoe Bay to Langdale takes 40 minutes, and then there is a short bus ride to the waterfront town of Gibsons. Call B.C. Ferries Corp for sailing times and fares if you are taking your car.

Gulf Islands

Sail to the peaceful Gulf Islands from Tsawwassen, perhaps to Galiano or Mayne, the two closest islands. Both are popular cycling destinations; Mayne is more compact and not as hilly. If you are taking a car, make sure you have a ferry reservation. See also Excursions from Vancouver (Gulf Islands).

Granville Island Ferries

See Sightseeing (Granville Island).

Special Tours

B.C. Ferries offers CirclePac travel packages, which give you a 15% reduction off regular, one-way fares on four routes: Horseshoe Bay to Langdale, Earls Cove to Saltery Bay, Powell River to Comox and return from Vancouver Island to the mainland. During summer, B.C. Ferries have added three northern routes that show off the wild beauty of the coastline. For example, one trip departs Port Hardy on the northern tip of Vancouver Island to take in magnificent fjords and small villages before landing in Bella Coola.

Vancouver International Airport

The airport is on an island at the mouth of the Fraser River, 13 km (8 miles) from downtown. It is Canada's second-busiest airport, with 343,000 takeoffs and landings handling some 15 million passengers a year. The major international and regional airlines that utilize the main terminals are: Air Canada, Air China, Air New Zealand, Alaska Airlines, All Nippon Airways, America West Airlines, American Airlines, British Airways, Canadian Airlines International, Cathay Pacific, Continental Airlines, Delta Air Lines, Japan Airlines, KLM, Korean Air, Lufthansa, Malaysia Airlines, Mandarin Airlines, Northwest Airlines, Philippine Airlines, Quantas, Reno Air, Singapore Airlines, Swissair, United Airlines, Air B.C. Canadian Regional, Horizon Air, NWT Air, SkyWest Airlines, and WestJet Airlines. Local and charter airlines using the main terminals are Cypress Airlines, Hanna Air, Harbour Air, Helijet Airways, K.D. Air, North Vancouver Air, Pacific Coastal Airlines, Shuswap Air and Wilderness Air, as well as Air Club International, Air Transat, Canada 3000, Royal Aviation and SkyService. The smaller South Terminal is located about a five-minute drive away but transportation between the two terminals is not regular. Call the connecting airline to arrange transportation, or take a taxi. Nine regional airlines fly from this location. See also Sightseeing (Touring Vancouver).

Getting There

Getting to the airport by cab costs about $23 from downtown. It's cheaper to take the Vancouver Airporter (946-8866) for $10. It leaves every 30 minutes from the major downtown hotels. You can also flag it down at Broadway and Granville or at 41st and Granville.

Airlimo provides a flat-rate, 24-hour limousine service between the airport and various locations ($29 to downtown). Phone 273-1331 to book.

Public transit buses to and from the airport unfortunately involve a transfer and so are not recommended if you have luggage. But if you decide to go by bus from downtown, take a #8 Granville south to 70th and Granville and then transfer

While waiting for a flight at Vancouver International, travellers are treated to Bill Reid's Spirit of Haida Gwaii. (Judi Lees)

to the #100 Airport, which goes to the airport terminal. Going into town, take the #100 New Westminster Station and transfer at 70th to the #8 Fraser.

For transportation to Whistler Village call Perimeter Transportation (266-5386). One-way fare on the Whistler Express is $45.

Getting Around Vancouver International

In 1996 a $456-million expansion saw the addition of a new international terminal, a state-of-the-art control tower, an additional runway, and a 2080-stall parkade. All international and U.S. traffic goes through the new International Terminal while the original terminal now handles domestic flights.

Whether arriving, departing or meeting people, take time to appreciate Vancouver International's unique works of art, soaring glass fa-

cades, large open spaces, and pillars of Squamish rock. All give a feeling of spaciousness to a facility that may see as many as 60,000 passengers using it on a busy day. A focal point of the airport is *Spirit of Haida Gwaii, The Jade Canoe*, a large bronze work by world-renowned Vancouver Haida artist, the late Bill Reid. The carving, which is approximately 4 m (13 feet) high and 6 m by 3 m (20 feet by 10 feet) in area, is located on the main floor of the International Terminal between the international and U.S. check-in counters. It is backed by floor-to-ceiling glass art depicting waves and is surrounded by an amphitheatre, an ideal spot to rest and enjoy this artistic wonder.

Should you require assistance of any kind, look for a "Green Coat," one of the 175 volunteers who cruise the airport from 7 AM to 10 PM and are happy to answer questions or give directions.

International Departures

International check-in is in the southwest wing (Concourse D), and U.S. check-in is to the south-east (Concourse E) of the Departures Level (this is the third level) of the International Terminal. There is an information centre here as well as a food fair (with mezzanine seating), lounge and restaurant, newsstands, retail outlets, duty-free shops and children's play areas. There are several currency exchanges and bank machines (near check-in counters in both wings, beside security in the east wing and in the international departure lounge). Throughout the terminal, five moving sidewalks ease movement. Airline lounges for first-class and business passengers are located past security on the Departures Level of the International Terminal.

Departing passengers must pay the Airport Improvement Fee, which varies according to destination—$5 for flights within B.C. and the Yukon; $10 for North American flights including Mexico and $15 for international destinations. The fee must be paid before going through security, and can be paid at machines that take credit cards or at staffed booths (which take cash or credit cards) located near the security gates.

Arrivals

Arriving passengers are greeted with superb views of the West Coast mountains through floor-to-ceiling windows at some gates. The walk to Canada Customs and the Arrivals Hall is enhanced by Musqueam art. *The Spindle Whorl*, a 4 m high (13-foot-high) cedar carving, which depicts eagles, man, salmon, the moon and the earth, dominates a wall; weavings hang from the ceiling; and water cascades beneath an escalator. At the bottom of the escalator, arriving passengers meet the *Welcome Figures*. Carved from one red cedar log, the 5.2 m high (17-foot-high) figures of a Native man and woman display a traditional Coast Salish welcome.

Goods and Services Tax rebate forms for non-Canadians are available from the Canada Customs office on the Arrivals Level (next door to the Elephant and Castle), at all YVR Customer Service Counters and from Duty Free shops.

Located directly outside the Customs Hall are tour operators and cruise ship information counters. Cruise passengers who are not participating in the direct baggage transfer process from their air carrier to the ship's port should go to this counter to have their luggage transferred. There is a currency exchange, tourist information, food and beverage outlets and a chapel in this area. Arriving passengers can enjoy the *Spirit of Haida Gwaii* from this level as well as it sits above the meet-and-greet lobby in an open area. Through the exit doors, the first curb is for buses, taxis and limousines, and the next curb is for general pick-up traffic.

Domestic Departures and Arrivals

The Departures Terminal for domestic travel contains concourses A, B and C. There is a children's nursery and large play area on the Departure Level located in the passageway that connects the Domestic and International Terminals. Domestic passengers arrive one floor down.

Airport Parking

Covered walkways connect the Domestic and International Terminals to a four-storey parkade. Rates begin at $2 per half-hour. Baggage carts are available inside beside the baggage carousels, curbside at the terminals and in the parkade. There are several nearby lots that run shuttle buses to and from the airport. There is an outdoor parking lot next to the parkade as well as several long-term parking lots (such as Park 'N Fly, 270-9476, whose rates start at $9.95 per day) that are serviced by shuttle.

Car Rentals

Car rental outlets are located on Level 1 of the Parkade. Companies here include Alamo (1-800-327-9633), Avis (606-2847), Budget (668-7000), Hertz (606-3700), National Tilden (1-800-387-4747), and Thrifty (1-800-367-2277).

Extra Time at Vancouver International

Time between flights? No problem in this airport. Get some fresh air and enjoy West Coast scenery. Just outside the Arrivals Level of the International Terminal is Chester Johnson Park, a pleasant retreat with benches, a variety of local plant life and a short walk between trees. In autumn 1997 another lush landscaped area was added on the east end of the International Terminal. A gravelled walkway is bordered by West Coast growth—60 mature trees were transplanted—that includes rhododendrons, wild roses, shrubs and ground cover. There are few airports in the world where a between-flights walk in the park is an option.

Flights to Victoria

Downtown Service

Harbour Air Seaplanes
688-1277
1-800-665-0212
In summer 20 daily flights on weekdays and 8 on weekends depart Vancouver Harbour to land in Victoria Harbour. The 35-minute flight costs $79. Flights also depart from Harbour Air near the airport (4760 Inglis Dr) on the Fraser River. If time allows, visit the restaurant/pub that adjoins the Harbour Air terminal. See Sightseeing (Touring Vancouver).

Helijet Airways
273-1414
A 12-passenger Sikorsky helicopter will transport you from the Vancouver Harbour heliport to the Victoria heliport, a few minutes drive from the city centre. A free shuttle service is provided to downtown Victoria. On a clear day this regularly scheduled trip shows off the city, mountains, Mt Baker, the Gulf Islands and Vancouver Island. The fare is $250 return, but book early for a reduced fare of $170.

Victoria Airport

Air B.C.
688-5515

Canadian Regional Airlines
279-6611

Both airlines fly from Vancouver International, Domestic Terminal, to Victoria International in Sidney on Vancouver Island. The flight is about 35 minutes long. The fare is about $266 return, but weekend and greatly reduced excursion rates are available. There is a 30-minute drive to and from the city at each end.

Sightseeing

The Sights

Thanks to the mountains, ocean and climate, as well as the history, there are sights that are unique to Vancouver. Listed below (in no particular order) are 10 not-to-be-missed attractions. Many are described in this section and elsewhere in the book. See as many of these as you can:

1. **Granville Island**; see this chapter
2. **The Royal Hudson**; see this chapter
3. **Grouse Mountain**; see Parks/Beaches/Gardens
4. **Museum of Anthropology**; see Museums/Art Galleries
5. **A walk in the forest**; see Parks/Beaches/Gardens
6. **A ferry ride**; see Getting Around (Ferries)
7. **Chinatown**; see this chapter
8. **Stanley Park seawall**; see Parks/Beaches/Gardens
9. **Dr Sun Yat-sen Classical Chinese Garden**; see Parks/Beaches/Gardens
10. **Jericho Beach to Spanish Banks**; see Parks/Beaches/ Gardens

Boats and bridges are part of the Granville Island scene. (Judi Lees)

Granville Island

In many ways, this island (connected to the city by a causeway) comprises the best of Vancouver. It is rich in history; showcases some of the area's best agricultural products, crafts and art; is busy with marine activity; is home to several theatres; and has no lack of eateries and good views.

The island boomed with industry in the '20s and '30s, but after the war many of the large plants left. It remained unnoticed until 1973, when the federal government got involved. Most of the remaining industries were persuaded to leave, but buildings were kept and given a facelift. The public market opened in 1979 and became a raging success. Now Granville Island is a hub of enjoyment for locals and visitors alike. It's a hodge-podge of unusual buildings—the exteriors of the industrial structures are jazzed up with bright blues, greens and yellows, and the blend of old and new works. During 1999, in honour of the island's 20th anniversary, a year-long celebration will take place.

Granville Island is a people place. It is not too trendy or touristy, and there is far more to do than just shop. One can spend hours wander-

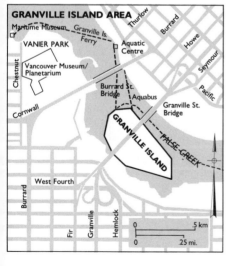

GRANVILLE ISLAND AREA

Maritime Museum
Granville Is. Ferry
VANIER PARK
Aquatic Centre
Vancouver Museum/ Planetarium
Burrard St. Bridge
Aquabus
Granville St. Bridge
GRANVILLE ISLAND
FALSE CREEK
West Fourth
Thurlow
Burrard
Howe
Seymour
Pacific
Chestnut
Cornwall
Burrard
Fir
Granville
Hemlock

0   5 km
0   25 mi.

A fruit grower's day stall at Granville Island Public Market. (Judi Lees)

ing the craft and art galleries, enjoying the waterfront scenes and simply being part of the easygoing atmosphere.

What to See

Granville Island Information Centre
1592 Johnston St near the Public Market
666-5784
There is an excellent map of the island, brochures and helpful information officers here, as well as a continuous 12-minute slide presentation on the island's history. Open daily 9 AM–6 PM. There is a currency exchange and bank machine in the same building.

Granville Island Public Market
Nothing can beat the market for one-stop food shopping. If you're making a picnic (perhaps to take to Kits Beach, a few blocks away), here is a cornucopia. On a dull day, the market building is dry, warm and full of fragrances, bright colours, lively people and wonderful things to taste. In hot weather, huge glass doors lift so that you are right out on the shore of False Creek, where you

can sit, sample your purchases, enjoy buskers and watch tugs and sailboats go by. The market is open 9 AM to 6 PM every day in the summer (May to Sept) and is closed Mon in the winter. See also Shopping.

Art and Crafts Galleries
Some of the galleries on the island are in the Net Loft, which is across from the Public Market. Circle Craft displays jury-selected B.C. crafts, Kingsmill Pottery Studio showcases murals that are worth checking out, and Paperworks Gallery exhibits limited-edition prints.

As you wander the island, you will discover a superb mix of local crafts, and many artisans will welcome you into their studios. Some are the tapestry makers at Fibre Art Studio and silk painters at Maiwa Handprints (both in the Net Loft building on Johnston), weaver Diana Sanderson (15–1551 Johnston, tucked behind a narrow walkway near Mulvaney's Restaurant), the glassblowers at New-Small & Sterling (1440 Old Bridge), the quilters at Textile Context (1420 Old Bridge), the three women jewellers at Hammered & Pickled (1494

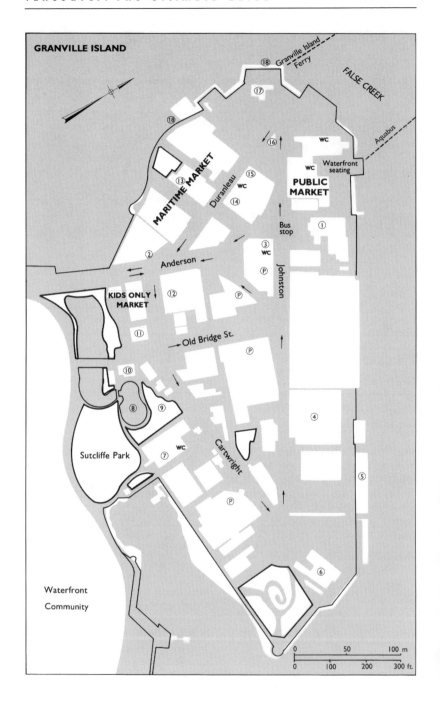

GRANVILLE ISLAND

FALSE CREEK

Granville Island Ferry

Aquabus

PUBLIC MARKET

Waterfront seating

WC

WC

MARITIME MARKET

Duranleau

WC

Bus stop

WC

Anderson

KIDS ONLY MARKET

Johnston

Old Bridge St.

Cartwright

Sutcliffe Park

WC

Waterfront Community

0   50   100 m

0   100   200   300 ft.

Old Bridge), the gold- and silver-smiths at Forge and Form (1334 Cartwright) and Joel Berman, maker of contemporary glass (1244 Cartwright). At Black Stone Press (1249 Cartwright) you can order specialized printing products.

Don't miss purchasing a gift that is typical of B.C., such as native masks or jewellery, or some locally made pottery or weaving. Go to the Gallery of B.C. Ceramics or to Crafthouse; both are on Cartwright. Federation Gallery (1241 Cartwright) features Canadian art—prints, water colours, photography—and Wickaninnish Gallery in the Net Loft has traditional and contemporary Native art.

See also Museums/Art Galleries (Craft Galleries).

Granville Island has boat rentals (see Sports/Recreation); a great water park for kids, tennis courts at the Community Centre and theatres.

1. Arts Club Theatre
2. Sport Fishing and Model Ships Museum
3. Granville Island Info Centre
4. Emily Carr College of Art
5. Sea Village floating homes
6. Granville Island Hotel
7. False Creek Community Centre
8. Water Park
9. Adventure Playground
10. Isadora's Restaurant
11. Waterfront Theatre
12. Granville Island Brewery
13. The Lobster Man
14. Net Loft
15. Blackberry Books
16. La Baguette et L'Échalote
17. Bridges Restaurant
18. Boat rentals
WC Washroom
Ⓟ Parking

Here are a few more highlights:

Granville Island Sport Fishing Museum/Model Ships Museum
1502 Duranleau
683-1939

New in 1998, these two museums in one are a delightful stop. The sport fishing section displays old, even antique, fishing gear, some fabulous sculpture and a simulator that allows you to reel in an 85-pound chinook salmon. If you've ever wondered what a 185-pound halibut looks like up close, there's a model here. At the back of the museum facing the water are exquisitely detailed, large-scale model ships of the 1900s. The *Bismarck* is here, and there's a dramatically narrated video of its sinking.

Sea Village
The only residents of the island live here in one of Vancouver's few houseboat communities.

Brewery Tour
Island Lager, made on the island by Granville Island Brewery, is the best beer in British Columbia. For more details, see Special Interest Tours later in this chapter.

Kids Only Market
Everything and anything for little people under 14.
    See With the Kids (Day Trips).

Places to Eat

As well as the many take-out stands in the market—you can get fish and chips, deli fare, Japanese, or even a good steak—there are more than half-a-dozen restaurants on the island.
    Don't miss taking the kids to Isadora's Co-operative Restaurant. (See Restaurants, Breakfast/Brunch.) There's plenty to amuse them, including a water playground next door. On a sunny day, eat outside at Bridges. (See Restaurants, Outdoors.)

It's a five-minute ride on a small ferry from the West End to Granville Island. (Judi Lees)

For a cool drink go to the Arts Club Backstage Lounge or Bridges Neighbourhood Pub.

Getting to the Island

By Boat

For those with their own boat, there is free two-hour moorage directly behind Granville Island Public Market.

Two companies run small ferries from downtown to the island.

False Creek Ferries (684-7781) run continuously from the south foot of Thurlow behind the Vancouver Aquatic Centre to Granville Island for $1.75 for adults, with discounts for children and seniors. The trip takes about five minutes. Daily service 7 AM–10 PM in the summer; 7 AM–8 PM in the winter. During summer, the ferry also goes to Vanier Park daily 10–8 (weekends only in the winter), and to Stamps Landing at False Creek 10–6. There is also service to Science World, 10–6 in summer and 10–5 in winter on weekends

only. Aquabus Ferries (689-5858) run from the south foot of Hornby St, leaving every two or three minutes, for Granville Island. During summer the hours are 7 AM–10 PM; during winter, 7 AM–8 PM. Price is $1.75 for adults, with discounts for seniors and children. Aquabus also does trips to False Creek, Science World and to the south end of Drake St near the Roundhouse Community Centre. In winter, some trips run only on weekends. Bikes travel for 50¢; there is one specially designed ferry that transports 12 cyclists and bikes.

By SkyTrain

Get off at Science World and take the False Creek ferry to Granville Island.

By Bus

Catch a #51 Granville Island bus at Broadway and Granville; it runs until 6:05 PM. The #50 False Creek South from downtown stops a five-minute walk away from the island and runs until 12:30 AM.

By Car

If possible, avoid taking your car to Granville Island. Line-ups and parking can be horrendous. Free parking has a three-hour time limit, and you have to be lucky to find a spot. Cars parked too long are towed. Covered pay parking costs $1.50 per hour; 6 PM–12 AM is a flat fee of $1.50. Credit cards are accepted by the machines. There is less traffic on weekdays (the earlier in the day, the better).

Chinatown

The Chinese are Vancouver's oldest ethnic group. They first came in 1858 to join the Fraser Valley gold rush and were later contracted in large numbers to construct the Canadian Pacific Railway. Many settled in this area of the city where Chinese clan associations or benevolent societies provided homes and welfare for new immigrants. (The best examples of the distinctive turn-of-the-century architecture, with the ornamental roof lines and curved roof tiles, are in the two blocks of Pender west of Main.) In these early days, the Chinese were not allowed citizenship, and they had no rights until 1949. Today there are over 230,000 people of Chinese origin who live in Vancouver and its bordering municipalities. They are active and respected in all aspects of city life.

A visit to Chinatown is a step into another culture. The sights, smells, sounds and tastes of China are all here. It's the street life that makes Chinatown distinctive—sidewalks are bustling, often jammed with curious foodstuffs spilling from the stores. And it's noisy with enthusiastic vendors calling out their specials. Lichee nuts, anyone? If you wish to experience this lively scene, go on a sunny weekend afternoon. For a leisurely stroll, go midweek in the morning.

To visit Vancouver's Chinatown is to visit another culture. (Judi Lees)

Getting to and Parking in Chinatown

Chinatown is a 20-minute walk from Georgia and Granville. You can take a bus (either #3 Main or #8 Fraser will take you to Main and Keefer) or the SkyTrain (get off at Main St station and walk north). Those with cars may find parking difficult, but there are several parkades— Chinatown Plaza at Keefer and Columbia, Sun Wah Centre on Keefer east of Main, and one on Union just off Main. There are also lots with meters; take change.

A Walking Tour of Chinatown

The heart of the Chinese community is Pender from Carrall to Gore, and Keefer from Main to Gore. Like the rest of the city, Chinatown has seen changes during the '90s, but care has been taken to blend the new with

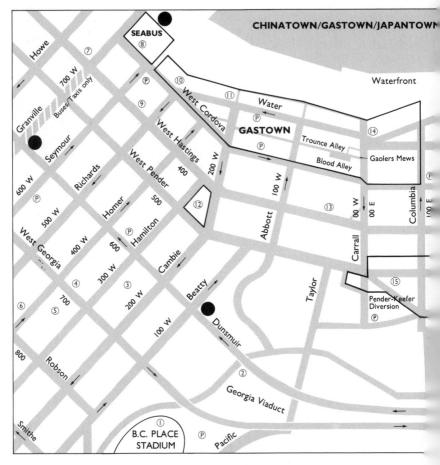

CHINATOWN/GASTOWN/JAPANTOWN

the old. Modern buildings, like the **Bank of Hong Kong** and the **Chinatown Plaza Parkade & Shopping Centre**, are finished in soft-toned red brick. (The latter, at 180 Keefer, houses shops and The Floata, a 1000-seat restaurant.) Apartments and a care facility were added to meet community needs, and the Bank of Hong Kong is in a tower at Main and Keefer.

A good place to start walking is on Pender west of Main. At 50 E Pender is the **Chinese Cultural Centre** (687-0729), which holds classes in English and Chinese, Chinese arts and crafts, and *tai chi*. The building is the entrance to **Dr Sun Yat-sen Classical Chinese Garden**. This garden was designed in the People's Republic and built with the help of $6 million worth of labour and materials donated by the people of China. The walled Ming Dynasty-style garden is the only classical Chinese garden outside China and is a lovely, tranquil stop. There is a small gift shop with some unusual items from China, like beautifully painted glass eggs. See also Parks/Beaches/Gardens.

Along Pender between Carrall and

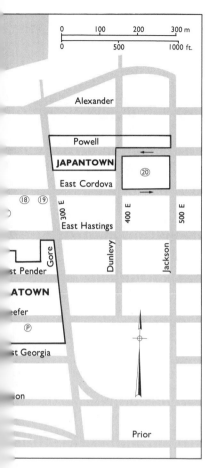

1. B.C. Place Stadium (B.C. Sports Hall of Fame
2. GM Place
3. Queen Elizabeth Theatre/Playhouse
4. Main Post Office
5. Library Square
6. Ford Theatre
7. Sinclair Centre
8. SeaBus Station
9. SFU Downtown Campus
10. The Landing
11. Steam Clock
12. Victory Square
13. Army & Navy Dept Store
14. "Gassy Jack" statue
15. Chinese Cultural Centre/Dr Sun Yat-sen Classical Chinese Garden
16. Carnegie Community Centre
17. Police Station
18. Vancouver Police Museum
19. Firehall Theatre
20. Oppenheimer Park
• SkyTrain station
→ Traffic direction
Ⓟ Parking

Main are stores selling rattan, porcelain, silk and inexpensive gifts. Stop in at **Ming Wo** at 23 E Pender, one of the best cookware stores in town, crammed with every imaginable kitchen utensil. (See Shopping, Kitchenware and China.) Along this block, some of the funky, old shops are disappearing, but except for a Mr Coffee cappuccino bar, most are still Chinese-oriented. At 51 E Pender is **Chinatown Art Gallery**, where all the works of art are imported from China. Some tiny hole-in-the-wall shops are treasure chests of cheap toys and novelties. These are excel-

lent places to pick up small, unusual treats for children. Throughout your walk you will notice outlets where herbalists work behind counters and mix herbs for whatever ails you.

In spring 1998 the Chinese Cultural Centre opened a new complex on Columbia St just south of Pender. Done in the same gracious Chinese architectural style, this two-storey building has a museum on the second floor where changing exhibits portray Chinese-Canadian history. Admission is $5 for adults. On the ground floor is the **East West Gallery** with Canadian Chinese art exhibits.

Just before Main is **New Town Bakery** at 158 E Pender, a favourite of the Chinatown bakeries. You can

Library Square

The Vancouver Public Library is worth a visit both for its bold, Colosseum-style architecture and because it is a fine place to be among books. While its design may resemble an ancient Roman structure, it is a library fashioned for the future, with everything from electronically controlled conveyors to move books to a state-of-the-art language section that allows self-tutoring in 90 languages. True bibliophiles should not miss the Special Collections on the 7th floor, where rare, historic books are kept in a glass-enclosed area. The vast, six-storey, circular building was designed by renowned architect Moshe Safdie and opened in 1995. You can take a self-guided architectural tour by picking up a brochure at the library's Central Information Desk.

Attached to the library are retail shops, espresso bars, kiosks and a bookstore. The book'-märk has gift items and is run by Friends of the Library. A row of shops are located under an atrium-style roof between the library and an attached office building. Library Square is a lively hub in the city. Locals love to enjoy the sun on its wide sweep of steps and mingle in its casual eateries.

Visitors may obtain a temporary library card (call 331-3670). For general information: 331-3600.

Located at 350 W Georgia at Homer St, the library is open Mon to Thurs 10–8; Fri and Sat 10–5; closed Sun during the summer. Sept to May, Sun 1–5.

---

take out or sit at the back and have baked goods and tea. Near the corner, on the north side at 173 E Pender, is **Yeu Hua Crafts.** Go downstairs to view a huge selection of Chinese ceramics and rosewood furniture.

Once you cross Main you are in the thick of the food markets. Prices in Chinatown are cheaper (and quality often higher) than anywhere else, especially for produce, fish, poultry and meat. Stop at one of the bigger markets (try **Yuen Fong** at 242 E Pender) and you'll find cans, bottles and packages of foods you've never seen before. Yuen Fong also has a large selection of Chinese cooking and eating utensils.

On this block you can watch butchers skillfully wield their cleavers to chop up barbecued pork or duck in the windows of the meat markets.

Turn right at Gore, walk past more markets and then turn right at Keefer. At the corner of Keefer and Main is the **Ten Ren Tea and Ginseng Co**, which sells an enormous variety of Chinese teas that promise simple refreshment or a cure of all ailments—and cost up to $68/kg ($150/lb.). Ginseng is a specialty here. The store also sells a range of attractively packaged teas that make great gifts. Another perfect gift is the Chinese tea sets found here and in other small shops.

The best Chinese restaurants unfortunately are no longer in Chinatown, but a couple of outstanding spots remain. Try **Hon's Wun Tun House**, 268 Keefer in Sun Wah Centre, for noodles, and the **Phnom-Penh**, 244 E Georgia, the best Vietnamese/Cambodian restaurant in town. (See Restaurants, Chinese, Vietnamese/Cambodian.)

The Symphony of Fire

Each summer the four nights of fireworks, called the Benson & Hedges Symphony of Fire, are bigger, splashier and more expensive, attracting more than 500,000 spectators. They are set off in the middle of English Bay and can be seen from Kitsilano, the West End and West Vancouver. Traffic used to be horrendous in the West End that evening; now the area is closed to cars on fireworks nights. Take transit, park downtown and walk, or watch from Kitsilano or West Vancouver.

Touring Vancouver

In Vancouver you can see the sights by bus, trolley, horse and carriage, steam locomotive, helicopter, Rolls-Royce, float plane or a variety of boats.

By Air

Harbour Air
688-1277
1-800-665-0212 (Canada and U.S.)
Trips range from a 30-minute tour of the city ($72 a person) to a 2¼-hour outing to a secluded alpine lake with a picnic lunch ($229 per person, but the price is reduced when more people attend).

In the spring and summer there are daily commuter flights to the Gulf Islands from Vancouver Harbour. From Harbour Air's terminal, located at Vancouver Airport's South Terminal, there are flights to Galiano and Salt Spring Islands.

Don't miss Harbour Air's Flying Beaver restaurant/pub. It's worth the drive to the South Terminal. In summer you can watch the float planes

land as you eat on a sunny deck that juts over the river. In colder weather, there's a fireplace, comfy seating and the same terrific views. There's finger food, pastas, fresh seafood and beer on tap.

See Getting Around (Flights to Victoria).

Vancouver Helicopters
270-1484
1-800-987-4354 (Canada and U.S.)
Tours leave from either the Vancouver Harbour heliport or from Grouse Mountain. City and mountain tours from Grouse Mountain start at $45 a person for an 8-minute tour; a 45-minute North Shore Discovery tour costs $195 a person.

By Land

A bus tour can be a fine introduction to a city. Bus tour companies seem to fall into two categories: the big companies that use big buses, where you'll find yourself with about 50 people, or smaller companies with small buses that hold about 20 people.

The trips themselves don't vary that much between the big and the small companies, although some have specialities that may include meals or a ride on a ferry. Check the itineraries. The city tours will include downtown, Gastown, Chinatown, Robson Street, Canada Place, Stanley Park, Shaughnessy, Queen Elizabeth Park and Granville Island. There are also excursions that include the North Shore, taking in Grouse Mountain, the Capilano Suspension Bridge, salmon hatchery and perhaps Lonsdale Quay market.

The two largest tour companies are:

Pacific Coach Lines
662-7575
1-800-661-1725 (Canada and U.S.)

A horse-drawn carriage tour is one of the many ways to enjoy Stanley Park. (Judi Lees)

Gray Line of Vancouver
879-3363
1-800-667-0882 (Canada and U.S.)

See also Getting Around (Public Transit, Taxis).

The small bus companies are:

West Coast City and Nature Sightseeing
451-1600
"Nature" is a little misleading here. These are city tours. Tours available in German and Mandarin.

LandSea Tours
255-7272
Excursions to Whistler and Victoria as well as city tours in 24-passenger coaches. This company also has a variety of water tours.

Some Unusual Land Tours

Captain Billy's Magical Tours
687-2220
A luxurious six-passenger van is your transportation, Captain Billy, a Vancouver native, is your guide, and you customize your own tour. Chat with Billy and he'll help you decide what you'd like to see in his city. He'll show you the best. Cost is $60 per hour for a minimum of 2½ hours.

Fridge's Early Motion Tours
687-5088
See the city in a 1930 Model A Ford Phaeton touring convertible. A one-hour tour of downtown, Stanley Park, Chinatown and Gastown costs $80. Follow the suggested route or devise your own. The car holds four passengers.

Stanley Park Horse Drawn Tours
681-5115
A one-hour narrated tour of Stanley Park takes you through the forest, past the rose gardens and along the waterfront in a 20-passenger carriage. It leaves every 20–30 minutes from the information booth in the first parking lot from the Georgia St entrance. Cost is $12 for adults, with discounts for seniors and students. Private tours (there are also two- to six-person carriages) can be booked. Horse-drawn tours run March 15 to October 31 but private bookings are available during December.

Vancouver Trolley Company
801-5515
1-888-451-5581 (Canada and U.S.)
The turn-of-the-century trolleyless trolley cars you occasionally see on Vancouver streets let you take a tour

Sea Lions at Steveston

Since 1980 Steller sea lions from as far north as Alaska, and California sea lions from as far south as Baja, have been congregating on the Steveston jetty at the mouth of the Fraser River. Each spring more and more sea lions arrive, possibly lured by the warm currents of El Niño. Most recently more than 700 were counted sunning themselves on the jetty. Eulachon (a smeltlike fish of the northern Pacific) have been particularly plentiful in the Fraser River lately, and the sea lions keep coming back for more. All the visiting sea lions are males, here to fatten up before returning home to breed. Some mature Stellers reach 1120 kg (2500 pounds).

Unlike the territorial hostility between the males at the breeding grounds, or rookeries, confrontations at Steveston are usually limited to a dominant male shoving a smaller one off a choice sunning rock. It can get to be a lively and social scene, with the Californias barking and the Stellers growling like bears, but mostly the sea lions are intent on lazing in the sun. They feed at night, and during the day at the height of the season every boulder on the end of the 8 km (5-mile) jetty has a sea lion draped over it. (Similar to the beach at Fort Lauderdale during spring break!)

Sea lions are protected but are hated by fishermen because of their voracious appetites and the damage they do to nets—California sea lions off Vancouver Island alone consume 600 tonnes of salmon a year, and that's just 10 per cent of their diet. In recent years the numbers of Californias have been increasing; the Steller population is stable.

of the major attractions at your own speed. They cover a two-hour circuit including 16 stops and have a guide who narrates the trip. You can get out at each stop and reboard a subsequent trolley—they come every 30 minutes. Fares, $20 for adults with discounts for children, can be paid to the driver and are good for one circuit. Cash, traveller's cheques and U.S. dollars ($16) are accepted.

By Water

Vancouver has myriad water tours, from dinner cruises of 200 people to chartering your own sailboat. (See *Yellow Pages* under Boat Charter.) We recommend the following:

Starline Tours
272-9187, 522-3506 (seasonal)

If you're in Vancouver in the spring, the sea lion boat trips from Steveston are a must. The trips are 1½ hours long and cost $20 for adults, with discounts for seniors and children. Phone to check times. The sea lions—you may see as many as 700—generally arrive in March and leave in May.

Starline Tours' 5½-hour Historic Steveston excursion plys the Fraser River to its mouth, where the George C. Reifel Migratory Bird Sanctuary is located. At the fishing village of Steveston you have time to explore museum, shops, galleries and have fish and chips on the boardwalk. The cost is $42 for adults. There is also a relaxing and scenic 6-hour cruise on Pitt Lake that costs $53. The Starline crew is knowledgeable about the

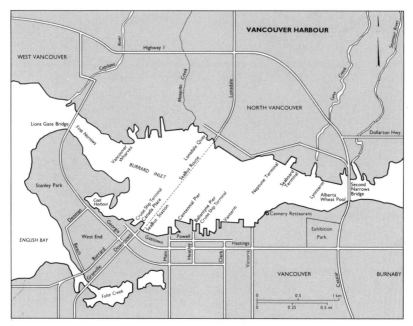

rivers, local history, and flora and fauna. These trips depart from New Westminster Quay across from the New Westminster SkyTrain station.

Harbour Ferries
687-9558

Board the MPV *Constitution* and step back into yesteryear. The paddle wheeler takes you on a 75-minute cruise of Burrard Inlet to view Lions Gate Bridge, Stanley Park, the city skyline and the workings of a busy port. Cost is $16 for adults, with discounts for seniors and children. There is also a sunset dinner cruise. Both tours run May to October.

Aquabus Ferries
689-5858

Chug along in these cute water taxis for a 30-minute mini-cruise that shows off False Creek, the city skyline, mountains and beaches. Cost is $6; discounts for children and seniors. Kids love this trip. See also Getting to the Island, this chapter.

Paddlewheeler River Adventures
525-4465

Go churning upriver on the mighty Fraser aboard the MV *Native*. This paddle wheeler follows the route of hundreds of boats of earlier times. Your destination is Fort Langley, where lively and informative narrations by guides in turn-of-the-century outfits help you relive B.C.'s history. As well, you are treated to the ever-changing waterway traffic and chances to view wildlife. Day and evening cruises depart from New Westminster Quay across from the New Westminster SkyTrain station. The Fort Langley Adventure costs $54 for adults, discounts for seniors and students. Prices are lower when large groups book.

Lotus Land Tours
684-4922

For a quick entry into wilderness, take a day trip kayaking in Indian Arm, a spectacular glacial fjord. Lotus Land will pick you up and

The Pacific National Exhibition

Classified as an agricultural fair but really much more, the PNE has been held every summer since 1910. It opens mid-Aug and ends on Labour Day. Originally a gala parade took place on the streets of Vancouver to start the popular event; today there is a daily on-site parade to set the mood.

This fair is one of the largest in North America. You'll see horse shows, prize livestock, some horticultural displays and craft shows. There is a petting farm, an international food fair and entertainment that features local and international performers on a variety of stages. Events like "Super Dogs" (where canines show us how smart they are) and the Motor Sport Bowl (a takeoff on a demolition derby) draw large crowds. You can wander through educational and cultural exhibits or eat corn on the cob on the midway after a wild ride on one of the few wooden roller coasters in North America.

Phone B.C. Transit regarding special PNE buses. For the daily schedule of events, check the newspaper or phone 253-2311. Gates are open daily 10:30–10:30; grounds are open until midnight and the casino until 2 AM. Admission is about $6 for adults. After 1999, the PNE will leave its Hastings and Renfrew location. Future plans will be announced. (Information: 253-2311. Website: <www.pne.bc.ca>.)

See also With the Kids (Playland).

transport you to Deep Cove for a six-hour trip that includes paddling a wooded marine park. Harbour seals, cormorants, herons, eagles, starfish, jellyfish—there are many bonuses on this soft adventure. There's a barbecued salmon lunch on Twin Island and time to explore the beach and forest—all less than an hour's drive from city centre. No kayak experience is necessary. Cost is $120.

Princess Louisa Tours
1-888-566-7778 (Canada and U.S.)
This excursion departs from Porpoise Bay on the Sunshine Coast. To reach Princess Louisa Inlet, a 32-foot customized yacht takes you up Sechelt Inlet through the famous Skookumchuck Rapids and into a green-shrouded wilderness. For those who revel in water journeys and glorious scenery, this trip is a must. It runs Apr to Sept on Sun, Wed, Fri, takes about 10 hours, and costs $245, which includes continental breakfast and gourmet lunch. To do this as a day trip, take your car on the ferry from Horseshoe Bay to the Sunshine Coast, or take a bus or helicopter from Vancouver.

See also Sports/Recreation (Cruising/Sailing).

Walking/Hiking/Cycling Tours

Historical Walking Tours of Gastown
683-5650
Gastown's namesake, *raison d'être* and first non-Native inhabitant was a saloon owner named Gassy Jack Deighton back in 1867. After the 1886 fire that destroyed Vancouver, the area was rebuilt with warehouses and hotels. Once the depression hit, it became a skid row and remained derelict until the late 1960s, when it was declared a historic site. Gastown underwent a beautification program and today is attractive, containing

Mountain bikes offer an exciting way to explore Grouse Mountain. (C.J. Relke)

the city's oldest architecture (some buildings predate 1900). It's a pleasant place to stroll and shop. Water St from Richards to Columbia is where you want to be.

At the corner of Water and Cambie is an odd contraption, the world's first steam clock. It is powered by an underground steam system used to heat the neighbouring buildings. Every quarter-hour the whistle blows, and on the hour, steam spews from its works. A statue of the loquacious Gassy Jack stands in Maple Tree Square.

A popular walking tour of Gastown is conducted daily mid-June to the end of Aug. The free, 90-minute tour leaves from the Gassy Jack statue in Maple Tree Square (Water and Carrall) at 2 PM.

Rockwood Adventures
926-7705

To enjoy a guided walk with a naturalist on some of the city's finest trails, call Manfred Scholermann. He combines his knowledge of the outdoors with his background as a chef to offer his half- or full-day trips to Lighthouse Park, Bowen Island and other nearby locations. Walks go ahead rain or shine (umbrellas and ponchos provided). Wear good walking shoes and don't forget your camera. A four-hour excursion to Lighthouse Park includes a snack and

costs $45; a Bowen Island trip with a gourmet lunch is $85. Rockwood also does several city walking tours for groups only; for example, a Chinatown walk includes *dim sum*.

Hike BC
540-2499

Experience some of Vancouver's high mountain trails accompanied by first-aid-certified guides. Hike BC provides transportation and picnic lunch along with panoramic vistas on full- or half-day hikes, May through Oct. Treks are designed for a variety of hiking levels. Cost for half-day picnic hike is $55.

From Dec through Apr, snowshoe tours can be booked. Cost $35–$55. A special add-on combines a downtown spa visit with one of the outdoor trips.

Urban Adventures Vancouver Cycle Tours
831-0367

A guided cycling tour is a wonderful way to explore Vancouver. This company offers three- and five-hour excursions that start and end in downtown. Two-wheeling at a comfortable pace, you can take in the Stanley Park seawall, English Bay, Granville Island, and the Kitsilano beaches. You purchase lunch at the Granville Island Public Market and later enjoy a picnic overlooking the water. Urban Adventures also customizes tours so that people of "average" fitness level can enjoy the sights around UBC and the Capilano Suspension Bridge. Cost is $50 for five hours; $30 for three.

Velo-City Cycle Tours
924-0288

This is your chance to have an unusual, high-mountain cycling adventure. The Grouse Mountain West Coaster takes you from the top of Grouse to the Seymour River, 25 km

(15.5 miles) below. Suited to novice mountain-bikers, this guided trip is a commune with nature. As you traverse mountain trails you may spot eagles, grouse, owls, woodpeckers, black bear and deer. There is time to enjoy flower-rich alpine meadows and views of a miniature Vancouver far below. Cost is $95 for this five-hour descent; a shorter excursion is $75. Prices include tram, all equipment, snack or lunch and guide. Trips run May to Oct, rain or shine (rain gear provided) and Velo-City picks up from downtown. Another option is the Sunrise Express, which captures the rising sun from atop Grouse Mountain.

Train Trips

Royal Hudson/
MV *Britannia* Excursion
688-7246

This is the best day trip from Vancouver. In fact, this combination train and boat excursion along a spectacular stretch of coast is arguably one of the best city day trips in the world. The Royal Hudson is a regal steam locomotive that runs up the coast to the logging town of Squamish, 64 km (40 miles) north of Vancouver. The train steams out of the B.C. Rail train station in North Vancouver at 10 AM and chugs through picturesque West Vancouver—beach cottages and lavish waterfront mansions perched on cliffs and surrounded by mammoth Douglas firs. Then you're in the wilds of the Coast Mountains and the train tracks are hanging onto a cliff with the ocean 30 m (100 feet) below. Waterfalls plummet beside you and hawks circle above.

Find a seat at the back of the train so that you can see the engine as you round curves, and be sure to sit on the left side for the journey north.

As if the scenery isn't enough, the

A walk in a rain forest sometimes calls for an umbrella. (Rockwood Adventures)

Royal Hudson's Parlour Class offers fine dining (lunch en route to Squamish and tea and desserts on the return) in the grandeur of a historic railway car.

The trip to Squamish takes about two hours, and you have 1½ hours to explore or have lunch before the return trip. Unless you're from a small B.C. town and have seen it all before, use the time to wander around and have the barbecued salmon buffet later on the boat. There are several optional side trips from Squamish: try a guided walking tour of Shannon Falls Provincial Park or—a favourite with train buffs—the West Coast Railway Heritage Park.

Don't miss a 20-minute flightseeing excursion from Squamish over the glaciers of the Coast Mountains. It's a once-in-a-lifetime experience. You glide above dramatic peaks studded with vast fields of ice.

The boat MV *Britannia* has two

10 Best Buildings

This list favours big landmark buildings on Vancouver's downtown peninsula. Only Simon Fraser University's Burnaby campus is beyond walking distance of the core.

1. **Marine Building**, 1930
   355 Burrard at Hastings
Vancouver's only art deco skyscraper, carefully detailed with period-transportation bas reliefs and a sumptuous lobby.

2. **St James Anglican Church**, 1937
   Cordova at Gore
Go inside. Sir Adrian Gilbert Scott's essay in concrete is a masterpiece outside, a spiritual redoubt within.

3. **Daon Building**, 1981
   888 W Hastings at Burrard
Carefully massed to maximize the view to the north and honour the Marine Building opposite, this modestly proportioned temple of commerce exhibits good manners and design finesse.

4. **MacMillan Bloedel Building**, 1969
   1075 W Georgia at Thurlow
A return to load-bearing walls, Arthur Erickson's most Ionic building was the most elegant corporate headquarters of its time.

5. **Robson Square**, 1979
   800 block Robson
By knitting together law courts, government offices and the Vancouver Art Gallery over three blocks, Erickson gave the city its heart.

6. **Toronto-Dominion Bank** (now SFU Downtown), 1920
   580 W Hastings at Seymour
A romantic Mediterranean temple by the best architect of Vancouver's pre–World War I boom, New York–trained Marbury Somervell.

7. **B.C. Hydro and Dal Grauer Substation**, 1957, 1954
   570 Burrard at Nelson
In top form, Vancouver's greatest firm of architects (Thompson Berwick Pratt) brings modern architecture uptown.

8. **Sylvia Hotel addition**, 1987
   1861 Beach at Gilford
Richard Henriquez sets a new standard with this sympathetic but utterly contemporary extension to a formerly ordinary character building on a landmark site.

9. **Sinclair Centre**, 1986
   757 W Hastings at Granville
Henriquez fuses four significant heritage buildings of different styles and structures into more than the sum of their parts.

10. **Simon Fraser University**, 1965
    Burnaby Mountain
Erickson's most seditious work, cradle of student rebellion, risks livability in search of timelessness.

—*Sean Rossiter*

seating levels with huge windows and a sun deck on top. It follows the same route as the train, but the view from the water is entirely different. (Bring binoculars.) You cruise through Howe Sound, Burrard Inlet, English Bay and Vancouver Harbour, sailing past Stanley Park and downtown, and then dock at Coal Harbour by the Bayshore Inn at 4:30 PM. A free shuttle bus will take you to the train station in North Van to retrieve your car, or you can

One of the last operational steam locomotives in Canada, the Royal Hudson, on a trip up the coast to Squamish. (Province of British Columbia)

walk downtown in 10 minutes.

The pacing of the train and boat excursion is perfect—you are never bored, left waiting or rushed.

We recommend taking the train up and the boat back because the boat can be cool in the morning, but you could reverse this. Cost is $72.

It is also possible to take the Royal Hudson both to and from Squamish ($42 adult, return fare), but the boat is definitely worth the extra money.

The boat/train day trip is operated by Harbour Cruises (688-7246). Tickets must be purchased 48 hours before departure; this can be done over the phone with Visa, MasterCard or American Express. You can also purchase tickets from the Harbour Cruises' dock at Coal Harbour beside the Bayshore Inn, at the B.C. Rail Station in North Vancouver (1311 W 1st St) or from the Vancouver TouristInfo Centre at 200 Burrard (663-6000). The train runs Wed to Sun from June to mid-Sept. Reserve well in advance for weekends.

Avoid taking your car to the B.C. Rail Station by catching the #740 Royal Hudson bus, which runs from downtown to the station and back. It stops at some hotels. Get more bus information when you buy your tickets.

Pacific Starlight Express
984-5500
1-800-363-3373 (Canada and U.S.)
In the summer of 1997 B.C. Rail added this delightful dinner train. Although it covers part of the same route as the Royal Hudson, this evening excursion is a totally different experience. Nine vintage cars refurbished in art deco style depart the North Vancouver station at 6:30 PM to ramble along the coast to Porteau Cove. The send-off at the station by a Dixieland band sets a party mood, and the elegance of the cars gives a glimmer of early-day luxurious train travel. At times you are in a corridor of glorious evergreens; other times you overlook the sparkling blue Pacific or gape at ritzy West

Vancouver homes. Along the way you dine—entrées of salmon, beef, chicken or pasta—and sip wine while the sun slips and the moon rises. Fine dining aboard a train is a challenge but the award-winning chef does a pretty fine job. There's a 45-minute stop at Porteau Cove while the train engine is reversed, and you can even dance as the band sets up at the small station. Advance bookings are necessary; prices of $71 for salon service and $86 for dome service includes the train and meal. (Gratuities, taxes and drinks are extra.) The Pacific Starlight runs Wed to Sun, May 1 to mid-Oct. Hints: Dome-car service is worth the extra, especially if there is a full moon. Book a table with a water view. If you don't request a table for two, you may dine with strangers.

Special Interest Tours

Granville Island Brewery
1441 Cartwright, Granville Island
687-2739
This high-tech brewery run by a German brewmaster has expanded—you can tour the brewhouse, taste a variety of beers and receive a souvenir glass. There is a retail outlet featuring beer, souvenirs and a good selection of premium B.C. wines as well as other labels. Half-hour tours are offered daily; call ahead as times vary by season.

Seymour Demonstration Forest
987-1273
This 5600 ha (14,000-acre) wilderness is for outdoor enthusiasts. For a family outing, take the 90-minute walk with a professional forester, who will identify local vegetation and discuss forest management techniques. Tours are conducted during the summer; call for times. This Ecology Loop Trail is an easy one,

but others, like the 22 km (14-mile) hike to Seymour Dam, are more challenging. Opened to the public in 1987, this area has 50 km (30 miles) of paved and gravel trails and draws mountain bikers and in-line skaters as well as walkers and hikers.

Take the Lillooet Rd exit from the Upper Levels Hwy. A handy, guide-yourself brochure is available. See also Sports/Recreation (In-Line Skating).

University of British Columbia
822-8687
Located on a wooded finger of land that juts into the Strait of Georgia, this campus, home to more than 40,000 students, combines wilderness, beaches, gardens, theatres and a mix of grand and basic architecture. It's well worth a visit. Free walking tours leave from the south entrance of the Student Union Building, directly north of the bus loop on University Blvd. Tours are twice a week during Sep to Apr, Tues 9:30 AM; Thurs 12:30 PM. May to Aug tours run daily. Call to check times.

TRIUMF
222-7355
The science-minded should check out TRIUMF, a research centre at UBC. Discover the many uses of subatomic particles and view the world's largest cyclotron. Free 90-minute tours are given Mon to Fri, twice daily in summer, twice weekly in winter. There are also drop-in tours. No reservations necessary except for large groups. Located on Wesbrook Mall 1 km (0.6 mile) south of 16th Ave. Free parking.

Calendar of Events

January 1 Polar Bear Swim Club members dip into the frigid waters of English Bay; 665-3424.

January Pacific International Auto Show: A grand event for car buffs and a chance to view the new models. Held at B.C. Place Stadium; 294-8330.

Late January to mid-February (date varies) Chinese New Year: Celebrated with the traditional Dragon Parade in Chinatown on a Sunday afternoon. Chinese Cultural Centre; 687-0729.

February Spring Home Show at B.C. Place Stadium; 433-5121.

March Vancouver Storytelling Festival: A wonderful mix of ethnic stories; translators assist in five different languages. Held for three days at the Roundhouse Community Centre; 876-2272.

Mid-March to mid-May Sea lions at Steveston jetty; 272-9187.

March or April Vancouver Playhouse International Wine Festival: Over 150 wineries are represented at this fundraiser for the theatre. A chance to sample some 600 wines. Vancouver Trade and Convention Centre; 873-3311.

April Bradner Daffodil Festival: Welcome spring at this festival of flowers. Geraniums, orchids and home cooking also featured. To reach Bradner go east on Hwy 1 to the Aldergrove cutoff and follow signs; 856-2794.

May Vancouver International Marathon: This AIMS-certified marathon changed its route in 1998 to include a Jericho Beach section. It's a spectator-friendly marathon that draws some 6000 runners; 872-2928. Vancouver International Children's Festival: Starts third Monday of May. A seven-day extravaganza that includes entertainment, crafts,

games and fun under tents in Vanier Park; 708-5655. X-SITE: Arts festival for young adults held at Vancouver East Cultural Centre. By the same producers as the Children's Festival; 687-7697. Music West: From alternative rock to folk music, featuring international performers as well as new names. Four-day event at a variety of downtown venues; 684-9338. The Cloverdale Rodeo: The second largest in the country. May 24th weekend at the Exhibition Grounds in Cloverdale; 576-9461.

Late May New Westminster Hyack Festival: Celebrates Queen Victoria's birthday with parades; 522-6894.

June Canadian International Dragon Boat Festival: About 100 local and international paddlers compete in decorative boats on False Creek; 688-2382.

June through September Bard on the Beach: Shakespeare performed in tents in Vanier Park; 737-0625.

Late June to early July Du Maurier International Jazz Festival: Two-week celebration of jazz and blues in a variety of downtown locations; 872-5200 (Jazz Hotline).

July 1 Canada Day Celebrations, Canada Place: Family fun that ends with fireworks. Plaza of Nations; 666-7200. Steveston Salmon Festival: Culmination of a variety of events held in June in this small fishing village in Richmond; 277-6812.

July Dancing on the Edge: Dance of every kind with performers from across Canada in a ten-day festival. Firehall Arts Centre; 689-0926.

Mid-July Vancouver Folk Music Festival: Folk music lovers gather beside the beach to enjoy the best. Jericho Beach Park; 602-9798.

Mid-July to Mid-August Early Music Festival: Concert series featuring period instruments. UBC Recital Hall; 732-1610. Vancouver Chamber Music Festival: Up and coming classical artists perform. Crofton House School; 602-0363.

Late July Symphony of Fire: International fireworks competition on four specified nights. English Bay; 688-1992. Vancouver International Comedy Festival: Ten days of laughter, thanks to comedians from around the world. Granville Island; 683-0883. Caribbean Days Festival: Music, food and entertainment from the colourful Caribbean. Lonsdale Quay; 303-1455.

Early August Abbotsford International Airshow: Every second year; 1-604-852-8511. Powell Street Festival: Two-day celebration of Japanese-Canadian arts and culture. Oppenheimer Park, Powell St; 739-9388. Street Fare: Sidewalk entertainment by buskers from around the world. Robson Square and Art Gallery; 685-7811.

Late August Pacific National Exhibition Agriculture: Midway, musical shows and much more. See Pacific National Exhibition, this chapter; 253-2311. Wooden Boat Festival: Enjoy the beauty of wooden boats. Granville Island; 688-9622.

Early September Indy Vancouver car race: Three days of racing fea-

turing the world's best. Concord Pacific Place; 684-4639.

September Vancouver International Fringe Festival: Alternative theatre and performance art. Five hundred productions in ten days. Variety of venues; 257-0350.

Late September or October Vancouver International Film Festival: Films from more than 40 countries. Variety of venues; 685-0260.

Late October Vancouver International Readers and Writers Festival: Authors, playwrights and poets please audiences. Granville Island; 681-6330.

November Snow Goose Festival: Popular event now held for the whole month—the spectacle of thousands of migrating snow geese. George C. Reifel Migratory Bird Sanctuary; 946-6980.

Mid-November Hycroft Christmas Fair: Christmas crafts displayed in a lovely manor. Hycroft Manor; 731-4661. Circle Craft Co-op Christmas Market: Held in Trade & Convention Centre; 669-8021.

Early December Carol ships in English Bay and Burrard Inlet; 878-9988. Christmas Under the Sails: Lovely yuletide scenes. Canada Place; 666-8477.

December Festival of Lights: Thousands of lights create a magical wonderland. VanDusen Garden; 878-9274.

Parks/Beaches/Gardens

Dr. Sun Yat-sen offers tranquil moments in the midst of bustling Chinatown. (Bob Herger)

Parks are places where people go to commune with nature and escape the city. In Vancouver you don't have to go far. The equivalent of 20,000 blocks is devoted to green space where, rain or shine, Vancouverites walk, jog, cycle, picnic, play and just generally have a good time. Some parks are manicured; others are wilderness. Some stretch along the waterfront; others offer panoramic views. There are unique parks and ones with ethnic origins. Pack a picnic and head for a park.

IN THE CITY

Dr Sun Yat-sen Classical Chinese Garden

This serene walled garden at 578 Carrall near Pender in Chinatown is a significant local treasure. The Ming Dynasty-style garden is the first classical Chinese garden to be built outside of China. In 1985, 52 artisans from China spent 13 months creating the garden, using only traditional methods and materials. Most of the materials came directly from China (donated by the Chinese government, as was the labour), and no nails or screws were used in the construction.

You leave the hustle and bustle of Chinatown behind when you enter this enclosed sanctuary. Its emphasis is very different from that of Western gardens—there are no flashy displays of brightly coloured flowers. The garden reflects the Taoist philosophy of yin and yang: light elements are balanced with dark; rugged objects are complemented by soft, flowing ones. Craggy evergreens and unusually shaped limestone rocks suggest a miniature landscape, contained within architecture boasting ornate "leak" windows, curving tiled roofs and shiny lacquered beams. The garden is tiny, only 1300 m² (⅓ of an acre), yet as you stroll through pavilions and over bridges and pebble-mosaic pavement, you'll feel a spaciousness created by the careful arrangement of rocks, plants, water and architecture.

To understand the garden's symbolism, join one of the guided tours that are offered from 10:30 to 6 in summer and from 10:30 to 3 in winter. Hours are from 10 to late afternoon, depending on the season. Admission is $6.50 for adults, with discounts for children, seniors and families. Call 689-7133 for information.

Adjacent to the classical garden is Dr. Sun Yat-sen Park, which is a free public park. Although somewhat less elegant than its neighbour, the park is also a walled enclosure that is a very pleasant place to stroll or rest. It features a Chinese pavilion (the Pavilion of Gratitude), set in a large pond, and walkways through local

A morning walk on Vancouver's beaches is peaceful and offers views of the cityscape and mountains. (Judi Lees)

and Asian shrubbery. The park also has an entrance on Columbia at Keefer. Hours are the same as at the classical garden.

Don't miss an Enchanted Evening at Dr. Sun Yat-sen. The program is held on Friday evenings July through Sept. You listen to Chinese music, sip tea and stroll the classical garden under the soft light of hand-made lanterns. This is especially magical on a moonlit night.

Jericho Beach to Spanish Banks

The chain of beaches from Jericho to Spanish Banks is active with wind-surfers, swimmers, sailors, picnickers and sun-bathers but is over 3 km (2 miles) long and so is never congested.

Start your walk at the foot of Alma at Point Grey, where there is a small wooden structure, the Hastings Mill Museum. (See Museums.) Cross the

small park and go past the Royal Vancouver Yacht Club, the Jericho Tennis Club and Brock House (a restaurant and senior citizens' centre). Jericho Beach Park is straight ahead. There are paths through the park and around a duck pond, or you can walk along the beach.

Jericho Sailing Centre is next, and then Locarno Beach and Spanish Banks. Directly across Burrard Inlet are the Point Atkinson Lighthouse and Bowen Island. Keep going around the farthest point, Point Grey, if you want to sun-bathe nude at Wreck Beach.

There are concession stands and washrooms en route.

Don't miss the sunset from the small bay at the west end of the Spanish Banks seawalk. There are two or three prime beach spots to catch this daily spectacle, but this is the most private one.

From downtown take the #4 UBC bus or the #7 Dunbar. Get off at 4th

and Alma, and walk four blocks north to the Hastings Mill Museum.

Queen Elizabeth Park/Bloedel Conservatory

Queen Elizabeth Park is a spacious, beautifully landscaped park with ornamental flowerbeds, shrubs, trees and lots of grass. The park is on Little Mountain, the highest spot in the city. At the top are two abandoned quarries that have been transformed into huge sunken rock gardens full of blossoms and shrubbery, with ponds and waterfalls at every level.

The park facilities include Seasons in the Park, a restaurant with a smashing view (see Restaurants, With a View), tennis courts, a pitch and putt golf course, lawn bowling, a roller hockey court, basketball area, disc golf and picnic spots. The big attraction at Queen Elizabeth Park is the Bloedel Conservatory at the top of the mountain. The building is a Plexiglas dome, 43 m (140 feet) in diameter, covering a small rain forest and desert. It is a multisensory experience: you feel the heat and humidity, see and smell the lush tropical growth, watch a hundred brightly coloured tropical birds flying freely, and hear parrots squawking and a stream rippling beside you. A path takes you on a short circular walk and ends up in a desert. Guaranteed

to cheer you up on a rainy day.

Queen Elizabeth Park is off Cambie, between 29th and 37th Ave. The conservatory is open every day but Christmas; in summer Mon to Fri, 9–8, and Sat and Sun, 10–9; and in winter 10–5 daily. Admission is $3.30 for adults, with discounts for seniors, children and families. Phone 257-8570 for more information. From downtown, take the #15 Cambie bus.

Stanley Park

This park is one of a kind. While it has the lawns, picnic tables, civic monuments and gardens that you usually find in a civic park, it also has wilderness and the ocean. Stanley Park is *huge*. It combines the best of manicured gardens and tidy public areas with a dense, natural forest that has only paths and a road cutting through. The ocean almost encircles the park, and along the shore are sandy beaches and a seawalk that offers spectacular views.

The aquarium is the biggest attraction, but there are dozens of other activities for exercise, fun or relaxation. Stanley Park is one of the largest inner-city parks on the continent, and it is a mere 15-minute walk from downtown. Originally its 400 ha (1000 acres) were swamp and rain forest. The forest was a dense growth of Douglas fir, cedar and hemlock; the swamp that filled the low-lying area is now Lost Lagoon. Several culturally important Coast Salish villages were once on the land, and former Native trails have become park paths.

Getting there: catch the #135 Stanley Park downtown on Pender, (also #123 Stanley Park in the summer) and it will take you to the park entrance. If you're on foot, Alberni or Beach Ave are the best entrances.

Siwash Rock on the Stanley Park Seawall is a popular stop for cyclists, anglers, walkers and joggers. (Judi Lees)

Stanley Park is very popular. It is not advisable to take your car into the park on summer weekends unless the weather is bad. If you do drive around the park, remember that vehicle traffic runs one way, counter-clockwise, so you must use the Georgia St entrance. There is a charge for parking in the park—on the roadside as well as in the lots. The cost is $1 per hour during summer and $5 for all day. There are many parking meter machines scattered throughout the park; they take coins and credit cards. Park attractions are well marked.

On Foot in Stanley Park

The park is a peninsula rimmed by a seawall. A walk introduces you to the ocean, the harbour and the forest, and provides fabulous views of the mountains and the city—all this within the two hours that it takes to walk the 8.8 km (5½ miles).

If you do only one thing in Vancouver, walk around the seawall. It gives you the best idea of what living in this city is like. Go on Sunday if you want to be part of the parade of joggers, cyclists, dogs (which must be leashed), anglers and hundreds of people out strolling. Go on a weekday morning if you prefer quiet. The seawall path is clearly divided—one side for pedestrians and the other side for cyclists—but look out anyway.

Start at either English Bay or the park entrance at the foot of Georgia. Walking east from the Georgia St entrance, you pass by the Vancouver Rowing Club and the Royal Vancouver Yacht Club. A causeway leads to the naval reserve training base, called the HMCS *Discovery* (the last remnant of the original military base), on Deadman's Island, a former Salish burial ground. Hallelujah Point is next, where Salvation Army revival meetings were once held.

On the water side of the path is a large metal box enclosing a cannon, the Nine O'Clock Gun. Beginning in 1894, the gun was sounded to signal the curfew that ended weekend fishing. Now it is a time signal electronically fired at 9 PM.

At Brockton Point, once a pioneer cemetery and now occupied by a small lighthouse, you can see Lions Gate Bridge ahead. At lower Brockton Oval is a display of totem poles. These poles represent a variety of different B.C. nations and are an ideal picture spot. You are now walking west; there is a grassy area used for cricket, field hockey and rugby. Next is Brockton Oval, a cinder jogging track.

The seawall path passes the *Girl in a Wetsuit*, a statue sitting on a rock off the shore. You'll notice a similarity between it and the famous mermaid statue in Copenhagen Harbour.

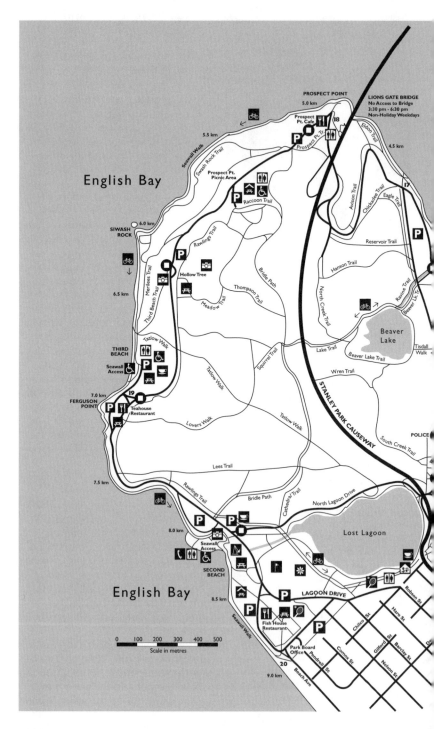

English Bay

PROSPECT POINT
5.0 km

Prospect
Pt. Cafe

Prospect Pt. Tr.

18

LIONS GATE BRIDGE
No Access to Bridge
3:30 pm - 6:30 pm
Non-Holiday Weekdays

4.5 km

17

5.5 km

Seawall Walk

Swash Rock Trail

Prospect Pt.
Picnic Area

Eldon Trail

Avison Trail

Chickadee Trail

Eagle Trail

Raccoon Trail

Reservoir Trail

SIWASH
ROCK

6.0 km

Rawlings Trail

Hanson Trail

North Creek Trail

Ravine Trail

Beaver Lk. Tr.

Merilees Trail

Hollow Tree

Bridle Path

6.5 km

Third Beach Trail

Meadow Trail

Thompson Trail

Beaver
Lake

Tisdall
Walk

Tatlow Walk

THIRD
BEACH

Seawall
Access

Lake Trail

Beaver Lake Trail

Squirrel Trail

Wren Trail

7.0 km
FERGUSON
POINT

19

Teahouse
Restaurant

Tatlow Walk

Tatlow Walk

STANLEY PARK CAUSEWAY

Lovers Walk

POLICE

South Creek Trail

Lees Trail

7.5 km

Rawlings Trail

Bridle Path

Cathedral Trail

North Lagoon Drive

Lost Lagoon

8.0 km

Seawall
Access

SECOND
BEACH

English Bay

8.5 km

LAGOON DRIVE

Robson St.

Chilco St.

Haro St.

Gilford St.

Barclay St.

Fish House
Restaurant

Comox St.

Nelson St.

Park Board
Office

Pendrell St.

20

Seawall Walk

Beach Ave.

9.0 km

0   100   200   300   400   500
Scale in metres

Burrard Inlet

al Harbour

Seawall Access
3.0 km
Kinglet Trail
Avison Way
Mallard Trail
Brockton Oval Trail
Brockton Point Trail
RV's
RV's
Bus
Brockton Oval
Totem Poles
Seawall Walk
2.5 km
Seawall Access
1.5 km
1.0 km
Royal Vancouver Yacht Cub
Deadman's Island
BROCKTON POINT
2.0 km
HALLELUJAH POINT

LEGEND

P	Parking
?	Information
	Restroom
	Wheelchair Access
	Telephone
	KODAK Photo Spot
	Concession Stand
	Restaurant
	Picnic Area
	Picnic Shelter
	Playground
	Gardens
	Wildlife Management
	Variety Kids Farmyard
	Variety Kids Water Park
	Miniature Railway
	Aquarium
	Nature House
	Pitch and Putt Golf
	Tennis
	Horse Drawn Tram
	Cycle/Roller Route and Direction
——	Pedestrian Trail
O	Stanley Park Shuttle Stop (Summer only)

MONUMENTS

1 Lord Stanley
2 Robert Burns
3 Queen Victoria
4 Shakespeare Garden
5 Garden of Remembrance
6 Harding Memorial
7 Japanese Monument
8 Hallelujah Point
9 Harry Jerome
10 HMS Egeria
11 9 O'clock Gun
12 Port of Vancouver
13 Chehalis
14 Edward Stamp
15 Girl in a Wet Suit
16 SS Empress of Japan
17 Stanley Park Centennial
18 SS Beaver Cairn
19 Pauline Johnson
20 David Oppenheimer
21 Lumberman's Arch

The sculptor who made this piece was inspired by the Danish work but transformed it to show a more modern, adventurous and down-to-earth figure.

Next is a replica of the figurehead of the *Empress of Japan*, a trading vessel that sailed at the turn of the century to and from Asia. At Mile 2, a children's water playground is on your right. On your left is Lumbermen's Arch, made of rough Douglas fir and erected in 1952 to honour workers in the logging industry. This was the site of one of the original Native villages. **Don't miss** fish and chips from the snack stand at Lumberman's Arch. It may be the salt air, it may be fact that it's so convenient to buy them and settle on the large lawn and enjoy the view, but these are mighty tasty fish and chips.

Pauline Johnson (1862–1913)

This legendary Indian "princess" was born in Ontario, the daughter of a Mohawk chief and an Englishwoman. She gained acclaim for her poems about Native life and spent much time touring North America and England giving recitations. She settled in Vancouver and learned local Native legends from Chief Capilano; she retold these in a collection entitled *Legends of Vancouver*.

Pauline Johnson often went canoeing at Lost Lagoon in Stanley Park, and her ashes are buried near Ferguson Point, where there is a memorial to her. She is best known for her poem "The Song My Paddle Sings" and a poetry collection entitled *Flint and Feather*.

Lions Gate Bridge marks the halfway point of the walk around the park. Slightly beyond is Prospect Point, named for the stunning viewpoint 60 m (200 feet) above. Just past the point are cormorants nesting on the rock cliff.

The seawall turns to the southwest, and along this section you will see the impressive Siwash Rock. The story of Siwash Rock is Vancouver's best-known Native legend. Long ago, a young Native man was about to become a father. He decided to swim the waters of English Bay until he was utterly spotless so that his newborn child could start life free from the father's sins. The gods were so impressed that they immortalized him in the form of Siwash Rock. Two smaller rocks, representing his wife and son, are up in the woods overlooking Siwash Rock.

There are often anglers fishing for bottom fish, and occasionally you see them get lucky. The first beach you encounter is Third Beach. If you're hungry and prefer eggs Benedict to fish and chips, walk up to the lovely Teahouse Restaurant at Ferguson Point for lunch. (See Restaurants, Outdoors.) Back on the seawall, the view is soon of English Bay, Kitsilano and the conical roof of the planetarium at Vanier Park.

About 800 m (½ mile) past Ferguson Point is the swimming pool at Second Beach. If you've had enough walking and want to return to your starting point, cross the road behind the pool and head back to Lost Lagoon. Water birds on the lagoon include Canada geese, trumpeter swans, mallards, wood ducks and coots. Pictures on a signboard on the west side of the lagoon help identify them. Lost Lagoon, originally a tidal inlet, was so named by Mohawk poet Pauline Johnson because the water often disappeared at low tide. Today the main road through the park acts as a dike to keep the lagoon at a constant level.

If you want to continue along the water, the seawall extends for several kilometres to English Bay. Or you can take advantage of the sports facilities between Second Beach and the lagoon. There is an inviting pitch and putt course and putting greens where you can rent equipment. **Don't miss** a short walk on the north side of the pitch and putt to see the remains of the ancient fir trees that were logged in the 1870s. You can clearly see springboard holes in some large stumps. This is also a display of glorious greenery and flowers.

The Lawn Bowling Club is open to visitors, and there are also tennis and shuffleboard courts. The Fish House Restaurant (see Restaurants, Seafood) by the tennis courts has both casual and more elegant dining rooms as well as outdoor decks for lunch and dinner.

In this same area, between the road and seawall, is an old fire engine for children to play on, and nearby there is an adventure playground. The tarmac here is used for ethnic dancing and square-dancing on summer evenings, and everyone is welcome to join in. On weekday afternoons in July and Aug (weather permitting), the Vancouver police run the Kids' Traffic School at this site for children 5 to 8 years old. It starts at 12:30; show up early because it's first come, first served.

If you walk the northern edge of Lost Lagoon and follow trails on the east side of Pipeline Rd, you'll find other attractions for children. The Children's Farm Yard is heaven for small children. Most of the animals are in a large open area and are free to move around together and with the children. All the usual barnyard animals are there, eager to be patted. Beside the Children's Farm Yard is a miniature steam locomotive that takes children and adults on a ride through the forest. Come early in the day; it's popular. The train runs daily in the summer and on weekends in the winter, weather permitting.

Directly south of the Children's Farm Yard is the cafeteria-style Dining Pavilion with a view of colorful flowerbeds and an outdoor theatre, Malkin Bowl, which stages Broadway productions in the summer. (See Entertainment/Culture, Theatre and Concert Venues).

Getting around the Park

There is a free Stanley Park shuttle bus that operates mid-May to mid-Sept. It picks up and drops off at 10 well-marked stops throughout the park. The bus arrives about every 10 minutes so you can hop off and on and enjoy the sights.

Stanley Park Horse Drawn Tours offer a pleasant alternative to walking. (See Sightseeing, Some Unusual Tours.) They leave from the parking lot closest to the Georgia St entrance.

Don't miss one of the park's finest views. It is from Prospect Point lookout; unfortunately it's not easily reached on foot. If you are cycling or walking, there is a steep gravel path that traverses up from the first turn in the paved road. The view of the North Shore is unforgettable.

Vancouver Aquarium

The Vancouver Aquarium (268-9900), Canada's largest, has more than 8000 animals. You will find displays of B.C. marine life in the Sandwell North Pacific Gallery. Living exhibits depict specific coastal regions such as Vancouver shores, the West Coast of Vancouver Island and the rocky bottom of the Strait of

Georgia. A new exhibit highlights B.C.'s salmon and provides a transition between this gallery and the Rufe Gibbs Hall, where you'll come face to face with pikes, sticklebacks, frogs and salamanders from the lakes, rivers and wetlands of B.C. Interactive exhibits in the Ducks Unlimited Wetlands Discovery Centre help visitors understand wetlands that are home to thousands of creatures.

The MacMillan Tropical Gallery presents marine life from the tropical Pacific: sharks, sea turtles and a rainbow of coral reef fish from Indonesia, Micronesia and the Philippines. From here you enter the Graham Amazon Gallery—a tropical rain-forest experience. Colourful songbirds fly, tropical plants grow around turtle-filled pools, and exotic bugs, such as giant cockroaches and hairy tarantulas, crawl around behind glass. You'll see big anacondas, poisonous frogs and schools of piranhas. Once an hour thunder, lightning and the deluge of a tropical rainstorm shatter the calm. It's a short but gripping walk.

The aquarium has outdoor pools for marine mammals large and small: a graceful killer whale, curious beluga whales, roaring sea lions and playful sea otters. The aquarium staff interact with these animals frequently, and you can watch feeding, play and research sessions throughout the day. The best experience of all is being eyeball to eyeball with these rarely encountered marine mammals through the underwater viewing windows.

The Jean MacMillan Southam Arctic Gallery not only provides underwater viewing of the belugas but also highlights the unexpected richness of Lancaster Sound off Baffin Island in the Canadian High Arctic. Innovative exhibits entice the whole family to explore how animals from Arctic cod to belugas live in an ecosystem dominated by freezing winds and shifting ice.

In spring 1998 the aquarium introduced WhaleLink, an exhibit in the H.R. MacMillan Gallery of Whales that chronicles the ongoing research on killer whales. As part of this exhibit, you can tune in to the world's first all-whale radio station: ORCA FM88.5.

Admission is $12 for adults in summer and $10 for adults in winter, with discounts for seniors, children and families. Open daily year-round. Summer hours are 9:30–7; winter hours are 10–5:30.

Note that the ClamShell Gift Shop in the aquarium is the best spot in town for souvenirs. You can pick up sandwiches and snacks at the Upstream Cafe.

VanDusen Botanical Garden

Originally a golf course, VanDusen Botanical Garden (878-9274) covers 22 ha (55 acres) and has been named one of the 10 best botanical gardens in the world by *Horticulture* magazine. Tranquillity envelops you as you wander around the ponds, lawns and thousands of varieties of trees, shrubs and flowers. Some of the walks are wonderful as well as educational. The rhododendron walk, with one of the best collections in Canada, is spectacular in its prime in May and illustrates botanical relationships.

All of the plants are well labelled and are arranged by species and place of origin for those interested in horticulture; for the rest of us, it's an enjoyable stroll.

This is a year-round garden. Each month showcases floral highlights.

Nitobe Memorial Garden exudes tranquillity. (June West)

A favourite with children is the Elizabethan hedge maze planted with a thousand pyramid cedars —don't worry; it's only 1.5 m (5 feet) high, and parents can watch from a grassy knoll. Families also enjoy trying to find turtles that bask around the lakes or experiencing the gentle motion of the floating bridge in Cypress Pond.

The garden opens daily at 10 AM; closing time varies according to daylight hours. In December, the Festival of Lights takes place with 20,000 lights twinkling amid the greenery from 5–9:30 PM daily.

Guided tours (and cart tours for those with limited walking ability) are offered every afternoon from Easter to Thanksgiving, weather permitting. Seasonal self-guided tour sheets are available at the entrance. Apr to Oct admission is $5.50 for adults, with discounts for seniors, children and families. The rest of the year, rates are half price. There is a restaurant with an open-air deck at the entrance.

The garden is at Oak and 37th Ave; from downtown, take the #17 Oak bus.

AT THE UNIVERSITY OF BRITISH COLUMBIA

Nitobe Memorial Garden

The Nitobe garden (822-6038) at the University of British Columbia is a gem. It is an authentic Japanese tea and stroll garden complete with teahouse. Japanese landscaping objectives of harmony, balance and tranquillity are clearly met by the blend of indigenous fir and cedar with classical arrangements of shrubbery, waterfalls and small bridges over gurgling streams. The garden was started more than 37 years ago and has an established, serene feeling. The ground cover is moss so you must stay on the paths, but there are benches on which to pass a quiet moment.

The garden is off NW Marine, a short walk west from the Museum of Anthropology, so go to both; they are fine examples of Pacific Rim cultures. From mid-Oct until mid-Mar, Nitobe is open weekdays 10–2:30;

J.K. Henry Lake is in the UBC Botanial Garden. (June West)

during the summer, daily 10–6. Admission is $2.50 for adults, with discounts for seniors, students and children. Combination tickets to Nitobe and the UBC Botanical Garden are available for $5.75.

For access by public transit, see UBC Botanical Garden.

UBC Botanical Garden

The beauty of this garden is more subtle than that of display gardens like VanDusen. The purpose is to inspire gardeners by showing new and creative ways to use plants. The garden also displays and sells new and rare varieties and is known for its fine examples of espalier fruit trees and

for its giant 4 m (13-foot) Himalayan lilies. In all, 10,000 types of trees, shrubs and flowering plants are displayed here.

There are several parts to this 28 ha (70-acre) garden. The Asian Garden is on the west side of Marine; Moongate tunnel, a pathway under the road, leads you to the Food, Physick, Contemporary, Arbour, Winter, Alpine, Perennial Border and B.C. Native Gardens. The Asian Garden is a unique combination of native cedar forest underplanted with Asian plants: 400 varieties of rhododendrons, the giant lilies, climbing hydrangeas, magnolias and more. The Food Garden has an unusual display of espalier fruit trees—imagine an apple tree hedge thick with fruit but no higher than your head. The Physick Garden is a formal 16th-century herb garden with plants from the Chelsea Physick Garden in London. In the B.C. Native Garden you can walk from a coastal rain forest into the semiarid environment of the interior of the province, all within 3 ha (7½ acres).

The shop at the garden has the best selection of gardening books in town, plus gardening gizmos and unusual plants for sale. Tours of the garden are strongly recommended because they allow you to catch the seasonal highlights that you might otherwise miss. During the summer tours are offered at 1 PM on Wed and Sat. Admission to the garden is $4.50 for adults, with discounts for seniors, students and children. Call 822-4208 for more information. The entrance to the botanical garden is off NW Marine, 3 km (1 mile) south of Nitobe Memorial Garden. In the summer the #42 Chancellor bus takes you right to Nitobe and the Botanical Garden from 10th and Alma. From downtown take the #10 UBC bus to this transfer point.

Pacific Spirit Regional Park

Pacific Spirit Regional Park is a haven of wilderness that encompasses 753 ha (1800 acres) of forest and foreshore. Located in the city's west side, it borders the University of British Columbia and was formerly part of the endowment lands before being established as a park in 1989. This park is considerably larger than Stanley Park, but it's used by relatively few people. Even though the 53 km (33 miles) of trails are perfect for hiking, jogging, mountain biking and horseback riding, you can sometimes meander through the forest and not encounter a soul. No need to worry about getting lost; the park is cut by three major roads that provide landmarks, and every trail junction is signed. There are also park volunteers, who wear yellow armbands.

The wildlife is varied but elusive. Squirrels, chipmunks, voles, moles, bats, weasels, mink, raccoons, otters, owls, skunks and coyotes all live in the park, but you will see them only if you are a keen observer. Bald eagles are often spotted.

There is a park information centre at 4915 W 16th Ave. There are interpretive programs led by naturalists; inquire at the park centre or phone 224-5739 for times. The centre is the best place to pick up maps; there is also parking.

If you are heading out without a guide, you will find Pacific Spirit a welcoming place with fairly easy trails. Trail #24, Swordfern (in the southwest corner of the park), is recommended as a typical B.C. coastal forest with cedar and fir trees. The trail starts from sw Marine opposite the viewpoint and historical monument (marking Simon Fraser's 1808 trip down the Fraser River). On the same side of the street as the monument, another trail descends sharply to the Fraser and the largest log-boom grounds in Canada. Here you will pass a remnant of old-growth forest.

Pacific Spirit Regional Park is simply a refreshing walk in the forest, a chance to get away from the city, just 20 minutes by car from downtown traffic.

By public transit from downtown, take the #10 or #4 UBC bus to campus or the #25 UBC from Brentwood Mall in Burnaby to enter the park via 16th Ave.

ON THE NORTH SHORE

Capilano River Regional Park

This North Shore park is on a strip of land along the Capilano River running from Grouse Mountain to Burrard Inlet. The park is wide at the top and very narrow from the middle down. The river is tempestuous (it is used for whitewater kayaking) and has gouged a deep canyon along its course. Although park trails are well kept, the surroundings are dramatically wild: rapids, plunging cliffs and huge timber, all in a misty rain forest setting.

At the very top of the park is the Cleveland Dam, which separates Capilano Lake from the river and regulates the city's water supply. Park your car at the dam. You can walk across the top of the dam for a view in either direction. Maps of the trails are available at a signboard near the parking lot. **Don't miss** the Giant Fir Trail. It leads to the biggest tree in the park—2.4 m (8 feet) in diameter and 61 m (200 feet) tall—and is thought to be over 500 years old. It is truly an awesome sight.

A salmon hatchery is a 10-minute

hike down the path on the east side. It hatches about 3 million salmon eggs a year and releases the finger-lings into the Capilano River and other local waters. The outdoor dis-plays and fish tanks are open 8–8 in summer; they close earlier in winter months. (Call 666-1790 to check hours.) A brochure is available for self-guided walks. In late summer and fall, if the river is high enough, you may witness coho jumping up the fish ladders at the hatchery.

From the dam you can hike the trails on either side of the river above Dog's Leg Pool. On the west side you can hike all the way down to the mouth of the river, about 7 km (4½ miles), but the park itself is sometimes not much wider than the trail, which occasionally goes through residential neighbourhoods. If you hike about halfway down on the west side you will reach a bicycle barrier. From here you can hike back up the same side. The round trip takes about 90 minutes.

Farther along is Capilano Suspen-sion Bridge, a well-publicized attrac-tion that is a swinging wood and cable bridge that hangs 70 m (230 feet) above the canyon. Unfortu-nately, it costs $8.25 to walk across. Although the bridge is spectacular and is an easy walk for people who don't want to negotiate the paths, the views from Capilano River Regional Park are free. If you must walk across a swinging bridge, there's no charge for the one at Lynn Canyon Park. See With the Kids (Day Trips).

There are two ways to get to the park by public transportation. From downtown, take the #246 Lonsdale Quay/Highland. At Edgemont and Ridgewood, transfer to the #232 Grouse Mountain. The #236 Pemberton Heights/Grouse Moun-tain bus leaves from Lonsdale Quay and goes right by the park. You can get to Lonsdale Quay easily from downtown via the SeaBus.

Grouse Mountain

At night, look for the brilliant arc of lights that adorns the dramatic North Shore mountains and you'll have found Grouse Mountain. Twelve hundred metres high (4100 feet), it towers over Vancouver and offers a phenomenal view of the city and its surroundings. Year-round, Grouse is a must-visit.

In winter it is a popular close-to-the-city ski spot and the rest of the year it is a quick escape from the city. Grouse is ideal for families; there's a whole mountain to keep the kids amused. Go on a clear day to best enjoy the astonishing view.

The Skyride is a 100-passenger tram that glides you up the steep moun-tainside, skirting treetops. Far below, Vancouver and all of the Lower Mainland are laid out in miniature. In eight minutes you're 1100 m (3700 feet) above sea level and near the top of Grouse Mountain. The Skyride is $17 for adults, with dis-counts for seniors, children and fam-ilies. The price may seem a bit steep but in all seasons it includes extras. When you arrive, you will find the area around the tram is developed and probably bursting with activity, but there is plenty of wilderness. Pick up trail maps and directions from Alpine Guest Services on the main floor of the Chalet. For that top-of-the-world feeling, take the Peak Chairlift (included in the Skyride price) up another 120 m (400 feet) for a panoramic view that in-cludes Mt Baker, Vancouver Island and the Pacific Ocean sprinkled with islands.

In summer there are picnic tables and lawns where you can find a

A horse-drawn sleigh ride is a favourite winter excursion on Grouse Mountain. (Grouse Mountain)

quiet place to sun-bathe or read. Just behind the chalet an adventure playground made of logs and ropes, with a kid-size suspension bridge and a hand rope tow, is a hit with the younger set.

For a hike on a well-marked interpretive trail try the one around Blue Grouse Lake, north of the Skyride; it takes less than an hour. For a more strenuous workout, there are intermediate trails that begin just behind the Peak Chairlift. Sturdy footwear is recommended for mountain trails. The ultimate challenge is the Grouse Grind. See Sports/Recreation (Hiking/Mountaineering/Indoor Climbing Walls).

For a walk in the woods combined with art, tour Tribute to the Forest, a 40-minute, free, guided or self-guided stroll that features 26 giant Douglas fir chainsaw sculptures. This easy trail celebrates the importance of the forestry industry to B.C., and the tour departs from the tram terminal.

Grouse is one of the few places that features a logger sport show. These competitions highlight traditional loggers' skills such as springboard chopping, axe throwing and races between hand-saws and power saws. Held twice daily, the shows take place in a grass amphitheatre near the Peak Chairlift.

Included in your Skyride ticket price is *Born to Fly*, an acclaimed 30-minute video presentation that gives an eagle's-eye view of B.C.

Don't miss Grouse's newest addition, the Hiwus Feasthouse, which opened May 1998. It is a traditional native long house located on the banks of Blue Grouse Lake. Guests are greeted by a welcoming totem and then enjoy dance, stories and a five-course feast. Each visitor takes home a native gift of friendship. There are seatings at 5:30 and 7:30; cost is $69 for adults Sun to Thurs, and $79 Fri and Sat. Reservations are recommended and may be made by calling Grouse Mountain Catering at 984-0661, ext. 362.

Helicopter tours of the mountains and lakes behind Grouse Mountain leave from the platform at the top of the mountain. Costs range from $45 to $95 a person, depending on the length of the tour. Phone Vancouver Helicopters, 270-1484.

Another exciting option to a Grouse adventure is to take a mountain-bike excursion. See Sightseeing (Walking/Hiking/Cycling Tours).

The Rusty Rail, an outdoor beer garden beside the Peak Chairlift, is a pleasant place to eat or sit in the sun with a cold drink. As you might expect, the main restaurant, Grouse Nest, has a knockout view. It's open for dinner and is expensive, but if you make advance reservations for dinner the Skyride is free. Phone 984-0661 for more information. The Bar 98 Bistro is a casual restaurant (burgers, nachos and the like) open for lunch and dinner. It is less costly but still has the view.

In winter Grouse is a popular ski spot—there are lots of lessons for skiers and boarders and, on clear, crisp nights, the after-work crowd rushes here. The price of the Skyride also includes a Snocat-drawn sleigh ride. There is a skating pond and skate rental near the Skyride terminal, and snowshoe rentals and an extensive network of snowshoeing trails for all fitness levels. See also Sports/Recreation (Skiing and Snowboarding).

From downtown, take the SeaBus to North Vancouver. The #236 bus leaves from the SeaBus terminal on the North Shore for Grouse Mountain. Another way to get there from downtown is to catch the #246 Lonsdale Quay/Highland bus on Georgia St. It goes over Lions Gate Bridge. At Edgemont and Ridgewood, transfer to the #232 Grouse Mountain.

For information on Grouse, call 984-0661.

Lynn Canyon Park

See With the Kids (Day Trips).

Lighthouse Park

Point Atkinson Lighthouse, built in 1912, sits at the tip of a wilderness area not far from the city centre. Park trails take you past mammoth Douglas firs, rocky cliffs and smoothly sloping granite rocks that line the shore (a perfect sun-bathing and picnicking area). The water is not as warm as at the city beaches, but after you've lain in the sun on the hot granite it feels just right.

A notice board in the parking area has maps that show the many trails, including the two main ones to the lighthouse. Follow one path down and the other back for a round trip of about 5 km (3 miles) that takes less than an hour. At the point, you can see Point Grey and the University of British Columbia campus directly across Burrard Inlet; to the southwest across the Strait of Georgia are the mountain tops of Vancouver Island, visible on clear days.

Watch for bald eagles and their large, ragged nests in the forks of tall trees. The largest Douglas fir trees here, 61 m (200 feet) tall and 500 years old, are the best accessible example of virgin forest in the Lower Mainland. The arbutus, an unusual tree recognizable by its smooth, peeling, orange-red bark, is the only broadleaf evergreen native to Canada.

The Point Atkinson Lighthouse is a working one and is not open to the public.

To drive to the park, go west on Marine 10 km (6 miles) past Park Royal Shopping Centre. On your left at Beacon Lane is a large, wooden sign directing you into Lighthouse Park.

From downtown, take the blue West Van bus #250 Horseshoe Bay.

Point Atkinson Lighthouse in Lighthouse Park, a good hiking and swimming spot with one of the last stands of virgin timber in the Lower Mainland. (Rosamond Norbury)

Mount Seymour Provincial Park

Mount Seymour is convenient for your first taste of hiking in the mountains because it's close to the city and a road goes part way up the mountain. Even if you don't feel like hiking, drive up the 13 km (8-mile) parkway for a picnic and the splendid views.

There are several good hiking trails on the lower section of the mountain. Around the 1 km signpost on the road up, there is access to the Baden-Powell Trail, which can be followed to Indian River Rd and eventually to Deep Cove. This covers about 3 km one-way. This trail intersects with Old Buck Trail, which is used for mountain biking as well as hiking. As a precaution, don't hike any mountain trails without a map.

Most of the trails start at the top parking lot, which is at the end of the road. A signboard at this parking lot shows the paths and their distances. Trail maps are available at the signboard and the park office, which

is located at the bottom of the mountain. The main trails are well maintained but can be wet, so wear sturdy shoes for walking and hiking boots for the more rigorous trails. Snow lingers until June at this altitude, so the best time to hike is from July to late Oct. Exercise caution as there may be bears in the vicinity. Remember that you are in very different climatic conditions than in the city. Clouds can move in quickly and reduce visibility dramatically. Pack a rain jacket, wear warmer clothes than you would down below, and keep to the trails.

The Goldie Lake Trail is the easiest. A 1½-hour walk will take you around the lake through a hemlock and cedar forest. The large Douglas firs in the park are 250 years old, and lower down on the slopes are a few 800-year-olds.

On your way back down the mountain parkway, stop at the Deep Cove lookout, just past the 8 km sign. On a clear day this gives panoramic views of Washington state's Mt Baker and, towards the northeast,

Ten Favourite Walks in the Forest

Because 90 per cent of B.C. is covered in trees, you won't truly experience the West Coast until you've gone for a walk in the forest. Although there is virtually no old growth in the Lower Mainland, you may see a solitary tree left because it was not choice material or because it grew on too steep a slope. Second growth is not as dramatic as old growth but some trees are now 130 years old and are quite impressive. Here are suggestions for accessible trails that are easy family walks unless otherwise noted:

1. **Pacific Spirit Park, Swordfern Trail.** The trailhead is across sw Marine Dr from the viewpoint and historic monument. Less than an hour for the return trip. See Pacific Spirit Regional Park.

2. **UBC Botanical Garden, B.C. Native Garden.** This is a pretty tame walk, but it is pleasant. Green-thumbers will love it. Half an hour for the return trip. Admission charge for the garden. See UBC Botanical Garden.

3. **Stanley Park, Siwash Rock Trail.** The trail starts on the water side of Park Dr just past Prospect Point, parallels the shoreline on the cliff above the seawall and ends at a viewpoint of Siwash Rock and English Bay. (See map in Stanley Park section.) Less than an hour return.

4. **Mount Seymour Provincial Park, Mystery Lake Trail.** Many people are not happy unless they hike a mountain trail. This trail head is at the end of the parking lot located at the end of the road. This is a pleasant area with picnic tables, washroom facilities and maps.

On Mystery Lake Trail you are instantly among stands of Douglas fir, cedar and hemlock. It's an uphill, occasionally rocky route with a few view spots. You reach the pretty little lake in less than an hour, a great spot for a picnic. You can return by the same route or go east around the lake and follow several well-marked trails that continue up the mountain or go back to the parking lot. Take a jacket, since weather changes quickly in the mountains, and wear good walking shoes or hiking boots. Be cautious if it is wet. See Mount Seymour Provincial Park.

5. **Lynn Headwaters Regional Park, Lynn Loop Trail.** Drive over Lions Gate Bridge to the Upper Levels Hwy, go north on Mountain Hwy and follow signs to the park. As in all Greater Vancouver Regional District parks, trails are very well maintained and marked, and maps are available at the park entrance. Walk the loop trail in a counter-clockwise direction so that you are going downhill at the steep section. Don't miss the short detour to the viewpoint (it's marked) at the top of the loop. Some sections may be a bit steep for seniors and small children. Two hours return.

6. **Cypress Provincial Park, Yew Lake Trail.** Drive over Lions Gate Bridge, go west on the Upper Levels Hwy and take the turn-off to Cypress Park. The traversing road up the mountain has magnificent views of the city and as far as Mt Baker and Vancouver Island.

The Yew Lake Trail leaves from

the top parking lot across from the ski-lift ticket office. This is an easy 1.5 km (1-mile) interpretive trail (signs point out flora and fauna indigenous to the area) looping through forests of Douglas fir, mountain hemlock and yellow cypress, which the park is named for. At times the trail skirts the shore of the lake before returning you to the base of the black chair ski lift. This is a leisurely walk of about 45 minutes. Be alert for black bears; they are a possibility on any mountain trail. If you want a more demanding hike, dozens of trails are marked on the map. Some depart from this area; others are in the Hollyburn area (they are cross-country trails in winter), which is lower down the access road.

7. **Capilano River Regional Park.** Park your car at Cleveland Dam. The Capilano Pacific Trail takes you down the west side of the Capilano River. Take detours to a viewpoint that shows off the dam and rushing river as well as to see the Giant Fir. Then continue on the Capilano Pacific Trail. You will pass one bridge; further along go left on Shinglebolt Trail to Pipeline Bridge. Cross to the other side and you are just below the salmon hatchery. Return to the dam on a trail just beside the hatchery. At a leisurely pace, this takes about an hour. See Capilano River Regional Park.

8. **Lighthouse Park.** The Valley Trail, parallel to but on the east side of the road, takes about an hour for the return trip to the lighthouse side. See Lighthouse Park.

9. **Belcarra Regional Park.** Take the Barnet Hwy, turn off to Port Moody and turn west on Ioco Rd. Following signs to the park, you drive along the new Tum-ta-mahy-tun Dr. It's about a 45-minute trip from city centre. There are trail maps in the kiosk in the park.

Admiralty Point Trail hugs the shoreline above rocky outcrops and beneath an umbrella of evergreens. The one-hour walk to Admiralty Point has view spots overlooking the water, and the point is perfect for a picnic.

For more of a workout, take Jug Island Beach Trail. It's occasionally steep and takes about 1½ hours to reach a rocky beach that looks out on Jug Island. There's a lovely mix of greenery—evergreens, alders, maples, ferns and bush. Avoid Belcarra on warm summer weekends; it's best midweek or during spring and fall weekends.

10. **Buntzen Lake.** Take Hastings St to the Barnet Hwy and go through Port Moody to Ioco. Watch for signs to Anmore and Buntzen Lake. It's an hour's drive from downtown, but this lake in the midst of the forest and mountains is a slice of wilderness heaven. From the picnic area take the interpretive loop trail on a half-hour walk. The park is very busy on weekends; go midweek if possible. For a more ambitious but very rewarding walk, you can circumambulate the lake in about 3½ hours, not including stops.

See also Sports/Recreation (Hiking/Mountaineering/Indoor Climbing Walls).

The exotic-looking wood duck can be seen at the George C. Reifel Migratory Bird Sanctuary. (Judi Lees)

the glacier-formed fjord of Indian Arm.

Please remember that you are not allowed to remove anything from a provincial park and that pets must be leashed at all times.

In winter here you can ski downhill, snowboard, enjoy snowshoeing and tobagganing or, if you are equipped, access the backcountry. There is a cafeteria, day lodge, ski and snowshoe rentals, and ski lessons. See also Sports/Recreation (Skiing and Snowboarding).

Access is by car only, via the Second Narrows Bridge and Mt Seymour Parkway.

OTHER

George C. Reifel Migratory Bird Sanctuary

946-6980

Located on Westham Island at the mouth of the south arm of the Fraser River, this sanctuary is for birders and families. At the entrance you can buy a bag of seed and get a map of the 3.2 km (2 miles) of paths, and then you are on your own. Bring a bird book, binoculars and a warm jacket. Remember that this is a wildlife refuge, so the amenities are for the birds. Take the path on the dike to see the marshy flatlands of the delta—it's dramatic country. A four-storey observation tower and several blinds (wooden shelters with viewing slats) give you views of the tidal marshes and of birds you may not spot anywhere else. The refuge is heavily populated in fall, winter and spring but is pretty quiet in the summer. One of the best times to visit is between mid-October and late November, when Westham Island is visited by some 25,000 snow geese. They can be viewed in the fields and flying to and from the shoreline, where they feed and roost. The Snow Goose Festival is held annually in November. Choose another time to visit if you don't like crowds.

Open daily 9–4. Admission is $3.25 for adults, with discounts for children and seniors. There is a guided walk every Sun at 10. All the paths are wheelchair accessible, and there are picnic tables.

Reifel is not accessible by public transit. To get there, drive south on Hwy 99, and after the George Massey Tunnel take the second exit (marked Hwy 17). At the lights, go right on Ladner Trunk Rd and follow through a 4-way intersection on to 47A which becomes River Rd. Follow this road to the sign and over a bridge that leads to Westham Island.

Museums/Art Galleries

Major Museums

Museum lovers will revel in the variety that awaits them in this city, from world-class museums housed in architectural wonders to small, cosy ones tucked into a quiet space.

Vancouver's Favourite Museum

Museum of Anthropology
6393 NW Marine, University of British Columbia
822-3825

This museum is lauded as the city's favourite, and it is stunning in its exhibits, venue and setting. The museum houses artifacts from all over the world but focusses on the arts of the First Nations peoples of the Pacific Northwest. The award-winning building is an architectural stroke of brilliance, designed by Arthur Erickson and inspired by Native cedar houses. Its setting is a lofty bluff overlooking the ocean and mountains.

As you walk through the carved front doors and into the Great Hall, you will be awe-struck by the monumental totem poles and carvings. You can almost feel the power of the spirits depicted on the poles in the form of ravens, bears, frogs and humans. The back of the Great Hall is a 13.5 m (45-foot) glass wall that overlooks more totem poles, traditional Haida houses and the unspoiled cliffs of Point Grey. It is easy to imagine that you have stepped into another time and another culture.

This entrance through the impressive Great Hall sets you up for hours of enjoyment. Northwest Coast Native works on display include exquisite gold and silver jewellery, intricate sculptures of argillite (a jet-black slate found in British Columbia's Queen Charlotte Islands), bone carvings, baskets and a collection of amazing ceremonial masks.

Also featured is contemporary First Nations art such as the massive

The Museum of Anthropology's Great Hall offers a magical moment with totem poles. (Museum of Anthropology)

sculpture *The Raven and the First Men,* designed and carved by Bill Reid. (This world-renowned artist died in spring 1998. The Museum of Anthropology has the largest collection of his Haida art; that alone makes this museum a must-visit.) Finished in 1980, it was created from a block of 106 laminated yellow cedar beams and took five people more than three years to complete. The carving is an enormous, menacing, smirking raven perched on a partially open clamshell. Teeming inside the shell are human figures struggling either to emerge or retreat; it is the Haida legend of the beginning of man.

The Museum of Anthropology's permanent collection is not locked away as in other museums but is completely accessible. Visitors are encouraged to pull out the glass-topped storage drawers.

Join a guided walk for an introduction to the collection (phone 822-5087 for times) or use the excellent booklet called "Guide to the UBC Museum of Anthropology." You should walk to the Great Hall and experience the totem poles for a few minutes before doing anything else.

A variety of special events takes place throughout the year, often on Sunday afternoons. There are also special changing exhibits, so the museum definitely warrants return visits.

The museum is on the University of British Columbia campus. To drive there, go west on 4th Ave until the road forks at NW Marine. Take the right fork and follow it until you are on the campus; then watch for the museum, which is on the north side of the road. Or take the #4 or #10 UBC bus, which will let you off in the middle of the university campus; the museum is a 10-minute walk northward (there is a map at the bus stop when you get off). Admission is $6 for adults, with discounts for children, seniors and families. Free on Tues, 5–9. Open daily, 10–5; Tues, 10–9. Closed Mon in winter.

Don't miss the First Nations Longhouse, which is used by First Nations students. It is not open to the public but is worth seeing as it's a hybrid of Northwest Coast architecture with mixes of contemporary and Salish styles. Cross Marine Dr and walk south on West Mall. It is built into a hillside at 1985 West Mall and is about a five-minute walk from the Museum of Anthropology.

Vanier Park Museum Complex

To take in several museums and attractions at one stop, head for Vanier Park, a scenic stretch of waterfront on the Kitsilano end of the Burrard St Bridge. As well as green spaces and a shoreline walk, the park is the home of the Vancouver Museum; the H.R. MacMillan Planetarium and the Gordon Southam Observatory, which are both part of the Pacific Space Centre; the Maritime Museum; and the City of Vancouver Archives. The museum and planetarium are in the same building, a distinctive landmark because of its conical roof. The roof shape is patterned after the woven cedar-bark hats worn by the Northwest Coast Native people, a reminder that the land surrounding the museum was once the site of a Native village. Outside the building is a huge, stainless steel sculpture of a crab, which, according to Native legend, guards the entrance of the harbour.

Vanier Park is easily reached by driving (there is parking) or walking over Burrard Street Bridge. From the city centre, take bus #2 or 22 south

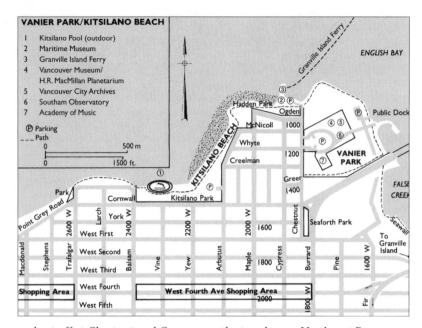

VANIER PARK/KITSILANO BEACH

1 Kitsilano Pool (outdoor)
2 Maritime Museum
3 Granville Island Ferry
4 Vancouver Museum/
   H.R. MacMillan Planetarium
5 Vancouver City Archives
6 Southam Observatory
7 Academy of Music

ⓟ Parking
--- Path

and get off at Chestnut and Cornwall; walk north on Chestnut. Vanier Park can be reached by False Creek Ferry (684-7781) from Thurlow St or Granville Island; they run daily in summer and on weekends the rest of the year.

Don't miss Vanier Park on a windy day. The large lawn is the best place in the city to fly kites. On a wild day you will see some of the city's best kite flyers doing their tricks here. There is a great kite store in the Kid's Market at Granville Island, a short walk away.

Vancouver Maritime Museum
257-8300

Look for the tall Kwakiutl totem pole to find the Maritime Museum, one of the city's best loved and most visited. A favourite with families, it is just the right size—there is no museum burnout after a visit.

A highlight is the completely restored *St Roch*, a 1928 two-masted schooner that was the first ship to sail

the treacherous Northwest Passage from west to east. (It took the captain and eight crew members more than two years to complete the voyage.) The *St Roch*, a Royal Canadian Mounted Police patrol boat, was also the first ship to circumnavigate North America. It is now an official National Historic Site, and you can take a self-guided tour. The ship is just as the crew might have left it—rum on the table, laundry by the bunks and huskies on deck.

Other exhibits reflect the maritime heritage of coastal B.C. The Children's Maritime Discovery Centre is an interactive display where youngsters can learn about boats and the sea using computer games, an underwater robot and telescopes. In the Pirates Cove exhibit you hear tales of wild pirates, and young swashbucklers can board *Shark*, a kid-size pirate ship, to take an imaginary journey complete with treasure chests of jewels. There is an excellent exhibit of ship models and a working model shop. In the *Man the Oars & Map the Coast* exhibit there is a chronometer and original maps from George Vancouver's ship. Everyone who has ever yearned to run away to sea loves this museum.

There are temporary exhibits, and many special events take place at the Maritime Museum, particularly in the summer. Restored heritage vessels are moored at Heritage Harbour, in front of the museum, and can be explored.

Open daily in summer 10–5; closed Mon in winter. Admission is $6 for adults, with discounts for children, seniors and families.

Vancouver Museum
736-4431

The heritage, culture and natural history of the Lower Mainland are depicted in this museum. In the recently opened Orientation Gallery, a multi-layered Timeline Wall uses artifacts from the museum's collection to depict Vancouver's history. There is even a Toy Timeline to keep the younger set interested. This museum is a story in progress—as well as featuring the past, it looks at current issues and the future of Vancouver. The excellent gift shop specializes in First Nations art and jewellery.

The museum holds many special events evenings and on weekends: concerts, workshops, cultural demonstrations and lectures. Children's programs focus on natural history, storytelling, and arts and crafts.

Between 1998 and 2000, the museum is renovating all of its galleries as well as creating new exhibits. Although regular hours will be maintained and there will always be areas open to the public, it is best to call ahead for the current program and exhibition schedules.

Open daily, July and Aug; but

Vanier Park is home to several popular museums. (Pacific Space Centre)

closed Mon the rest of the year except holidays. Hours are 10–5. Admission is $6 for adults, with discounts for children, seniors and families. The combined price for the Vancouver Museum and the Pacific Space Centre is $15 for adults, with discounts for children, seniors and families. Parking is free, but the lot can fill up quickly when special events are held at Vanier Park.

The Pacific Space Centre
738-7827

Come and explore the universe. At this state-of-the-art centre you can fly through space on the Virtual Voyages flight simulator; see dramatic multimedia shows in the H. R. MacMillan Star Theatre; learn about the solar system and beyond in the Cosmic Courtyard interactive exhibition gallery and discover the latest in space in the GroundStation Canada mission control theatre. If a flight simulation is too scary for you, then try some of the audio-visual shows. Many of the exhibits in the Cosmic Courtyard are hands-on, and you may find yourself planning a voyage to Mars or battling an alien.

Evening Rock Laser Shows take place

Science World, along with the Omnimax Theatre, is housed in a geodesic dome on the shores of False Creek. (Science World)

in the Star Theatre Wed, Thurs and Sun at 9 PM (10 PM July and Aug) and Fri and Sat at 9 and 10:30 (9:30 and 11 July and Aug). Be forewarned, this rock music/laser light show is loud. Best for children over 8; teens love it.

The Pacific Space Centre is open Tues to Sun, 10 AM–5 PM (Sept to June) and Mon to Sun 10–6 July and Aug. Admission is $12 for adults, with discounts for children, seniors and families. Children under 5 are free. Admission to the rock music show is $8 with no discounts.

Gordon Southam Observatory at the Pacific Space Centre
738-2855

The observatory is the small domed building beside the museum/planetarium complex and is open for public stargazing. An astronomer explains how the 50 cm (19½-inch) reflector telescope works and how to use it. If you have a 35-mm SLR camera, phone for details on the observatory's "shoot the moon" program—you can take your own

pictures of the full moon on clear evenings.

Open every evening during the summer (depending on the weather). During the winter, open Fri, Sat and Sun, 12–5 and 7–11 when the sky is clear. Call ahead to check. Admission is free.

City of Vancouver Archives
736-8561

The building behind the Southam Observatory that looks like a concrete bunker is the City of Vancouver Archives. Walking into it is like entering another world. The atmosphere is positively serene—it must be the most tranquil government office in the city. If you are a history buff, this is the place to spend a few hours poring over Vancouver's past.

In the main foyer is a changing exhibit, usually of wonderful old Vancouver photographs. The archives house public records from city hall, private papers of historical value, maps, newspaper clippings, books and, most interesting of all, historical photographs. Everything is indexed if you're looking for something specific, but the photographs are displayed in binders that you can leaf through for hours.

Open Mon to Fri, 9:30–5:30.

Don't miss a chance to visit a city gem as well as stretch your legs. From Vanier Park you can walk to the tiny Hastings Mill Museum (see below). Go west along the oceanside walk. Follow the curve of Kits Beach and pick up a snack at the beachfront stand, then meander on to Vancouver's oldest building.

The courtyard outside the Canadian Craft Museum is a restful, secluded spot. (Producer's Workshop/Images B.C.)

Other City Museums

Science World
1455 Quebec near Terminal and Main
268-6363

This hands-on museum located in a geodesic dome blends entertainment with education. Many "please touch" exhibits help both kids and adults understand science while having a whole lot of fun. Demonstrations are offered daily on such diverse topics as bubbles, illusions, water, air and fire.

In the Sara Stern Search Gallery, which is devoted to natural history, you can crawl through a beaver lodge, climb inside a hollow tree and watch a beehive in action. There's no end to the wonders—you can play a tune on a giant walk-on synthesizer, light up a plasma ball in the Matter and Forces exhibition or search for gold in the Mine Games section.

The Alcan Omnimax Theatre, the world's largest domed screen, can take you on journeys into space or to the top of Mount Everest; feature films change about every six months. The gift shop is the ideal place to purchase gifts for science buffs—young and old.

Admission to the museum is $10.50 for adults, with discounts for seniors and children; admission to the museum and Omnimax is $13.50 for adults, with discounts for children and seniors. Located across from the Main St/Science World SkyTrain station. Summer hours are daily, 10–6. Winter hours are weekdays, 10–5; and Sat and Sun, 10–6. Science World can be extremely busy—if you can't take crowds, go after 2 PM during the school year, on a sunny day in the summer.

Canadian Craft Museum
639 Hornby near Georgia
687-8266

The museum is located on the ground level of Cathedral Place, a prestigious downtown office tower. The adjacent courtyard is one of the city centre's most pleasant resting spots; during summer there is often entertainment here, but it's still a peaceful retreat. The museum entrance is off this courtyard.

Crafts are said to combine the best aspects of pure art with function. This belief is embodied in exhibits that showcase Canadian and international crafts and feature contemporary as well as traditional works of everything from jewellery to furniture. The gift shop is worth a stop. The museum is open Mon to Sat, 10–5; Sun and holidays, 12–5. Closed Tue, Sept to May. Admission is $4 for adults, with discounts for children, seniors and groups. Thurs 5–9 admission is by donation.

B.C. Sports Hall of Fame and Museum
B.C. Place Stadium, Gate A1
687-5520

It is apt that Canada's largest sports museum is located in British Columbia, where sports are, for many, a way of life. Although the history and development of sports are illustrated through photos, Olympic medals, trophies, personal mementos and equipment from all the big-name athletes, this museum is also about action.

In the Participation Gallery you can run, climb, throw, ride or row (perfect for wild kids on a rainy day), and in the Discovery Gallery you learn what makes a champion. There is also a Hall of Champions; galleries dedicated to Terry Fox and Rick Hansen; a salute to the province's coaches, referees, and others in the world of sports; a theatre where films focus on sports highlights; temporary exhibits; and a History Gallery, which chronicles sports from the 1890s to the present. As you walk through each decade, you follow the progress of sports. Guided tours are available.

Open daily, 10–5; $6 for adults; concessions for students and children (children under 5 free).

Vancouver Aquarium
See Parks/Beaches/Gardens (Stanley Park).

Vancouver Police Museum
240 E Cordova at Main
665-3346

The history of Vancouver's finest, along with mystery and intrigue, is told through displays on gambling, weapons, counterfeit currency and some of Vancouver's more infamous criminals. Open Mon to Fri, 9–3; Sat 10–3, May to Aug. Closed Sat Sept to April. Admission is $5 for adults; discounts for seniors and children.

B.C. Golf Museum
2545 Blanca near University Blvd
222-4653

Appropriately, the entrance of this museum overlooks the 16th green and 17th tee of the University Golf Course. Housed in the original clubhouse of this picturesque course, the beamed 1920s building filled with antique furniture contains information on most courses in the province, golf paraphernalia—it's fun to compare today's equipment with that of the early-day clubs— a library of over 1200 volumes that cover history as well as everything you would like to know about this sport, and a video viewing area. There are also rotating exhibits. Admission is free, but donations are welcomed. Open Tues to Sun, 12–4.

Hastings Mill Museum
Point Grey at Alma
734-1212

Built in 1865, this is the oldest existing structure in Vancouver and one of the few buildings that survived the 1886 fire. Lots of artifacts—photos, Native baskets, early clothing and furniture, all jumbled together. Worth a stop if you're in nearby Jericho Park or Vanier Park. Open seven days a week from June to mid-Sept, 11–4; winter hours are Sat and Sun afternoons only, 1–4. Admission by donation.

See also Sightseeing (Granville Island).

Museums Outside the City

Burnaby Village Museum
6501 Deer Lake, Burnaby
293-6500
You walk a pathway lined with fragrant flowers and then cross a rustic bridge to enter a peaceful 1920s village. This museum is a walk through history complete with costumed "townspeople" who chat about their everyday life. The dining room table is set for guests at the Elworth residence, a Charlie Chaplin flick is on at the Central Park Theatre, type is being set by hand in the print shop, the blacksmith heats iron bars at the forge . . . the scenes unfold in over 30 authentically restored buildings.

This is a wonderful place for children. They can take part in activities, like playing games from the 1920s, and in summer, there are zany vaudeville shows on Sun afternoon. Christmas is one of the best times, with strolling carollers, musicians and traditional decorations and crafts. **Don't miss** the beautifully restored 1912 carousel. Young and old enjoy this musical ride, which is truly a work of art. There are also lakeside walks and the Shadbolt Centre for the Arts.

From downtown, it's a 20-minute drive to the museum. Take Hwy #1 east and exit at Kensington South. By public transit take a #123 New Westminster Station bus from Granville and Hastings directly to the museum, or take the SkyTrain to Metrotown Station and then the #110 bus to city hall; the museum is a short walk when you turn left on Deer Lake Ave.

Open seven days a week from May to Sept, and Dec. Closed the rest of the year. Admission is $6.35 for adults, with discounts for children, seniors and families.

Buddhist Temple
9160 Steveston Hwy, Richmond
274-2822
An impressive example of Chinese architecture that houses an active Buddhist temple. Leave your shoes outside to enjoy the traditional artwork in the heavily incensed interior. Open daily, 10–5. No admission charge; donations appreciated.

Canadian Museum of Flight
5333–216 St, Langley (Langley Airport)
532-0035
A collection of vintage aircraft, including a Tiger Moth, a CF-100 Canuck and a Lockheed Starfighter, as well as a technical library and gift shop. An open house is held usually in June. Open daily, 10–4. Admission is $5 for adults; discounts for children and families.

Public Art Galleries

Information about current shows at both public and private galleries can be found in the *Georgia Straight*, *Vancouver Magazine*, the *West Ender*, and the What's On column of Thursday's *Vancouver Sun* and Friday's *Province*. Another source is the Arts Hotline, 684-2787, a 24-hour information source.

Vancouver Art Gallery
750 Hornby at Robson
662-4719
Vancouver's old courthouse, built in 1911, was transformed into the Vancouver Art Gallery in 1983. It is a grand building, designed by the famous architect, Francis Rattenbury, who is best known for Victoria's Empress Hotel and the Legislative Buildings. The elegance of the original courthouse remains: ornate plaster work and a glass-topped dome over a majestic rotunda that showers

the centre of all four floors with natural light. The neoclassical style was popular for administrative buildings because of the weight and authority lent to them by Greek and Roman architectural features in the form of imposing columns, domes and entries guarded by lions. The main entrance has been moved to Robson St, but notice the grandeur of the stately old entrance and square on the Georgia St side.

Off the main lobby is the gift shop, the Annex Gallery and access to the restaurant upstairs. Past the Annex Gallery is a stairway up to the gallery library (housed in the former law library). You can feel the tranquil atmosphere of the old law chambers here in the annex, with its quiet marble halls and heavy wooden doors. The former Supreme Court chamber, largely intact, is now the gallery boardroom.

The reference-only library is well stocked with art books, more than 100 different art magazines, files on contemporary Canadian artists and gallery catalogues from all over the world.

Don't miss the permanent gallery on the third floor that showcases the work of Emily Carr, British Columbia's best-known artist. Her paintings from the early part of this century depict the power and mystery of nature as reflected in looming forests, foreboding skies, magnificent totem poles and abandoned Native villages.

The gallery is closed Mon and Tues in winter, but the restaurant and gift shop are open every day. Gallery hours are Mon, Tue, Wed and Fri, 10–6; Thurs, 10–9; Sat 10–5 and Sun 12–5. Admission is $7.50 for adults. Thursdays between 5 and 9 admission is $3. The Gallery Café has the best outdoor seating downtown.

Other public galleries listed are found in nearby municipal centres and at universities and art schools.

Burnaby Art Gallery
6344 Deer Lake Ave, Burnaby
205-7332

Charles H. Scott Gallery
Emily Carr Institute of Art and Design
1399 Johnston, Granville Island
844-3811

Contemporary Art Gallery
555 Hamilton near Dunsmuir
681-2700

Morris & Helen Belkin Art Gallery
1825 Main Mall, University of British Columbia
822-2759

Richmond Art Gallery
7700 Minoru Gate, Richmond
231-6440

Simon Fraser Art Gallery
Burnaby Mountain, Burnaby
291-4266

Surrey Art Gallery
13750–88th Ave, Surrey
501-5580

Private Art Galleries

The arts community in this city is proud of its fine showing of local, Canadian and international artists. Sprinkled throughout Gastown, Yaletown and city centre are many welcoming galleries. In particular, Granville St between 6th Ave and 15th Ave has well over a dozen to wander through. Call for hours.

Art Beatus
888 Nelson near Hornby
688-2633

Bau-Xi Gallery
3045 Granville at 14th
733-7011

Buschlen-Mowatt Fine Arts
1445 W Georgia near Nicola
682-1234

Crown Gallery
1515 W 6th near Granville
730-9611

Diane Farris Gallery
1565 W 7th near Granville
737-2629

Equinox Gallery
2321 Granville at 7th
736-2405

Heffel Gallery
2247 Granville at 7th
732-6505

John Ramsay Contemporary Art
2423 Granville at 8th
737-8458

Artist-Run Galleries

Some of Vancouver's eclectic local artists join together to show off their work and their working space. This list includes the most intriguing artist-run galleries. Call for hours.

Federation of Canadian Artists Gallery
1241 Cartwright, Granville Island
681-8534

Or Gallery
112 W Hastings near Abbott
683-7395

Helen Pitt Galleries
882 Homer near Smythe
681-6740

Students' Concourse Gallery
Emily Carr College of Art and Design
1399 Johnston, Granville Island
844-3811

Western Front
303 E 8th near Kingsway
876-9343

Photo Galleries

Exposure Gallery
851 Beatty near Robson
688-6853

Presentation House
333 Chesterfield, North Van
986-1351

Indian or Inuit (Eskimo) Galleries

Vancouver is particularly rich in galleries (and shops) featuring dramatic native art. Call for hours.

Images for a Canadian Heritage
164 Water near Cambie
685-7046

Inuit Gallery
345 Water near Richards
688-7323

Knot-La-Cha
270 Whonoak off Marine Dr, beside the Capilano Indian Reserve, North Van
987-3339

Leona Lattimer Gallery
1590 W 2nd at Fir
732-4556

Marion Scott Gallery
481 Howe at Pender
685-1934

Wickaninnish Gallery
1666 Johnston St, Granville Island
681-1057

Craft Galleries

Circle Craft
1666 Johnston, Granville Island
669-8021

Crafthouse Gallery
1386 Cartwright, Granville Island
687-7270

Gallery of B.C. Ceramics
1359 Cartwright, Granville Island
669-5645

Oh Brothers
2356 W 41st near Vine
263-2122

Robert Held Art Glass
2130 Pine at 6th
737-0020

Susan Clark Gallery of Gem Art
The Penthouse, 555 W Georgia at Seymour
688-3553

See also Other City Museums (Canadian Craft Museum).

Entertainment/Culture

The best places to check for entertainment listings are the daily newspapers (Thursday's *Vancouver Sun* and Friday's *Province* have detailed event listings) and the *Georgia Straight*, Vancouver's free entertainment weekly.

The Arts Hotline (684-ARTS) provides information about arts events. Call Mon to Sat, 9:30–5:30. Or check the Vancouver Cultural Alliance's website: <http://www.culturenet.ca/vca>. Tickets for most major events are sold through Ticketmaster outlets and can be purchased over the phone with MasterCard, Visa or American Express. Call 280-4444.

Movie Theatres

There are many first-run movie theatres downtown within a few blocks of each other. Vancouver Centre Cinemas (669-4442), Capital 6 Famous Players (669-6000) and Granville Cineplex Odeon (684-4000) are all on Granville St between Georgia and Nelson.

Theatres catering to the growing enthusiasm for foreign and independent works include Varsity Theatre (4375 W 10th near Trimble), the Fifth Avenue (2110 Burrard near 4th) and the Park (3440 Cambie near 18th). To find out what's playing at all three, call 290-0500.

The Ridge (3131 Arbutus at 16th, 738-6311) is a popular repertory movie theatre.

Pacific Cinematheque
1131 Howe near Helmcken
688-8202
This nonprofit society is dedicated to developing and enhancing the understanding of cinema and contemporary media practice. This means viewers see art, foreign, and experimental films rather than mainstream movies.

Cinematheque schedules are available at public libraries and Duthie

Books, among other places. Membership is required (you must be 18) and can be purchased at the door. Cost is $6 annually; admission price, starting at $6.50 for adults, is discounted the night membership is purchased. Discounts for students and seniors.

Large-Screen Theatres

Omnimax Theatre (268-6363) is located at Science World. See Museums/Art Galleries (Science World).

CN IMAX Theatre (682-IMAX) is at Canada Place.

Both theatres were built for Expo 86. These are the places to see thrilling shows that will literally take your breath away. Check the newspapers for showings.

Theatre and Concert Venues

Arts Club Theatre
1585 Johnston, Granville Island
Granville near 12th
687-1644
The most active theatre in town, the Arts Club began in 1964 in a renovated former gospel house on Seymour. The location may have been peculiar, but the productions were consistently good, with a mix of classic plays, drama, comedy and musicals. Under the leadership of Bill Millerd, the Arts Club has burgeoned into the city's theatre success story. Theatre-lovers now have a choice of two venues in which to view Arts Club productions.

The first is the 450-seat Granville Island Stage, a spacious, modern theatre that was converted from a chain forge and warehouse at the edge of False Creek. Located beside the Granville Island Public Market, this theatre offers light comedies and

This festival tent allows rain-or-shine summer performances of Shakespeare on the shore of English Bay. (David Cooper)

musicals. It also houses the Backstage Lounge, a casual, fun hangout as well as a place to see the who's who of theatre in the city. (See Nightlife, Lively Bars.)

In the fall of 1998, the Arts Club opened its second venue, the Stanley Theatre on Granville. Originally a vaudeville theatre in the '30s, then a movie house until the early '90s the Stanley's exquisitely detailed art deco has been refurbished, and its 650-seat theatre features state-of-the art sound and lighting.

For reservations and tickets to the Stanley Theatre or the Granville Island Stage, call the box office at 687-1644, Mon to Sat, 10–7, or TicketMaster, 280-3311.

Bard on the Beach Shakespeare Festival
Vanier Park
737-0625
Shakespeare in the summer is a special event in Vancouver, when the backdrop of sea, sky and mountains adds magic to the performances. Productions run in repertory, rain or shine, in an airy, festival-sized tent behind the Vancouver Museum mid-June to mid-Sept. Ticket prices are

reasonable and shows generally sell out; reserve by calling the box office at 739-0559. Bring a sweater.

The Chan Centre for the Performing Arts
6265 Crescent Rd, UBC
822-9197
The Chan Centre opened in 1997 and instantly won praise from critics, performers and audiences alike. Cited in *TIME* magazine as the city's new cultural mecca, the facility is nestled into a lovely forest setting on the University of British Columbia grounds and comprises three performance venues. The crown jewel is the cello-shaped Chan Centre Concert Hall, which has a 37-tonne acoustical canopy that can be adjusted to accommodate a variety of performances. The BC Tel Studio Theatre has flexible stage configuration and seats up to 288 people. Surround-sound technology is one of many unique features of the intimate 160-seat Royal Bank Cinema. To order tickets, call TicketMaster (280-3311), or purchase tickets at the venue.

Don't miss the Chan on a warm evening. You can wander into the garden at intermission to experience

The Chan Centre's soaring windows provide an uninterrupted view of its verdant setting. (Wayne Thom)

the marvellous melding of unusual architecture with nature's lushness.

Firehall Arts Centre
280 E Cordova at Gore
689-0926
Until 1975, 280 E Cordova was the original No. 1 Firehall. It's now a 150-seat theatre and the home of the Firehall Arts Centre. The Firehall produces three theatre productions each season as well as an exciting contemporary dance series and the always-popular Dancing on the Edge Festival. This unusual venue also houses a spacious dance studio, an outdoor stage for summer events and an intimate lounge/gallery. For tickets, call the box office, 689-0926, Mon to Sat 1–6 PM.

The Ford Centre for the Performing Arts
777 Homer at Robson
602-0616
The Vancouver theatre scene reached new heights with the opening of the Ford Centre in 1995, and the fact that world-class, large-scale productions play to packed houses is testimony to its success.

Designed by Moshe Safdie, who also created Library Square across the street, the three-level venue offers patrons exceptional viewing as its 1,824 seats surround the stage on three sides, creating an intimate ambience. The modernistic lobby has an eye-catching glass cone and an intriguing mirrored staircase—during intermission, you may spot someone you know several storeys below.

All of the biggest and best productions appear here—*The Phantom of the Opera*, *Riverdance* and *Ragtime* are examples of shows that have thrilled Vancouver audiences. For tickets call the Live Entertainment number: 280-2222.

Orpheum Theatre
Smithe at Seymour
665-3050
The magnificent Orpheum, built in 1927, is known as the grand old lady of Granville Street. Dramatically ornate, it features gilt ornamental plaster work, a painted dome ceiling, sparkling chandeliers and the original Wurlitzer organ. When the 3000-seat theatre became unviable as a movie house in the '70s, Famous Players wanted to convert it into a modern movie complex. Vancouverites rallied, and after a successful "Save the Orpheum" campaign, the City bought the building and restored it to re-open in 1977.

It is home to the Vancouver Symphony and several choirs, plus hosts events from classical concerts to rock shows. Four hundred thousand patrons fill the theatre 200 nights a year to enjoy superb performances and the Orpheum's resplendent decor. The B.C. Entertainment

Hall of Fame and Starwalk are also based here. Groups can book guided tours of the theatre; call 665-3050. Order tickets through TicketMaster, 280-4411.

Presentation House
333 Chesterfield at 4th St, North Van
986-1351
A dynamic community arts centre combining a recital hall, a theatre, a museum, archives and a gallery specializing in photography.

Queen Elizabeth Theatre and Playhouse
630 Hamilton near Georgia
665-3050
The Queen Elizabeth Theatre complex houses the 2929-seat Queen Elizabeth Theatre and the 668-seat Vancouver Playhouse. Touring Broadway musicals, opera and dance frequently hit the stage of the Queen Elizabeth Theatre. In the more intimate Playhouse, the Vancouver Playhouse Theatre Company presents a six-play season between Sept and May; many recitals, chamber music and contemporary dance events are also staged here. Built in 1959, the QET features a glass-fronted façade, sweeping lobbies and a streamlined, acoustically superior auditorium. The large outdoor plaza is pleasant on warm evenings, and you can make reservations for dinner at the Queen Elizabeth Theatre Restaurant.

Tickets are available at Ticketmaster (280-4444). To check what's on, call 299-9000; local 8051 for the QET; 8052 for the Playhouse.

The Shadbolt Centre for the Arts
6450 Deer Lake Ave, Burnaby
291-6864
This modern, multi-use facility is surrounded by historic buildings (also part of the art complex) and located in picturesque Deer Lake Park. The

The Orpheum, home of the Vancouver Symphony Orchestra, is a mid-size theatre with excellent acoustics. (Glen Erickson)

performing arts season includes theatre, music and dance performances as well as visual arts exhibits. The Centre also provides instruction in a variety of artistic disciplines. Named for long-time Burnaby residents Doris and Jack Shadbolt, the Centre permanently displays two of Jack Shadbolt's stunning paintings. There is a heritage museum and art gallery nearby (see Museums/Art Galleries) as well as Hart House Restaurant, in a lovely heritage house.

Theatre Under the Stars
687-0174
For many, an evening under the stars at TUTS is an annual tradition. Malkin Bowl, the theatre in Stanley Park, was built in 1934 as a bandshell, and there is something wonderfully old fashioned about sitting outdoors and viewing lively musicals. The TUTS productions are usually popular ones such as *My Fair Lady* or *The King and I*, using professionals and amateurs. Shows are nightly, weather permitting, in July and Aug. Pick a dry

night, pack a blanket and enjoy. Curtain time is 8 PM.

Vancouver East Cultural Centre
1895 Venables and Victoria
251-1363

This turn-of-the-century East End church is one of Vancouver's more intriguing theatre and performing arts venues. It calls itself a neighbourhood theatre, but it would be unfair to leave the description at that. The VECC is one of the liveliest multipurpose performance spaces in the country, staging high-calibre theatre, music and dance, as well as a Saturday afternoon children's series.

All seats are general admission. Phone for information, 251-1363, Mon to Fri, 10–6 PM.

Vancouver TheatreSports League
Arts Club Revue Stage
1585 Johnston, Granville Island
738-7013

Vancouver TheatreSports League is synonymous with comedy improvisation and has been called "one of Vancouver's crown jewels." Since 1980, over 50,000 people annually flock to see grown men and women perform "acts" that would otherwise embarrass any rational human being. Classic TheatreSports has two teams of three actors competing against one another. They are judged by the audience and a referee makes the calls ("Two minutes for obscenity!"). Themes are set but there are no scripts. Audience participation is a must (though "we won't pick on you if you don't want us to!" applies). The Vancouver TheatreSports League has become a cult in the city; always reserve tickets. Shows Wed to Sat at 8:15 PM, with additional 10:15 PM shows on Fri and Sat. Red Hot Improv is a one-hour risqué comedy improv at 9 PM on Sat. Call 738-7013 for information or tickets, Mon to Fri, 9:30–5 PM, or TicketMaster (280-4444).

Waterfront Theatre
Cartwright at Old Bridge, Granville Island
685-6217

A number of production companies, such as Carousel Theatre, utilize this popular venue and present Canadian productions and theatre oriented towards families. There are musicals, improvisational theatre and special productions. It is a cosy theatre with 240 seats and a bar area. Some productions have preview performances that are pay-what-you-can.

Fringe Theatre
Vancouver has many small and innovative fringe theatre groups that perform in unusual venues. Vancouver Professional Theatre Alliance comprises 61 large and small theatre groups. For information, call 608-6799, or visit the website: <www.audience.com/theatre>.

Classical Music

New music, early music, choral music, symphony, opera, chamber groups, string quartets—the choice is yours. Information on current concerts is in the events listings in Thursday's *Vancouver Sun* and Friday's *Province* and at the two classical record stores in town, Sikora's and the Magic Flute; see Shopping (Recorded Music).

Music-in-the-Morning Concert Society
873-4612

If you love music and mornings, this concert series is for you. Or perhaps if you don't love mornings but love music, come to these concerts to experience a new way to greet the day. Held at the Vancouver Academy of Music, 1270 Chestnut St, the concerts showcase local as well as international talent. A good place to hear up-and-coming musicians. The Special

Composer and Coffee series features conversation after the performance. Both series run Sept to May.

Vancouver Bach Choir
921-8012

The Vancouver Bach Choir performs five major concerts in its regular season, including a Handel's *Messiah* sing-along each Christmas. The 150-voice choir, considered the most impressive nonprofessional choir in the city, tours extensively and frequently wins international competitions. The Bach Choir performs at the Orpheum Theatre.

Vancouver Chamber Choir
738-6822

The Vancouver Chamber Choir is one of only two professional choirs in the country. It has an extensive international touring schedule and records regularly. Concerts include a series of choral masterpieces at the Orpheum Theatre and Chan Centre for the Performing Arts, a chamber music series at Ryerson United Church (45th and Yew) and an annual candlelight and wine event in the Hotel Vancouver ballroom.

Vancouver New Music Society
606-6440

The New Music Society promotes contemporary classical concert music, multidisciplinary performance and new opera. The annual season of seven concerts features local, Canadian and international artists. Every second year the organization teams up with the city's major orchestras and ensembles, as well as guest artists, for a 10-day New Music Festival that spotlights innovative music in an accessible and affordable format. The Society performs in a variety of venues. Tickets available through TicketMaster (280-4444).

Vancouver Opera Association
682-2871

Vancouver Opera has been staging operas since 1960 and performs four major works a year, often with international stars. The season runs from Oct to May or June at the Queen Elizabeth Theatre. Popular works such as *La Traviata, Carmen* or *Madama Butterfly* are balanced by more adventurous operas.

Vancouver Recital Society
602-0363

Two of the most successful concert series in Vancouver are offered by this society. The summertime Chamber Music Festival features some of the finest young classical musicians in the world and is held in the parklike setting of Crofton House School. An optional dinner is served outdoors, or you are welcome to bring a picnic. Tickets are available at the door. Phone for information.

The main series (Sept to Apr) showcases internationally renowned musicians, and the society has built a reputation for bringing some of the world's best performers—both aspiring new musicians and well-established talents—to Vancouver. The Vancouver Playhouse, the Orpheum and the Chan Centre are the venues for this series of concerts.

Early Music Vancouver
732-1610

The aim of the society is to promote medieval, Renaissance and baroque music using the instruments of the time. Concerts are held at a variety of venues. Tickets are usually available at the door. The society also organizes an important summer festival of early music, held at UBC every July and Aug.

Vancouver Symphony Orchestra
684-9100

The VSO performs an eclectic mix of traditional symphonic works and pops. Guest soloists can range from local pianist Jon Kimura Parker to international performers like cellist Yo-Yo Ma. Most concerts are at the Orpheum, but there are some at the Chan Centre and other locations throughout the Lower Mainland. In summer, the vso performs several free outdoor concerts, at local beaches or parks. The culmination of the summer season is a mountain-top concert in the spectacular setting of Whistler Resort or Grouse Mountain.

Dance

The **Dance Centre** is a nonprofit organization that provides information about dance activities in the city; call 606-6400.

Ballet British Columbia
732-5003

Bold, innovative and sophisticated, artistic director John Alleyne has led his daring company to international critical acclaim. Ballet British Columbia's classically trained dancers were chosen for their power, strength and dramatic performance style. The company is based at the Queen Elizabeth Theatre and regularly tours Canada and the United States.

EDAM
876-9559

Experimental Dance and Music uses a multimedia presentation style. Productions are generally collaborations of choreographers, filmmakers, painters and musicians.

Karen Jamieson Dance Company
872-5658

Jamieson's award-winning choreography is bold, energetic and contemporary. The company makes a point of featuring Canadian composers, designers and artists and often presents cross-cultural collaborations.

As well as those listed above, there are many innovative resident companies, such as **Kokoro Dance, Mascall Dance, DanceArts Vancouver, The Holy Body Tattoo** and **Kinesis Dance.** Companies that combine dance with theatre are **Jumpstart, Dancecorps/Astrid, Battery Opera, DanStabat, Wild Excursions Productions** and **Vancouver Moving Theatre.**

Two popular multicultural dance companies are **Aché Brasil** (South American capoeira) and **Rosario Ancer Dance Company** (flamenco).

See also Sightseeing, Calendar of Events.

Nightlife

Complete entertainment listings are in the *Georgia Straight*, Thursday's *Vancouver Sun* and Friday's *Province*.

Jazz

Call the 24-hour **Jazz Hotline** at 872-5200 for current and upcoming jazz events.

Blue Note Jazz Bistro
2340 W 4th near Vine
733-0330
Live groups perform nightly at 8 PM; mainstream jazz while you dine. Minimum charge of $6.

Chameleon
810 W. Georgia near Howe (basement of Hotel Georgia)
669-0806
Jazz and funk; live bands Mon, Fri and Sat. Weekends, $5.

Cotton Club
1833 Anderson near 2nd Ave
738-7465
Nightly live performances of mainstream jazz; New York–style restaurant. Weekends minimum charge, $3.

Hot Jazz Society
2120 Main at 5th
873-4131
Dixieland, New Orleans and swing on Fri; big bands on some Sat nights. Dance floor. $25 annual membership fee; then $6 for members, $10 for guests.

Jazz Cellar Café
3611 W Broadway near Alma
738-1959
The Cellar has a romantic New York feel; modern, bebop jazz with some fusion. Open Mon to Sat, with live entertainment Wed to Sat. Thurs, some of city's top vocalists; Fri and Sat, top name trios and quartets. Snacky food. Thurs, Fri, Sat, $3 cover.

Latin Quarter
1305 Commercial at Charles
251-1144
Jazz, but also flamenco, jam, soft rock, latin guitar, you name it. Well worth a visit. One of Commercial's liveliest eateries.

Rossini's Pasta Pallazo
1525 Yew at Cornwall
737-8080
Jazz talent from all over North America, seven nights a week. Sat afternoon jam session, 3:30–6:30, a great time to stop by.

Rhythm and Blues

Yale Hotel
1300 Granville at Drake
681-9253
The home of R & B in Vancouver, great local and imported talent, seven nights a week. Jam sessions Sat afternoon and Sun evenings.

Fairview Pub
898 Broadway at Oak
872-1262
Located in a Ramada Inn but still lures crowds of R & B fans. Live performances seven nights a week; cover charge on weekends between $4–$8 depending on band.

Comedy

Yuk Yuks
750 Pacific Blvd, Plaza of Nations
687-5233
Standup comedy in a theatre setting, Wed to Sun, 9 PM. Wed is amateur night.

See also Entertainment/Culture (Vancouver TheatreSports League).

Quiet Bars

It's getting difficult to find quiet bars as so many of them have entertain-

The Four Seasons' Garden Terrace is rich in greenery. (Four Seasons)

ment and some of it's pretty lively. Here are a few where the tinkle of piano keys is usually unobtrusive and conversation reigns.

The Gallery
Hyatt Regency
655 Burrard at Melville
683-1234
A private-club atmosphere, soft background music. Two TVs but no sound. The comfy chairs around the bar are popular.

Garden Terrace
Four Seasons Hotel
791 W Georgia at Howe
689-9333
Sink into deep sofas and mellow out amid the greenery and soft piano music. Expensive and elegant.

Gérard Lounge
The Sutton Place Hotel
845 Burrard near Robson
682-5511
An elegant and comfortable gentlemen's-club atmosphere, complete with fireplace and piano music. A favourite with the movie set as well as the locals. Extra seating in the Promenade, which is usually quieter than the lounge.

The Park Royal Pub
Park Royal Hotel
540 Clyde, West Van
926-5511
The Tudor-style pub has quiet lounge atmosphere with a fireplace and piano music.

Sylvia Hotel
1154 Gilford, west of Denman
681-9321
Short on atmosphere but long on view. A West End institution that should be visited.

Lively Bars and Lounges

Bacchus Lounge
Wedgewood Hotel
845 Hornby near Robson
689-7777
A bright and airy lounge with a view of the street. Full of rather glamorous people after work and after the theatre. A pianist plays over cocktail hour and later a duo or trio may include a crooner.

Backstage Lounge
Arts Club
1585 Johnston, Granville Island
687-1354
A lively hang-out tucked at the back of one of the city's most popular theatres. Live bands Wed; variety of DJ music. One of the best selections of scotch in town. Cover charge on weekends. Great spot to mingle with the theatre set. Weekends $5; Wed $2.

La Bodega
1277 Howe near Davie
684-8815
This Spanish *tapas* bar has a European atmosphere and a following—clientele ranges from the fashion crowd to flamenco guitarists. The *tapas* are the best in town (don't miss the chorizos). Very crowded on weekends; come before 8 PM.

Joe Fortes
777 Thurlow near Robson
669-1940
Popular with the suit-clad set. The small bar and large restaurant are packed after work and on weekends. Piano player nightly.

Monterey Lounge & Grill
Pacific Palisades Hotel
1277 Robson at Jervis
684-1277
A comfy lounge with a California feel. Sit and watch the Robson St crowd wander by. Light jazz may be piano, soloist or vocal group. On warm evenings there's some patio seating and a great variety of snacks available from the adjoining grill. No jazz Mon. See Restaurants, Outdoors.

Pubs

Bridges
1696 Duranleau, Granville Island
687-4400
A lively, very casual Granville Island pub with a marine theme. Darts, three TVs tuned to sports.

Steamworks Brewing Company
375 Water near Seymour
689-2739
The main floor is the pub with book-lined walls, expansive windows, some outdoor seating and great pub food. Downstairs is a cozy lounge and fireplace, pool tables and a trendy restaurant. All this, and made-on-the-premises brew too.

Mavericks Sports Grill on the Waterfront
770 Pacific Blvd, foot of Robson
683-4436
DJ music—top 40 and classic rock. Large selection of ales and great pub fare. Popular with the sports crowd as it's a short walk to both B.C. Place and GM Place. The large outdoor patio buzzes on a summer evening.

See also the Railway Club, below.

Clubs

BaBalu
654 Nelson near Granville
605-4343
Martini cigar lounge with live entertainment—swing, big band—weeknights and Sun; DJ lounge music on Fri and Sat, 9 PM; Tapas and light dinner entrées; Cover charge at 9 PM when entertainment starts. Weeknights, $5; Weekends, $7.

Club Sonar
66 Water at Abbott
683-6695
A popular hang-out for the 19–24-year-olds. Mostly DJ but also live music—everything from hip-hop to jazz. Funky decor, casual crowd. Tues to Sat.

The Gate
1176 Granville near Davie
608-4283
Live music most nights. A popular place. Open nightly. Cover varies.

Kits on Broadway
1424 W Broadway near Hemlock
736-5811
Popular with those in their 20s. Top 40 and popular rock blasts and the dance floor is always frantic. Casual and fun place. Pool tables. Open nightly. There's also a Kits in New Westminster.

Located in Gastown, the popular Purple Onion Cabaret is a happening place for nightlife. (Purple Onion)

Luv-A-Fair
1275 Seymour at Drake
685-3288
Alternative rock plays to a bopping young crowd. Popular hangout; arrive early. Open nightly.

Palladium
1250 Richards (alley entrance)
688-2648
Loud music, young crowd. There are theme nights—Mon is DJ; Tue, disco; Wed, latino and hip-hop. Also live entertainment. There may be line-ups on weekends. Open nightly.

The Purple Onion Cabaret
15 Water near Carrall
602-9442
A lounge *and* a club. You may hit straight-up jazz (with cigars) in the lounge, then groovy DJ dance music in the club. A fun place, prepare for line-ups on weekends. Open nightly. (Cover charge, $5–$7, includes the club.)

The Rage
750 Pacific, foot of Robson
685-5585
This progressive dance and concert club is huge, with a high-tech look. Music blares, large screens flash and the 20–30s crowd grooves. Some big names perform here, like Spirit of the West. Open Fri and Sat. Cover charge varies.

Railway Club
579 Dunsmuir at Seymour, upstairs
681-1625
One of Vancouver's best and smallest clubs. A pleasant place to have a drink or play some darts, the Railway also books some of the best bands in town. Live music every night; rock-a-billy jam session Sat, 3–7:30 PM, during winter. Sun is movie theme night; screenings start at 7 and are free.

Technically this is a private club, so when you arrive at the door you sign in as a guest. People have been doing this for years, and the club's so pleasant that it's worth the bother. Annual membership is $10, which gets you a card-key for the door and discounts on show admission.

Richard's on Richards
1036 Richards at Nelson
687-6794
Still popular after all these years.
Splashy interior, valet parking; live
and taped top-40 music. Dress
code—no T-shirts or running shoes.
May be line-ups. Thurs to Sat.

The Roxy
932 Granville near Smithe
684-7699
The university crowd as well as other
classic rock-lovers are here for the
house bands and canned music. A
fun, casual club that has a following.
Open nightly.

Starfish Room
1055 Homer at Nelson
682-4171
Mainstream and alternative adult-
oriented music. Touring talent and
big-name local bands. A happening
place with a boppin' dance floor. DJ
music Wed; Thurs to Sat live bands;
Sun and Tues most likely to have visiting bands. Closed Mon.

Gay Clubs

Celebrities Night Club
1022 Davie near Burrard
689-3180
Touted as the largest gay club in
Western Canada. Two storeys, a huge
dance floor, good mix of DJ music.
May be long lineups on weekends.
Sat is Planet Drag on stage. Prin-
cipally gay crowd. Cover varies. Tues
to Sat.

Denman Station
860 Denman off Robson
669-3448
Friendly, subterranean neighbourhood bar. A social place with lots of

activities, including darts and
karaoke. Gay and lesbian crowd.
Open seven nights; no cover charge.

Heritage House Hotel
455 Abbott at Pender
685-7777
There is the Lotus Club for dancing,
Uncle Charlie's for an intimate drink
or Chuck's Pub for darts, billiards
and casual fare. Fri nights are
"women only" in Lotus Club. Gay
and lesbian crowd. Open seven
nights; cover Fri.

Ms T's Cabaret
339 W Pender near Homer
682-8096
Occasional live music; Sat is country
night. Mixed crowd—straight, gay
and lesbian. Mon to Sat. No cover.

Numbers Cabaret
1042 Davie near Burrard
685-4077
Good dancing, movies, pool tables.
Best club in town for cruising.
Mostly gay crowd. Open nightly. No
cover.

The Odyssey
1251 Howe near Davie
689-5256
Clientele is young and stylish and
predominantly gay. DJ, outdoor
patio, pool table. Open nightly.
Cover varies.

The Royal
Royal Hotel
1025 Granville at Nelson
685-5335
One of Vancouver's oldest hotel bars.
Clientele is mostly gay. Live bands
nightly—the best are on Fri, Sat and
Sun. Open nightly; no cover.

Vancouver's close-by mountain lakes and vistas please canoeists. (Judi Lees)

Vancouver is a sports-minded city and a perfect example of how geography and climate can shape people's lives. Balmy temperatures and the nearby wilderness lure people outdoors. It would be a shame to spend time in Vancouver and not partake in these wonderful assets. From a gentle walk in the park to view birdlife to paddling a wild river, it's all here.

Sport B.C. is an umbrella organization that can put you in touch with any sports association or give you up-to-the-minute information about any sport in B.C. The office is at 1367 W Broadway near Hemlock. Call 737-3000 during office hours.

Sports and recreational activities are listed here in alphabetical order.

Birding

The Lower Mainland is a birder's mecca. It is home to, or a stopover for, some 250 bird species, and another 150 are spotted occasionally. There are myriad sighting areas; the closest to downtown is Stanley Park's Lost Lagoon and forested trails. **Don't miss** George C. Reifel Migratory Bird Sanctuary, which has guided walks. (See Parks/Beaches/Gardens.) For information on birding in the area, call Vancouver Natural History Society, 737-3074. This is also the number for the Rare Bird Alert Line.

Canoeing/Kayaking/Rowing

Routes

False Creek
This trip is for the urban adventurer. Set off from Vanier Park, Sunset Beach or Granville Island and circumnavigate False Creek. From Sunset Beach, go under the Burrard, Granville and Cambie St Bridges, past the new developments that adorn the old Expo site and B.C. Place Stadium to the end of False Creek.

On the return trip, go along the south shore to pass by the waterfront

Kayaking in Deep Cove is an excellent escape into nature. (L. Cumming)

community of False Creek. Next is Granville Island and the public market, and then the commercial fishing docks between the Granville and Burrard St Bridges.

Now you are back where you started, having covered roughly 10 km (6 miles) in about three hours.

English Bay

The shores of English Bay, towards Stanley Park or by Kits Beach and Spanish Banks, are good paddling territory. *WARNING: Do not attempt to paddle under Lions Gate Bridge—the currents there are fierce.*

Deer Lake

Deer Lake is an urban park, but 5 km (3 miles) of wooded shoreline and wilderness surround the lake. Burnaby Art Gallery, Shadbolt Centre for the Arts and Burnaby Village Museum, a reconstructed pioneer village, are within a short walk. A great picnic place to take the children or spend a relaxing afternoon on the water.

Don't miss taking a walk along the shoreline paths on the north and northwest end of Deer Lake. You may see heron, eagles, towhee, and a wide variety of waterfowl. You can make a full day of it and have dinner at Hart House, a restaurant on the lakeshore in a lovely heritage house.

Indian Arm

Indian Arm is a dramatically rugged inlet about 1.6 km (1 mile) wide and 30.5 km (19 miles) long, surrounded by 1200 m (4000-foot) mountains. Rent a boat at Deep Cove and paddle across Indian Arm to Jug Island, Combe Park or Belcarra Park. Or paddle south to Cates Park at the mouth of the inlet.

Don't miss Honey Doughnuts & Goodies for a java or cold drink along with delectable sweets. It's located on Gallant St, the main drag of Deep Cove. Also in Deep Cove, fishing boats dock at the wharf and sell fresh salmon—excellent prices.

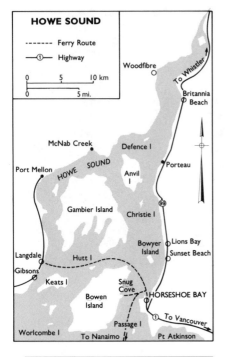

HOWE SOUND

------- Ferry Route

──①── Highway

0   5   10 km

0   5 mi.

Woodfibre

To Whistler

Britannia Beach

McNab Creek

Defence I

Port Mellon

HOWE SOUND

Anvil I

Porteau

Gambier Island

Christie I

Bowyer Island

Lions Bay

Sunset Beach

Langdale

Hutt I

Gibsons

Keats I

Snug Cove

HORSESHOE BAY

Bowen Island

Passage I

To Vancouver

Worlcombe I

To Nanaimo

Pt Atkinson

Rentals

Ecomarine Ocean Kayak
1668 Duranleau, Granville Island
689-7575
Double and single kayaks by the hour or day. A friendly crew will give you pointers if you're just beginning. Closed Mon.

Adventure Fitness
1510 Duranleau, Granville Island
687-1528
Canoes and kayaks for rent plus lessons and tours. Handy to False Creek and English Bay.

Deer Lake Boat Rentals
Deer Lake
255-0087
On the east side of Deer Lake in Burnaby. Kayaks, canoes, rowboats and pedal boats for rent by the hour. Open weekends April to June; daily June to Sept. It's a tricky entry to this

lake. Go along Canada Way to Burris; then right on Buckingham and left on Sperling.

Deep Cove Canoe and Kayak Rentals
Deep Cove
929-2268
Deep Cove is near the mouth of Indian Arm, a spectacular wilderness fjord in North Vancouver. Deep Cove Canoe Rentals is just south of the government wharf at the end of Gallant St. Canoes and kayaks for rent by the hour or the day. Lessons available. Mar to Sept.

Cruising

Routes

For a taped marine forecast, call 664-9032.

Howe Sound/Strait of Georgia

Howe Sound and the Strait of Georgia have some of the best cruising waters in the world and are the only protected saltwater cruising areas north of San Francisco. In addition, there are 28 marine parks between Vancouver Island and the mainland.

Howe Sound has many islands to explore, so bring a picnic lunch and find a secluded beach. Or cruise to Gibsons, where the CBC television series *The Beachcombers* used to be filmed. If you want to meet other boaters, try lively Snug Cove on the east side of Bowen Island, a short distance from Horseshoe Bay. There is a sandy beach at Deep Bay, the next bay north of Snug Cove. Chinook salmon fishing is good here all year.

Regular bus service (#250 Horseshoe Bay) takes you from downtown Vancouver to Horseshoe Bay, where you can rent a boat. Supplies are available within easy walking distance.

Burrard Inlet

For a marine view of the city, cruise up Burrard Inlet into the beautiful natural setting of Vancouver Harbour. You'll see freighters, float planes and cruise ships from all over the world, engaged in the varied activities of the continent's second-largest port. Then there is a quick transition into a wilderness area, with good fishing at the east end of the inlet.

Rentals

Granville Island Boat Rentals
1696 Duranleau, Granville Island
682-6287
U-Drive 15- to 19-foot speedboats by the day or long term.

Sewell's Landing Marina
6695 Nelson, Horseshoe Bay
921-3474
Motorboats by the hour, half-day or day; maps, fishing gear and licences also available here.

Cycling

Cycling B.C.
332–1367 W Broadway at Hemlock
737-3034
website: <www.cycling.bc.ca>
Cycling is popular in Vancouver. Cycling B.C. sells GVRD maps with bike routes marked. Cost is $3.15. Wearing a helmet is mandatory in the city, and riding on the sidewalks is illegal. Police will ticket cyclists for traffic violations. Bicycles are allowed on the SeaBus, and Aquabus (689-5858) transports cyclists and bikes from the foot of Hornby, downtown, to Granville Island and other points on False Creek.

Cyclists are not allowed in the George Massey Tunnel under the Fraser River on Hwy 99 south of the city, but from May through Sept a shuttle service will take you and your bike through the tunnel at designated times. Call 271-0337.

If you are travelling by ferry with a bike, bus #404 Airport/Ladner Exchange has a bicycle rack. The #351 Crescent Beach/Vancouver and #601 South Delta/Vancouver buses also have bike racks.

Routes

Although there are few designated cycling routes right in city centre, there are many excellent well-marked routes in and around the city.

Stanley Park
The seawall, an 8.8 km (5½-mile) paved path along the shore of Stanley Park, is a wonderful ride because of the spectacular views. The seawall is not a complete circle but connects with paths and roads. It is clearly divided in two: one side is for cyclists, the other for pedestrians. Cyclists must ride counterclockwise around the park and must dismount at a few designated busy spots. Start at the foot of Alberni or Georgia.

The seawall is a flat, easy ride that takes about an hour. If you must ride weekends, when the park is very busy, be patient and careful. During summer, members of the Bike Patrol (they wear bright yellow shirts) provide tourist information, give first aid and will even help fix a bike. They will warn fast cyclists as well.

There is also a perimeter road around the park, which is more challenging. The one formidable hill, underneath the Lions Gate Bridge, can be avoided by riding down to the seawall just after Pipeline Rd. The one-way road also goes counter-clockwise, so enter via Georgia and veer right. (See Stanley Park map.)

Port of Vancouver
This ride takes you past Bute Marina, Canada Place Pier, fish-packing plants, cargo docks and grain elevators. Start

*Experience the variety and vastness of Stanley Park the easy way—by bicycle.
(Rosamond Norbury)*

at the north end of Cardero, just east
of the Bayshore Hotel, where an un-
named asphalt service road runs close
to the water. (During the week there
may be some construction in this section, so you may want to start farther
east.) Ride east, picking your route
carefully to stay close to the water; it is
possible to ride almost to the Second
Narrows Bridge.

The return trip is 15 km (9⅓ miles).
The view is superb and the terrain
flat, but watch for oblique railway
tracks. Rentals are available nearby at
Denman and Georgia.

Shaughnessy

An exclusive old neighbourhood
with elegant mansions along quiet,
tree-lined streets, this is a perfect
area for a bicycle meander. From
downtown, take the Cambie St
Bridge south to 16th Ave; then turn
right and go along 16th until you
reach Tecumseh. Pick up picnic supplies at Max's Deli at Oak and 15th

and stop for a picnic at Crescent
Park. Osler, Angus and the Crescent
are the choice streets in Shaughnessy, but travel up the side streets as
well. The Hycroft mansion at 1489
McRae has been restored to its 1912
style and is sometimes open to the
public. Shaughnessy continues on
the other side of Granville.

To return downtown, use the
Burrard St Bridge; it's an easier ride.
Return trip is 13 km (8 miles).

Kitsilano Beaches

From downtown, cross the Burrard St
Bridge and keep right onto Cornwall.
Ahead a few blocks is lively Kits
Beach. Farther down Cornwall (it becomes Point Grey Rd) is Jericho Park,
which is quieter, Locarno Beach and
then Spanish Banks. Follow the
beach path through Jericho Park or
cycle along NW Marine. There are refreshment stands and washrooms at
the beaches. The few hills on this
route are not steep. Avoid rush hour.

The trip to Spanish Banks and back is 17 km (10½ miles).

University of British Columbia

The campus is separated from the city by the University Endowment Lands, a large wilderness area criss-crossed by hiking paths. Paved cycling paths run through the park alongside University Blvd, Chancellor Blvd and 16th Ave.

There is a very steep hill as you approach UBC, so use 8th Ave, which is the least arduous and from which you'll have one of the best views of the city (at 8th and Discovery). A good return route is along NW Marine Dr. Follow the seaside route along the beaches outlined above.

The round trip from downtown with a short stop would take about three hours.

Southlands

This wonderful, oasislike spot in the south end of the city resembles the English countryside. Southlands is the equestrian centre for the city, and you will encounter horses and riders on the bridle paths along the road. Great for a picnic, but there are no stores so pack a lunch. A good picnic spot is at the foot of Carrington.

There are hills on the route from downtown, 21 km (13 miles) return, but Southlands is as flat as can be. Taking the bus to Dunbar Cycles and renting a bike there would shorten the ride to 7 km (4⅓ miles) return.

See also Sightseeing (Walking/Hiking/Cycling Tours).

Rentals

Spokes Bicycle Rentals and Espresso Bar
1798 Georgia at Denman
688-5141

Bayshore Bicycles
745 Denman at Robson

688-2453
1601 Georgia near Denman
689-5071

Fishing

Charter Trips

The sure way to catch a fish is to join a chartered fishing trip. The charter company looks after the details while you sit back and wait for the fish to bite. Charters are available by the half-day, day or week. Call any of these companies for more details:

Bayshore Yacht Charters
1601 W Georgia at Cardero
682-3377

Granville Island Charter Centre
1808 Boatlift Lane, Granville Island
683-1447

Sewell's Landing Marina
6695 Nelson, Horseshoe Bay
921-3474

Information

If you'd rather go fishing on your own, you must check the local fishing restrictions. The tackle shops listed here are a good source of information. They will give you a current issue of the federal government's "B.C. Tidal Waters Sport Fishing Guide" and the provincial government's "B.C. Sport Fishing Regulations Synopsis for Non-tidal Waters." Any of these shops will sell you a saltwater or freshwater fishing licence and tell you where they're biting.

The Department of Fisheries and Oceans has an information service. By calling 666-2828 you can find out about restrictions, where and when to fish, and which lures to use.

The *B.C. Fishing Directory and Atlas*, available at most sporting goods stores, provides complete information about fishing locations.

See also Sightseeing (Granville Island Sport Fishing Museum).

Fishing Gear

Army and Navy
27 W Hastings near Carrall
682-6644

West Coast Fishing Tackle
2147 E Hastings near Victoria
254-0004

Three Vets
2200 Yukon at 6th
872-5475

Compleat Angler Tackle
4257 Fraser at 27th (rear)
879-8033

Ruddick's Fly Shop
1654 Duranleau, Granville Island
681-3747

Where to Fish

Burrard Inlet
Burrard Inlet is open all year.

Howe Sound/Horseshoe Bay
The Horseshoe Bay/Howe Sound area offers the best chance of catching salmon. This is one of the most popular fishing spots on the Pacific coast, and there are marinas all along the coast at Fisherman's Cove, Whytecliff, Horseshoe Bay, Sunset Beach and Lions Bay. Free boat launches in the area are at Fisherman's Cove and Porteau Beach.

Sunshine Coast
Another hot spot for salmon fishing, especially from Secret Cove to Egmont. It is a three-hour trip from Horseshoe Bay to the Sunshine Coast, including a ferry ride from Horseshoe Bay to Langdale.

Boat rentals and charters are available at Secret Cove, Pender Harbour and Egmont.

Fraser River
A saltwater licence is needed below the town of Mission; above the town you must have a freshwater licence. Information about access to the many Fraser River sandbars is in the B.C. fishing guides mentioned earlier. Fish the mouth of the Fraser for sockeye during late summer; pink salmon are available in odd years.

Lakes and Rivers
For freshwater angling, try the Squamish-Cheakamus River system, the Vedder-Chilliwack River, the lakes near the Sunshine Coast, or Pitt, Stave, Cultus and Harrison Lakes east of Vancouver. There is good fishing all year at Buntzen Lake east of the city.

On Vancouver's North Shore you can fish the Seymour River, the Capilano River and Lynn Creek, primarily for coho in late summer and early fall.

Golf

Vancouver is golfer-friendly. Courses are scenic as well as challenging, and although the season is Apr to Oct, many courses are open year-round. Several large tournaments—both amateur and professional—are held annually. The largest is the Greater Vancouver Open, which is played at the Northview Golf and Country Club in Surrey and features 156 of the world's top golfers.

For information on golf in the area call the **B.C. Golf Association** (294-1818) or **B.C. Professional Golfers Association** (536-7878) for details. There is a Last Minute Golf Hotline (878-1833), which allows discounts on last-minute bookings.

Don't miss a handy new service, The West Coast Golf Shuttle, which provides transportation and books tee-times to the top local courses.

The shuttle runs daily Apr to Oct and upon special request Nov to Mar. Call the 24-hour information line: 878-6800.

Public Courses

Listed here are some of the most popular courses close to the centre of the city.

Fraserview Golf Course
7800 Vivian at 54th
257-6923
This scenic municipal course may be Canada's busiest. A recent renovation of the course saw some of the large trees removed. Clubs and power carts for rent, cafeteria, bar, driving range. Par 71, 6346 yards.

Langara Golf Course
6706 Alberta near 49th
713-1816
Renovated in 1994, this is a new course with old-growth trees. Good intermediate golfing. It includes a clubhouse, a licensed restaurant and locker room facilities. You can walk or rent a power cart. Particularly pretty course in fall. Par 71, 6100 yards.

McCleery Golf Course
7188 MacDonald at Marine Dr
257-8191
Another picturesque course along southwest Marine Drive. This 18-hole course also has a driving range, pro shop, cafeteria, and you can rent power carts. Par 71, 6265 yards

Please note: The above three municipal courses have a central booking number for tee times. Call 280-1818 to play Fraserview, Langara or McCleery.

University Golf Club
5185 University Blvd
University of British Columbia
224-1818

This popular public course is the closest to the city centre. It is challenging but not punishing. The clubhouse has a dining room and bar; clubs and pull and power carts can be rented. Par 72, 6157 yards.

There are about 20 other public courses just outside Vancouver. Some particularly good ones are:

Burnaby Mountain Golf Course
7600 Halifax, Burnaby
280-7355

A beautiful mountain setting makes this course worth the drive. A wide open course, perfect for intermediates. Pro shop, driving range and rentals. Par 71, 6431 yards.

Gleneagles Golf Course
6190 Marine, West Van
921-7353
Nine holes. Located near Horseshoe Bay; the trip from Vancouver is one of the area's most scenic drives. Par 35, 2800 yards.

Mayfair Lakes
5460 No. 7 Rd, Richmond
276-0505
Beautifully laid-out with water absolutely everywhere. Very good facilities and restaurant. Par 71, 6641 yards.

Private Clubs

Many private clubs accept guests accompanied by members. Most also have reciprocal privileges, whereby you will be admitted if you are a member of another bona fide club. You must have a membership card and/or a letter of introduction from your club pro. Phone first for confirmation. The best private courses are:

Capilano Golf and Country Club
420 Southborough, West Van
922-9331
Fairly rigorous course, with a breathtaking view. Par 72, 6221 yards.

Shaughnessy Golf and Country Club
4300 sw Marine at Kullahun
266-4141
Very prestigious and very busy. Must be with a member to play. Par 73, 6320 yards.

Point Grey Golf and Country Club
3350 sw Marine at Blenheim
261-3108
Private club in the same area as Shaughnessy. Par 72, 6279 yards.

Pitch and Putt

Eighteen holes of golf the quick way, with a short fairway. Four public pitch and putt courses are centrally located; all rent clubs.

Queen Elizabeth Pitch and Putt
Queen Elizabeth Park
Cambie at 33rd
874-8336
Open Feb to Nov.

Stanley Park Pitch and Putt
Stanley Park
681-8847
Open year-round. Use the Beach Ave entrance.

Hiking/Mountaineering/ Indoor Climbing Walls

The **Federation of Mountain Clubs of B.C.** offers courses in all levels of mountaineering, guiding and rock climbing. They lead hiking and backpacking trips throughout B.C. and can provide you with a list of companies that offer shorter guided hikes. Also, ask for their excellent brochure, "Bus to Hiking Trails." Call 737-3053.

The Lower Mainland abounds with hiking trails, some with very easy access. There are several hiking guide books available; try *Easy Hiking Around Vancouver* by Jean Cousins. A good hiking guide grades trails from easy to difficult.

The ultimate challenge is the Grouse Grind, starting from the base of Grouse Mountain. Each year some 140,000 keeners scale the 2.9 km trail, which gains 900 m of vertical lift. Average hiking time is one hour and 15 minutes. The winning time at the annual Grouse Grind Hill Climb is just over 29 minutes!

See also Parks/Beaches/Gardens; Sightseeing (Touring Vancouver).

Cliffhanger Indoor Rock Climbing Centre
106 W 1st at Manitoba
874-2400
A climbing service for everyone from novice to expert. Children are welcome here.

The Edge Climbing Centre
1485 Welch St near Pemberton, North Vancouver
984-9080
Climbing walls and programs for adults and children.

Horse Racing

From Apr to Nov, thoroughbred races are run at **Hastings Park Racecourse**, at Hastings and Renfrew. Parade to post is 6:30 on Wed and Fri; 1:15 on Sat, Sun and holidays. The rest of the year racing fans can see simulcast racing from tracks in North America, Australia and Hong Kong.

You can dine and overlook the racetrack at Table Terrace Restaurant. Brunch is served on Sun at noon in the clubhouse. To reserve a table in the clubhouse, Table Terrace or in the dining room, phone 254-1631. Book well in advance for brunch or dinner. In the dining room you can also view the races on closed-circuit television.

From Sept to Apr, there is harness racing at **Cloverdale Raceway** at

176th St and 60th Ave in Surrey. Races are held at 7 PM on Wed and Fri and at 1:15 PM on Sat and Sun. Call 576-9141 for more information.

In-Line Skating

Vancouver's mild climate is ideal for this fast-growing sport. Officially, it is not allowed on sidewalks or streets, but as long as skaters are courteous and safety-conscious, authorities don't clamp down. Check with local skaters and those who work in the skate shops for the latest word.

Routes

Seymour Demonstration Forest
987-1273
A sanctioned 11 km (7-mile) route in North Vancouver called the Mainline. This is for experts only since there are some steep sections. One section must be walked due to the danger factor.

See Sightseeing (Special Interest Tours).

Stanley Park Seawall
There has been some controversy regarding skaters on the seawall; however, in-liners do share the bicycle path with cyclists and there doesn't seem to be a problem. During summer, the seawall is patrolled; fast skating is frowned on.

False Creek/Granville Island/Vanier Park
This is a popular route shared with cyclists. Start at the bottom of Denman and Beach and go east; the route goes around False Creek to Vanier Park. In a few places you are on the road, and near Granville Island there's a cobblestone section that's tricky. Or you can start just west of Granville Island and enjoy

the route along Vanier Park to Kits Beach.

See also Sports/Recreation (Cycling).

Rentals

Alley Cat Rentals
1779 Robson near Denman
684-5117

Jogging

Seawall, Stanley Park
The flat asphalt path along the seawall has stunning scenery to keep you going for all 8.8 km (5½ miles).

Lost Lagoon, Stanley Park
The path that circles the lagoon is accessible from the foot of Alberni. It is a level gravel pathway, about 1.6 km (1 mile) long, excellent for an easy run.

Seawall, False Creek
The seawall starts at Fisherman's Wharf by the Burrard St Bridge and runs past Granville Island and the community of False Creek to the Cambie St Bridge. The trip is 5 km (3 miles) return. If you need sustenance, stop at Isadora's on the edge of Granville Island near the seawall; see Restaurants (Breakfast/Brunch).

English Bay
A level pathway starts behind the Vancouver Aquatic Centre and follows the water's edge to Stanley Park, 2 km (1¼ miles) one-way.

Kits Beach/Vanier Park
A series of asphalt and dirt paths starts at Vanier Park on the Kitsilano side of the Burrard St Bridge. The paths follow the water around Kits Point, past the Vancouver Museum, the planetarium, the Maritime Museum, Kits Beach and the Kitsilano Yacht Club. This fairly flat route is about 5 km (3 miles).

Don't miss spending time at Kits

Beach, whether walking, jogging, cycling or in-line skating. On a warm summer's evening, this is Vancouver at its best. Families gather for barbecues, sporty types play volleyball and sailboats dot the ocean. This beach is among the finest places to watch the sun drop into the horizon.

Ambleside Seawall to Centennial Seawalk

The paths in Ambleside Park start at the east side and follow the water for the length of the park. You then have to pick your way along the beach and the road for a short distance until the beginning of the Centennial Seawalk. This 1.6 km (1-mile) path is asphalt and completely flat. The views are of the cityscape, Lions Gate Bridge, Stanley Park and the marine traffic.

Professional Sports

Vancouver residents are outdoor oriented and generally prefer to do, rather than watch, sports. But there are some diehard fans out there.

Tickets

Tickets for professional football, hockey and other sports events can be purchased from Ticketmaster outlets, which have branches in some Eaton's stores (the Pacific Centre store has one) and at the information booths of major malls. There is an outlet in the Farmer's Market on Granville Island. Or you can order your tickets by phone (280-4444) and charge them to Visa, MasterCard or American Express.

Auto Racing

Normally Pacific Blvd is a 50 km/h zone (30 mph), but on the Labour Day during the Indy Vancouver weekend this is upped to 300 km/h

(190 mph). The downtown track is about 2.7 km (1¾ miles) long, and cars do some 103 laps. The final race, on Sunday afternoon, takes only two hours; practices and time trials are held for two days before.

Odds are grandstand tickets will be sold out, but general admission tickets are usually available. Phone 684-4639.

Hockey

The Vancouver Canucks have been around since 1968, and like most professional teams, they've had their ups and downs. They took quantum leaps to respectability winning the Smythe Division in 1992 and taking the Stanley Cup Finals to seven games against New York in 1994. Just how popular hockey is in this city became obvious in summer 1997, when Mark Messier was drafted to the team; this made headline news for weeks in local papers. The Canucks are based in General Motors Place, where they draw crowds of more than 18,000. For information, call 899-4610.

Football

Since the team's beginnings in 1954, the B.C. Lions have won the coveted Grey Cup on three occasions: 1964, 1985 and 1994. The latter was a thriller as they defeated Baltimore in the last seconds of the game. Although there have been some less-than-thrilling seasons, the motto seems to be, once a Lions' fan, always a Lions' fan. The Lions play in B.C. Place Stadium downtown; their season starts in June and runs until late Oct. For information, call 583-7747.

Basketball

A Grizzlies' game is a happening place to be. Half-time is show time, and GM Place rocks with the antics of raucous fans. The Grizzlies, Vancouver's first professional basketball team, seldom win, but that doesn't seem to matter. NBA players like "Big Country" Reeves are familiar faces on the court as well as out in the community, as they support many events. Most games sell out. The season runs Nov to Apr. For information, call 899-7400.

Baseball

If you have fond memories of sunshine, hot dogs and Sunday afternoon baseball from when you were a kid, catch the Vancouver Canadians of the Pacific Coast League at grand old Nat Bailey Stadium. The highly popular Canadians are a cult in Vancouver and their games often sell out, so arrive early. Tickets are available at the door. The stadium is at Ontario and 29th, on the east side of Queen Elizabeth Park. The season is from Apr to Sept. There are afternoon and evening games. Take a cushion and, in evenings, a sweater. Phone 872-5232 for times or check the newspapers. See also With the Kids (Other Fun Places).

Soccer

The Vancouver 86ers play in the American Professional Soccer League (known as the A League). Highlights from the past decade include 46 undefeated games in a row, four league championships and one North American title. They are one of Vancouver's most successful teams. They play in Swangard Stadium in Burnaby; their season is May to Oct. Phone 930-2255 for information and tickets.

Don't miss a walk in Central Park, if you travel to Boundary and Kingsway to attend a soccer game. The stadium is in the corner of this lovely wooded park, and there are many trails, small ponds and a pitch and putt.

Rafting

If the daredevil in you wants to try whitewater rafting, companies in Vancouver organize trips that will take you through some incredible rapids—Hell's Gate, the Washing Machine, Devil's Cauldron or the Jaws of Death. The Thompson and Chilliwack Rivers are known for frothing white water and the Fraser for whirlpools and waves. Fraser River trips are also more historical, and most are on motorized rafts. Taking part in the paddling is the more exciting trip.

Some companies transport you from the city to the interior of B.C., or you can drive yourself to a meeting place in the area, a one- to three-hour trip from Vancouver. Rain suits are provided, but it's a good idea to bring a change of clothes.

It is also possible to raft rivers in the Squamish and Whistler areas—within a one- to two-hour drive from the city. Although these rivers do not have the phenomenal white water found in the interior rivers, these are fun trips. In winter one of these trips can be combined with eagle watching in the Squamish region.

There are many companies offering rafting trips.

Hyak Wilderness Adventures
734-8622

Offers paddling trips of one, two and six days on the Thompson, Chilliwack or Chilko Rivers. This company picks up from hotels and transports you to the rafting destinations.

Canadian Outback Adventures
921-7250
1-800-565-8735

Float trips on the lower Squamish

Setting sail off Jericho Beach into the waters of English Bay. (Rosamond Norbury)

and Cheakamus and whitewater rafting on the Elaho-Squamish, Chilko, Chilcotin and Fraser. (A float on the Cheakamus can be combined with eagle watching in Dec and Jan.)

Sailing

Cooper Boating Centre
1620 Duranleau, Granville Island
687-4110
Cooper offers everything from sailing lessons to a variety of excursions.

Day Cruises

During the summer, Cooper Boating Centre (see above) has three-hour cruises in English Bay on 6 to 12 m (20- to 40-foot) yachts. They leave from Granville Island; cost is $25 a person with a minimum of four people.

Cruise and Learn

This is a wonderful introduction to the world of sailing. Cooper's cruise-and-learn vacation is a five-day trip around the Gulf Islands on boats that are 9 to 12 m (30 to 40 feet) long. For about $890 you get sailing instruction, food and a berth. Trips run regularly from May to Oct with four students and an instructor. Advanced courses are also offered.

Considering the amount you could spend on hotels, restaurants and entertainment, this course offers a unique combination of sun, salt water, new territory and new skills. The bonus is finishing with a Canadian Yachting Association certificate.

Charters

If you are an experienced sailor you can rent a sailboat for an evening, half-day, day or longer. Blue Pacific (below), or Cooper will arrange charters, with or without a skipper. Please note that in False Creek sails are prohibited and the maximum speed is five knots.

Blue Pacific Yacht Charters
1519 Foreshore Walk, Granville
Island
682-2161

Scuba Diving

Divers in British Columbia encounter an incredible range of marine life: sea stars, anemones, coral, seals, sea lions, killer whales, the largest octopus species in the world, wolf eels, crabs, abalone, snails, prawns, 180 varieties of sponges and over 325 kinds of fish.

Around Vancouver most scuba diving is done in Howe Sound and Indian Arm. Both are steep-sided inlets formed by glacial activity. Indian Arm is at the east end of Burrard Inlet, and Howe Sound is the Horseshoe Bay region and beyond. It is highly recommended that visiting divers go out with a local expert the first time. The water here may be dramatically colder than the water they are used to diving in.

No diving is allowed in Vancouver Harbour between Lions Gate Bridge and Second Narrows Bridge. To dive in the outer harbour, advise the Vancouver Port Corporation at 666-2405.

Where to Dive

If you wish to dive with your own group, following are some suggestions for day trips. Because of the rugged, vertical shores, access may be a problem. All the spots listed here have shore access and are rated for beginners as well as advanced divers, except where indicated.

Whytecliff Park

This West Vancouver park has the province's only "Marine Protected Area." In fact it's the only one in Canada. You may get lucky and spot a resident octopus. The best visibility is from Oct to Apr. Follow signs to the park from Horseshoe Bay.

Lighthouse Park

This West Vancouver park is about 9.7 km (6 miles) past Park Royal Shopping Centre, and the entrance is off Marine Dr. A half-hour walk takes you from the parking lot to the shore. Lighthouse Park has been described as the "richest" dive in Vancouver. For intermediate and advanced divers.

Porteau Cove

This popular spot is a good place to meet other divers around a beach fire at the end of the day. On Hwy 99, 24 km (15 miles) past Horseshoe Bay, you will see an arched sign over the road saying Porteau Camp. About 1.6 km (1 mile) ahead is parking and beach access. Porteau Cove is a provincial marine park and has an artificial reef made from old ships' hulls, a wreck of a minesweeper, a campground, showers and a boat launch.

Gulf Islands

If you are willing to travel farther, diving in the Gulf Islands is spectacular. Try Beaver Point on Salt Spring. Take the ferry from Tsawwassen to Long Harbour on Salt Spring. Follow the signs to Fulford Harbour. Just before the town, take Beaver Point Rd for 9.7 km (6 miles) to Ruckle Park. Park at the end of the road and walk 800 m (875 yards) to the shore. Dive in the bay if you are a beginner or at the point if you are experienced.

Rentals and Charters

These stores all rent equipment by the day, and some even rent personal gear such as fins and masks to divers from out of town.

You need a 6 mm (¼-inch) neoprene wet suit in B.C. waters. The dive shops frequently organize day

Scuba diving is a year-round activity. (Gary Mallander)

trips as well as weekend and night dives. Occasionally, boat charters are available. The stores will arrange whatever is necessary—air, transportation or diving partners. Most trips are geared to beginners and intermediate divers. Proof of diving certification and tank inspection is necessary to obtain air.

Diver's World
1813 W 4th at Burrard
732-1344

Diving Locker
2745 W 4th near Macdonald
736-2681

Adrenalin Sports
1630 W 5th at Fir
734-3483

To charter a boat, contact:

Granville Island Charter Centre
1808 Boatlift Lane, Granville Island
683-1447

Skiing and Snowboarding

You name it, Vancouver's got it! There's handy, effortless skiing at Grouse, Seymour and Cypress, about a half-hour drive from downtown, and there's also world-class Whistler, a couple of hours away. With Whistler and Blackcomb Mountains now under one ownership, a day pass gets you two mountains for the price of one.

Don't miss the free tours at Whistler and Blackcomb, which are great introductions to the mountains. These tours are for good intermediate skiers, but don't be shy if you are a slower skier. Hang around, and one of the guides will put a group together for your skill level. Whistler's tours leave from the lightboard at the top at 10 AM and 1 PM. Blackcomb's are at the same times and leave from outside the Rendevous.

Downhill

Whistler
Vertical drop: 1530 m (5020 feet)
Base elevation: 652 m (2140 feet)
Lifts: 3 quad expresses, 3 triple and 1 double chairlifts, 2 T-bars, 2 gondolas. Capacity 23,500 people an hour
Runs: over 100; longest 11 km (7 miles)
Terrain: 20% novice, 55% intermediate, 25% expert
Average snowfall: 907 cm (357 inches)
Snow reports: Vancouver 687-7507, Whistler 932-4211
Facilities: A whole village supplies anything a skier could want: instruction, helicopter skiing, cross-country (rentals, instruction, unlimited terrain), paragliding, snowmobiling and two mountain-top restaurants. There is a half-pipe and "terrain park" for snowboarders.

Book accommodation through the

Whistler Resort Association (Vancouver 664-5625, Whistler 932-4222 or toll free from the U.S. or Canada 1-800-944-7853).

Getting there: Whistler is 120 km (75 miles) north of Vancouver on Hwy 99, a spectacular but sometimes hazardous road—keep your wits about you. Chains may be required.

There is daily train and bus service to Whistler from Vancouver. (Whistler/Blackcomb bus 662-8051).

Comments: Whistler, along with neighbouring Blackcomb (following), can only be described in superlatives: the largest ski area in North America, the longest ski season in western Canada, and so on. Not just the best skiing in this area, Whistler resort has been voted the number one ski destination in North America by several top ski magazines. The season runs from late Nov to April.

See also Excursions from Vancouver (Whistler).

Blackcomb
Vertical drop: 1609 m (5280 feet)
Base elevation: 675 m (2215 feet)
Lifts: 6 quad expresses, 3 triple chairlifts, 2 T-bars, 1 handle tow, 1 platter, 1 gondola. Capacity 29,000 people an hour
Runs: 100 plus; longest 11 km (7 miles)
Terrain: 15% novice, 55% intermediate, 30% expert
Average snowfall: 907 cm (357 inches)
Snow reports: Vancouver 687-7507, Whistler 932-4211
Facilities: Instruction, rental and repairs, three restaurants, plus all the facilities in neighbouring Whistler Village. A favourite with snowboarders. There are two half-pipes and the snowboard park has been enlarged to 16 acres.
Getting there: Same as Whistler.

Comments: The highest lift-serviced vertical drop in North America and the largest summer glacier-skiing operation.

No other resort on the continent offers skiing on two superb mountains beside each other, and most skiers are hard-pressed to say which mountain they prefer; both have thousands of enthusiastic fans. Winter season and hours are the same as Whistler. Blackcomb also offers summer skiing, 12–3:30 daily, on the Horstman Glacier.

See also Excursions from Vancouver (Whistler).

Grouse Mountain
Vertical drop: 365 m (1200 feet)
Base elevation: 885 m (2900 feet)
Lifts: 2 aerial trams to ski area, 4 double chairs, 2 T-bars, 2 rope tows
Runs: 22; longest 2.4 km (1.5 miles)
Terrain: 30% novice, 50% intermediate, 20% expert
Average snowfall: 488 cm (192 inches) with snow-making equipment
Snow reports: Vancouver 986-6262
Facilities: Rentals (984-0661), instruction, cafeteria, dining room, lounge and bistro, night skiing until 10.

Getting there: Grouse is 12 km (7.5 miles) north of Vancouver, a 20-minute drive from downtown via Lions Gate Bridge and Capilano Rd.

Public transit goes to Grouse from downtown. On Georgia catch the #246 Highland bus westbound, and at Edgemont and Ridgewood transfer to the #232 Grouse.

Comments: Grouse is popular with people who want to learn to ski after work, and there are many ski school programs. It's worth a trip up the mountain to ski—day or night—since the view from the Cut is spectacular. On a clear night, skiing is sublime. See also Parks/Beaches/Gardens.

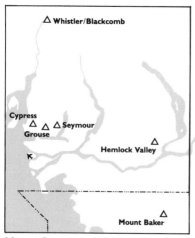

Whistler/Blackcomb

Cypress
Grouse Seymour

Hemlock Valley

Mount Baker

Mount Seymour Ski Resort
Vertical drop: 365 m (1200 feet)
Base elevation: 1010 m (3314 feet)
Lifts: 4 double chairlifts, 1 double rope tow
Runs: 25; longest 2.4 km (1.5 miles)
Terrain: 40% novice, 40% intermediate, 20% expert
Average snowfall: 255–305 cm (100–120 inches)
Snow reports: Vancouver 718-7771
Facilities: Instruction, rentals (986-2261), day lodge, cafeteria, night skiing until 10, snowshoe and cross-country rentals and instruction. No accommodation in park.
Getting there: This resort is in Mount Seymour Provincial Park, 16 km (10 miles) north of Vancouver. Take the Second Narrows Bridge, take the Dollarton Hwy (#23B) and follow the signs. Accessible by car only.
Comments: A family and learn-to-ski area. There are no groomed cross-country trails; beginners sometimes practice in open areas.

Cypress Bowl
Vertical drop: 533 m (1750 feet)
Base elevation: 980 m (3215 feet)
Lifts: 1 quad chair, 3 double chairlifts, 1 rope tow; capacity 5000 people an hour

Runs: 25; longest 4 km (2.5 miles)
Terrain: 23% novice, 37% intermediate, 40% expert
Average snowfall: 355 cm (140 inches)
Snow reports: Vancouver 419-7669
Facilities: Day lodge, cafeteria, 26 km (16 miles) of cross-country trails, rentals (926-5612), instruction, lounge. No accommodation.
Getting there: Cypress is a 30-minute drive from downtown Vancouver, 16 km (10 miles) away. Go over the Lions Gate Bridge and take the Upper Levels Hwy west.
Comments: The snow may be wet and heavy but it's easy access for some good terrain. This mountain is expanding. Plans include a gondola and a restaurant at the peak of Mt Strachan.

Mount Baker (In the U.S.A.)
Vertical drop: 457 m (1500 feet)
Base elevation: 1310 m (4300 feet)
Lifts: 2 fixed quads, 6 double chairlifts, 2 rope tows; capacity 8000 people an hour
Runs: 48; longest 3.2 km (2 miles)
Terrain: 30% novice, 42% intermediate, 28% expert
Average snowfall: 1511 cm (595 inches)
Snow reports: Vancouver 688-1595
Facilities: Instruction, rentals, cafeteria, daycare. There is 4 km (2.5 miles) of groomed cross-country track. No accommodation on mountain.
Getting there: Mount Baker is 120 km (75 miles) south of Vancouver, a two-hour drive. Take Hwy 99 south to Hwy 542; then go east. Or take Hwy 1 east to the Sumas exit; then go south. Take chains. Car access only.
Comments: Although Mount Baker is in the United States, it is a popular destination for skiers from Vancouver. Of the mountains close to Vancouver, Baker receives the

Grouse Mountain offers skiing half an hour away from downtown Vancouver.

heaviest snowfall. The season lasts until the end of Apr. Baker is popular with snowboarders and has a half-pipe. Accommodation is in tiny towns at the mountain base and is limited. Closed midweek in Apr.

Cross-Country

There are some cross-country ski areas within reach of Vancouver in the Lower Mainland. Cypress, Whistler and Manning are well groomed and well marked and provide the best skiing. The season for cross-country skiing generally runs from the beginning of Dec until the end of Mar.

Cypress Bowl
The closest to Vancouver, Cypress's Hollyburn Ridge on the North Shore has 16 km (10 miles) of groomed and track-set trails, of which 5 km (3 miles) are lit for evening skiing. Equipment rentals (922-0825) and hot food are available at Hollyburn Lodge. There are lessons in classical

and skate skiing. For information: 922-0825. Cypress is busy on weekends. For a snow report, call Vancouver 419-7669.

Whistler
There are two cross-country areas adjacent to Whistler Village. The best is the Lost Lake network, 22 km (13½ miles) of set trails. A day pass lets you take advantage of warming huts, trail maps and meticulously groomed trails. A 4 km (2½-mile) section is lit for night skiing. A free and more informal cross-country area is the golf course, which occasionally has about 6 km (3¾ miles) of set trails. These areas would appeal to beginners or those interested in a workout rather than a wilderness experience.

For back-country skiing try Cheakamus Lake Trail (a flat logging road not far from Whistler Village), the 14 km (8¾-mile) Singing Pass Trail, and Callaghan/Madeley Lake. For information or a cross-country snow report, call 932-6436 (seasonal).

Manning Park

The best cross-country area in the Lower Mainland is at Manning, where conditions compare favourably to those in Scandinavia. Back-country terrain trails total 190 km (118 miles), and 30 km (18½ miles) of trails are groomed for track and skating technique. There's a full range of lessons available. The inland location means drier snow and plenty of sunshine. For snow information, call 878-8900 in Vancouver.

The park is a three-hour drive east of Vancouver, via the Trans-Canada Hwy to Hope, then Hwy 3 to Manning Park. Accommodation is available at Manning Park Lodge (250-840-8822), which has a café, dining room and pub.

Don't miss a weekend of cross-country skiing with Sigge's Sport Villa (731-8818). Excursions (for the experienced and wanna-bes) are to Whistler and Manning Park. These offer excellent terrain and great fun. Manning Park trips usually run every Sunday from the beginning of Dec until the end of Mar. Whistler trips take place every second Saturday from the beginning of Jan until the end of Feb. The trips include return transportation by bus from Vancouver and trail ticket; rental equipment and lessons are also available. Call for the schedule.

Rentals

You can rent equipment at the ski resorts as well as at these outlets around the city:

Carleton Cycle and Outdoor Recreation
3201 Kingsway near Rupert
438-6371
Cross-country skis, telemark, snowshoes and mountaineering equipment. Closed Sun.

Destination Ski Rentals
1550 Marine near McGowan, North Van
984-4394
Downhill, cross-country, snowboards and snowshoes.

Sigge's Sport Villa
2077 W 4th at Arbutus
731-8818
Cross-country skis.

The Board Room
1911 Pine at 4th
734-7669
Snowboard equipment.

Spas

After a hard day of skiing, hiking or simply to indulge yourself, head to an urban spa for pampering. All those listed below are in the city and offer a full range of services.

Beverly's Skin Care on Fourth
732-4402

Le Spa at The Sutton Place Hotel
682-7490

Robert Andrew Salon & Spa (in the Hotel Vancouver)
687-7133

Spa at the Century
684-2772

Versailles Spa
732-7865

See also Excursions from Vancouver (Whistler).

Swimming

At the Beach

The city has 11 sandy swimming beaches. The water temperature is refreshing, peaking at 21°C (70°F) in the summer. The following beaches have lifeguards on duty from the Victoria Day weekend through

Labour Day: Second Beach and Third Beach in Stanley Park, English Bay, Sunset Beach, Kits Beach, Jericho Beach, Locarno Beach and Spanish Banks. There is also a lifeguard at Trout Lake.

Major Outdoor Pools

Kitsilano Pool
Kitsilano Beach
731-0011
The Kits Pool is gargantuan, modern and heated to 25°C (77°F). Both small children and serious swimmers use this pool because its depth is graduated and because it is so large. Open from Victoria Day (May 24) to mid-Sept; noon–8:45 weekdays until mid-June then Mon to Fri 7 AM–8:45 PM (7–9 AM adult swim); Sat, Sun and holidays, 10–8:45 all summer. Adults $3.75, with discounts for seniors and children.

Second Beach Pool
Second Beach, Stanley Park
257-8371
Located beside the seawall, this freshwater pool is large enough for a good workout, and there are three lanes designated for swimming laps. With a beach next door, this pool has always been a favourite with youngsters, and now there are three small waterslides. There is a lifeguard on duty, and there are children's lessons and aqua-fit classes for adults during July. Open Victoria Day to Labour Day weekend; weekdays noon–8:45 until mid-June; then until Labour Day weekend hours are 10–8:45 daily; some mornings there are early bird swims. Cost is $3.75 for adults, with discounts for seniors and children.

Major Indoor Pools

The two best indoor swimming facilities are the Vancouver Aquatic Centre in the West End and the University of British Columbia (UBC) Aquatic Centre. Both are Olympic-size pools with diving tanks, saunas, whirlpools and exercise gyms. There are also two smaller indoor pools downtown operated by the YMCA and the YWCA, and nine throughout the city operated by the Parks Board.

UBC Aquatic Centre
University of British Columbia
822-4521
During the school year, there is public swimming on evenings and weekends. The pool is also open to the public during the day in June, July and Aug. Phone to check times.

Vancouver Aquatic Centre
1050 Beach, south end of Thurlow
665-3424
On the shore of English Bay. Closed annually for maintenance the month of Aug. Public swim times vary, so phone ahead.

YMCA
955 Burrard near Nelson
681-0221
Open to men and women at co-ed swim times; there are some men-only swim times. Out-of-town YMCA memberships are honoured. Day passes for nonmembers are available and allow full use of all facilities, including the pool, sauna, drop-in fitness classes, weight room and racquetball, handball and squash courts.

YWCA
535 Hornby near Dunsmuir
895-5800
Open to men and women. Out-of-town memberships honoured, or you can purchase a day pass for access to the pool, sauna, whirlpool or weight room or any of the exercise or dance-fit classes.

Tennis

Vancouver is Tennis Town. The outdoor season runs from Mar to Oct, with the odd lucky day in the winter. Even 180 public courts are not enough, and you may have to wait on summer weekends.

Outdoor Courts

With one exception, all public courts are outdoors, are free and operate on a first-come, first-served basis. Popular courts are as follows:

Stanley Park

Twenty-one courts (17 by the Beach Ave entrance, and 4 by Lost Lagoon at the foot of Robson). From May to Labour Day weekend, 6 of the 17 courts at the Beach Ave location can be reserved for a small fee. Call 257-8489.

Andy Livingston Park
Pacific and Carrall
There are two courts at this recreational park close to the centre of the city.

Queen Elizabeth Park
33rd at Cambie
17 courts.

Kitsilano Beach Park
Ten courts.

Jericho Beach Park
Five courts behind Jericho Sailing Centre.

Night Tennis

The only lit public courts are on the Langara Campus of Vancouver Community College, on 49th between Cambie and Main, and at Killarney Community Centre, 6260 Killarney at 49th Ave.

Indoor Courts

Most indoor courts are at private clubs, but here are a couple where you can play on a rainy day.

University of B.C. Tennis Club
6184 Thunderbird Blvd at East Mall
822-2505
Four indoor courts (should book ahead) and 10 outdoors. Pay as you play.

Delta Pacific Resort & Conference Centre
10251 St Edwards off Bridgeport, Richmond
276-1140
Book same day for four indoor courts.

Windsurfing

Windsurfing schools operate at various beaches in town and will supply everything you need: instruction, board, wet suit and life jacket. The introductory rental/instruction packages vary from one to six hours, depending on the school. If you know anything about surfing or sailing, you are one step ahead; if not, the uninitiated can become competent after a few hours.

No sailboards are allowed at the mouth of False Creek between the Granville and Burrard St Bridges.

Windsure Windsurfing School
1300 Discovery
224-0615
Lessons and rentals at Jericho Beach.

Shopping

The public market and waterfront restaurants of Granville Island. (Bob Herger, Photo/Graphics)

Shopping Areas

Robson Street

Robson has changed drastically over the years. Most of the little European shops and services have been replaced by glitzy storefronts. However, as well as being a mecca for shoppers, Robson is pedestrian friendly with sidewalk cafés and street entertainment.

Granville Island

Don't miss Granville Island for the Farmer's Market, the wonderful arts and crafts and the Kids Only Market. There are many restaurants and small take-outs. On weekends the locals swarm here, so try to shop during the week.

See Sightseeing (Granville Island).

Kitsilano

The W 4th Ave storefronts stretch from Burrard to Alma and offer an eclectic mix of shops. There are kitchenware, clothing, home furnishing, book and sporting good stores—you can spend hours here. This is a great area to look for a unique gift. You can eat ethnic or sip espresso. Broadway, another busy thoroughfare in this popular neighbourhood, has good shopping but not the mix of shops that 4th does. There are also shops and eateries on a short block of 1st Ave west of Burrard.

Yaletown

Once a rowdy warehouse region—it boasted more saloons per hectare than anywhere else in the world during the late 1800s!—now Yaletown is hip. Architects and designers occupy loft apartments, brick heritage buildings house classy galleries, and brightly coloured awnings pretty up storefronts. Fashion and furniture are here; when you tire of shopping, *the* place to plop is the Yaletown Brewing Co. on Mainland. A super selection of microbrewery suds, pizza and pasta, billiards and a large outdoor patio.

South Granville

The shopping area on south Granville St stretches from W 7th to 16th Ave, offering Persian carpets, antiques, clothing and food stores and many excellent galleries. South Granville used to be an enclave of older, wealthier residents but now is trendy.

Gastown

Gastown, the oldest part of Vancouver, has been quite touristy for the last 20 years, but on weekdays around lunch hour it is also abuzz with members of the local design community, who have their offices there. Water St from Richards to Main is the heart of Gastown, and most stores are open Sundays in the warmer months.

Don't miss a visit to the Inuit Gallery. Even if you can't afford a native mask, carving or piece of jewellery, this place is a gem.

Kerrisdale

On W 41st from Maple to Balsam, you'll still notice well-heeled matrons in pearls. The area can be exclusive and expensive but has stores worth going out of your way for, such as Hager Books, Forster's Cheeses and Windmill Toys. Good bakeries and florists and a camera store.

West 10th Avenue

This shopping area on W 10th at Trimble is near the University of British Columbia campus and has some first-rate stores: several high-end women's clothing stores, Duthie Books, furniture and lots to eat. An excellent area to browse and one of the city's prettiest neighbourhoods.

Ethnic Neighbourhoods

Chinatown
Vancouver boasts the second largest Chinatown in North America, and Pender St for two blocks east and west of Main is its centre. Keefer, east of Main, is lively as well. The perfect place to purchase exotic teas, unusual herbs, fun knickknacks and fine silk. See also Sightseeing (Chinatown).

Punjabi Market
Main Street between 49th and 51st is the Indo-Pakistani heart of the city. At the Guru Bazaar or other sari shops, you will find floor-to-ceiling skeins of material—everything from fine silks to gaudy polyester; there are many stores in which you can pick up Indian spices and foods. A great place to spend a few hours.

Commercial Drive
Affectionately known as "the Drive," the section of this street between 1st Ave and Venables was originally Little Italy. You will still see Italian mommas shopping and men sipping espresso, but today this neighbourhood is an ethnic hodge-podge. There are many fun restaurants, a good magazine store, funky clothing and furniture shops and the city's best organic grocery store.

A Little Greek
Broadway from Trafalgar to Waterloo is a friendly neighbourhood shopping area that was once composed mostly of Greek shops. Like the rest of the city, it has become more diversified, but you can still purchase freshly made filo and sticky, sweet

baclava at several long-established bakeries here. Some good Greek restaurants remain.

Shopping Centres

Long established but always current with the times, both **Oakridge** (at Cambie and 41st) and **Park Royal** (on the North Shore just west of Lions Gate Bridge) have shops with high-quality merchandise.

Pacific Centre and **Vancouver Centre** are two downtown underground malls that join Eaton's and the Bay at Granville and Georgia. Pretty well everything you need is here, including a Holt Renfrew.

Metrotown, in Burnaby, comprises four major centres with a Holiday Inn, theatres, many stores and restaurants. In addition, the new Metropolis is a stadium-style theatre complex with 10 screens, giving Metrotown a total of 22 movie theatres. Playdium is an interactive entertainment centre with everything from virtual reality attractions to rock-climbing walls. It's the largest shopping complex in B.C., and is conveniently reached by SkyTrain.

Accessories and Extras

Gulliver's Travel Accessory Store
Arbutus Shopping Centre
4255 Arbutus near King Edward
733-0111
If you have a secret passion for poking around hardware or stationery stores, you'll love Gulliver's. There are hundreds of quirky little gadgets, all to make the life of a weary traveller a touch easier. Also in Park Royal North and Richmond Centre.

The Big Top Hat Shop
73 Water St near Abbott
684-7373
Go ahead, try on one of the unique creations of milliners Ellen Anderson and Renata Crowe. A funky hat for a funky party or an elegant topper for a fashionable soirée—if they don't have it on hand, they will custom create. Hats for men, women and children.

Satchel Shop
Pacific Centre, lower level
669-2923
1024 Robson at Burrard
662-3424
Superlative bags, small leather goods and luggage. Also in Metrotown.

The Umbrella Shop
534 W Pender near Seymour
669-9444
Umbrellas from elegant to utilitarian. If you came to Vancouver without one, go and get one, just in case. These are quality made and will outlast any shower.

Auctions/Antiques/ Oriental Rugs

Main from 20th to 35th Ave has many used-furniture stores, and you may find some antiques, particularly from Britain. Near the corner of 10th and Alma, as well as further along 10th, are stores specializing in Canadiana. For Oriental rugs and special items, go along Granville from 7th to 14th Ave.

Maynard's Auctioneers
415 W 2nd at Cambie
876-6787
Home furnishings auctions are held every second Wed at 7 PM. Phone for times of the art and antique auctions.

Love's Auctioneers
1635 W Broadway near Fir
733-1157
Auctions are held on Wed at noon and 7 PM.

Three Centuries Shop
321 Water, Gastown
685-8808
Precious and rare antiques from the
18th, 19th and 20th centuries.

Folkart Interiors
3645 W 10th near Alma
228-1011
Specializes in folk art and Canadiana
furnishings as well as locally made
reproductions.

Canada West Antique
4430 W 10th near Trimble
222-9190
Specializes in antique pine furniture.
There are also folk art, decoys and
quilts.

Peter Tolliday Oriental Carpets
2312 Granville near 7th
733-4811
The leading dealer in Oriental carpets, new and antique.

Books and Magazines

Banyen Books & Sound
2671 W Broadway near Trafalgar
732-7912
Books on alternative lifestyles, eastern religion, yoga, recovery, nutri-
tion, gardening—you name it. A
good place to browse and buy. The
sound section features New Age cassette tapes, videos and CDs.

Barbara-Jo's Books to Cooks
1128 Mainland near Davie
688-6755
A feast of books and periodicals for
cooks and food lovers. As well as
cook books, there are literary works
dealing with food. Evening cooking
classes, lectures and demonstrations.

Blackberry Books
1663 Duranleau, Granville Island
685-4113
Packed on weekends. A darn good
bookstore, with a commendable selection of guidebooks and local works.

Book Warehouse
632 W Broadway near Heather
872-5711
W 4th near Balsam
733-5721
Discounted best sellers and a huge
selection of bargain books. Hours
vary, but the stores are open until 9
or 10 nightly. Other locations.

Chapters
788 Robson at Howe
1-888-648-0889
This Canadian-owned, mega-book-
store stocks around 100,000 titles, as
well as an extensive selection of
magazines, out-of-town newspapers,
CD-ROMs and other multimedia
products. Visitors can enjoy readings, cooking and craft demonstrations, autographing sessions and
then pop into the in-store Starbucks
for a java. The staff is very helpful.
Other locations, including Granville
and Broadway, and Metrotown.

The Comicshop
2089 W 4th near Arbutus
738-8122
New and used comics and sci-fi,
probably the best this side of
Toronto. They also trade comics—
bring in your old for their old.

Duthie Books
650 W Georgia at Granville
689-1802
919 Robson at Hornby
684-4496
To find a good book, you go to
Duthie's. There are the two main
stores downtown, and branches
throughout the city, including one
at the airport. Excellent selection
and helpful staff. Open seven days a
week; hours vary.

Granville Book Company
850 Granville near Robson
687-2213
Things are often in disarray, but this
store does have books that other

stores don't. Excellent computer, sci-fi, mystery selection, as well as books on film and TV. Good place to kill time waiting for a movie to start. Open until midnight except Fri and Sat, when it's open until 1 AM.

Hager Books
2176 W 41st near Yew
263-9412
One of the best neighbourhood bookstores around. Good selection of classics, children's and travel books.

Little Sister's Book and Art Emporium
1238 Davie near Bute
669-1753
Quite possibly Canada's largest gay and lesbian bookstore, with over 11,000 titles plus paraphernalia that ranges from sex products to T-shirts.

Magpie Magazine Gallery
1319 Commercial Dr near Charles
253-6666
Best place in the city to browse for any type of magazine. Helpful staff, unusual stock and cosy atmosphere.

Manhattan Books and Magazines
1089 Robson near Thurlow
681-9074
Excellent choice of imported and domestic magazines. Large French section as well as other languages. Open seven days a week.

Mayfair News
1535 W Broadway off Granville
738-8951
A good place to get out-of-town and international newspapers. Also an excellent magazine selection. Open until 10:30 nightly.

Mystery Merchant
1952 W 4th near Cypress
739-4311
A bit of Olde England, with dark wood shelves and a sliding ladder—perfect for a mystery bookstore. It makes you want to hang around on a rainy afternoon. Both new and used books.

The NEWS Hound
2997 Granville at 14th
733-8868
Those with a voracious appetite for news head here. "If we can meet a request, no matter how obscure, we will," states co-owner Hilary Brooks-Hill. More than 5,000 titles of magazines, periodicals and newspapers from around the world.

Travel Bug
2667 W Broadway near Trafalgar
737-1122
You can't research for an upcoming trip without visiting the Travel Bug. Dwight and his staff have helpful tips, an excellent selection of books and all the travel paraphernalia (including maps).

Wanderlust
1929 W 4th near Burrard
739-2182
Kitsilano's other superb travel bookstore. If you're nutty about travel books, Wanderlust will give you that died-and-gone-to-heaven feeling. Thousands of books plus maps, packs and travel accessories.

White Dwarf Books
4367 W 10th near Trimble
228-8223
Sci-fi and fantasy buffs head here for a great selection.

Dead Write
4374 W 10th near Trimble
228-8223
Almost next door to White Dwarf, same phone number, same owner, but the specialty here is mystery books.

Wilkinson's Automobilia
2531 Ontario off W Broadway
873-6242
Wilkinson's sells automotive and motorcycle books, shop manuals and other collectible items.

Women in Print
3566 W 4th near Dunbar
732-4128
Fiction and nonfiction for and about women. Excellent selection on women's health issues. Open daily.

World Wide Books and Maps
552 Seymour near Dunsmuir
687-3320
Maps and travel books, as well as government publications. The place to go if you need a topographical map for hiking anywhere in B.C.

See also With the Kids (Shopping).

Books (Used)

If you enjoy secondhand bookstores, pick up a brochure called "Guide to the Secondhand & Antiquarian Bookstores of Greater Vancouver." It's available in secondhand book-stores.

Antiquarius
609–207 W Hastings at Cambie
669-7288
Vintage magazines, posters, photos, sheet music, books and a collection of other fascinating odds and ends.

Ashley's Books
3754 W 10th at Alma
228-1180
Particularly good for art and fiction.

Lawrence Books
3591 W 41st at Dunbar
261-3812
May be the best used-book store in town; worth going out of your way for. Specialties include Canadiana, children's books and military history. Open 1:30–5:30 daily.

MacLeod's Books
455 W Pender at Richards
681-7654
Very good general stock with specialties including western Canadiana, literature and antiquarian books.

Clothing

For Men and Women

A•Wear
350 Howe at Hastings (street level)
685-9327
A branch of the upscale Leone's that carries only Canadian-designed A•Wear. Large selection of men's and women's casual, sports, business and evening attire, all well priced.

Boboli
2776 Granville near 12th
736-3458
Hard to believe that clothes can be *this* expensive. Wide variety of high-end designer labels and imported shoes to swoon over. Smashing store-front.

Club Monaco
1153 Robson near Thurlow
687-8618
Trendy-looking clothes, well made and reasonably priced. Seven outlets, including one in Pacific Centre.

E. A. Lee
466 Howe near Pender
683-2457
Classic and traditional as well as contemporary clothing. Also men's shoes and some beautifully tailored women's fashions.

Holt Renfrew
Pacific Centre
681-3121
Canada's version of Saks Fifth Ave. Designer clothes for the whole family. It's a pleasure to shop surrounded by the best labels.

Jack & Jill Clothing
2911 Granville at 13th
738-2700
Danish-designed clothing for men and women. The Jackpot label is a find—all clothes are washable and each new season's clothes are designed to blend in with previous

years'. They also carry shoes; check out the comfy, waterproof walking shoes. Also on 4th Ave.

Knitwear Architects
City Square, 12th at Cambie
879-7010
Designed for people who knit, but you can order a custom-knit sweater. There are many sweaters on display, all the store's own designs. Knitters first pick a style and then select the yarn from a sample chart, and out comes the kit, ready to go. Modern styles and a super selection of yarn. A catalogue is available.

Leone
Sinclair Centre
757 W Hastings at Howe
683-1133
The most avant-garde (in the well-designed Italian way) retail space in town. The Sinclair Centre is ultra-grand and Leone's has ultra-high fashion. Bring money.

For Women

Aritzia
1110 Robson near Thurlow
684-3251
Vancouver-owned store, with five other outlets. Caters to the young and fashionable with designer labels like Talula Baton, Parallel and Kookai. Expensive, but it's quality that lasts.

Bacci Design
2788 Granville near 12th
733-4933
Casual European designer clothes and Italian shoes for the very fashionable. Expensive.

Catherine Regehr
111–1529 W 6th near Granville
734-9339
Vancouver designer Catherine Regehr's dramatic evening wear is in high-end U.S. stores and in Holt Renfrew in Vancouver. Now her elegant shop shows off her famous shimmering, rustling creations.

Edward Chapman Ladies Shop
2596 Granville near 10th
732-3394
Quality, conservative fashions from Europe for those who love the tailored look. Importers for over 100 years, Chapman's has a strong following. Three other stores.

DKNY
2625 Granville at 11th
733-2000
Quality designer collections. Also a store on W 10th; plan hours for a spree here as it has a children's play area and a cappuccino bar.

Laura Ashley
1171 Robson near Bute
688-8729
Romantic country-look fashions for you and your home. The small, floral print designs adorn pretty, feminine clothing, wallpaper, bed linens, fabrics and china.

LeslieJane
1480 Marine Dr at 14th, West Van
922-8612
The clothes are romantic and folksy, made of natural fibres, corresponding with the friendly, neighbourhood feel of the shop. Carries U.S. designers such as Margaret O'Leary and Babette.

Margareta
2448 W. 41st near Larch
264-4625
Casual, chic clothes from Vancouver designer Margareta are showcased at this location. Also accessories, including silk shells. A West Vancouver location carries the Margareta line as well as other designers such as Mondi and Votre Nom. Also stores in Richmond and Surrey.

Wear Else?
2360 W 4th near Balsam
732-3521
High-calibre fashion, including
sportswear, office clothes, evening
wear and accessories. Prices medium
to high. There are five other locations in the city, including a clear-
ance centre at 78 E 2nd at Quebec.

Maternity Wear

Hazel & Co. Maternity & Kids
2209 W 4th near Yew
730-8689
Hazel & Co. maternity clothing is
designed and manufactured in
Vancouver. Knitwear, suits, festive
—it's all here. Also children's wear,
sizes 0–10.

For Men

Edward Chapman Men's Wear
833 W Pender near Howe
685-6207
Conservative selection of quality
clothing, accessories and gifts. Also
carries the Chapy's line. Other stores
in Bayshore Inn and Oakridge
Shopping Centre.

Finn's Clothing
3031 W Broadway near Macdonald
732-3831
Large selection, with emphasis on
quality dresswear and dress casual.
Also a store on 41st that sells
women's clothing as well.

Mark James
2941 W Broadway at Bayswater
734-2381
Business and fun clothes, featuring
American and European imports at
medium to high prices. Good range
of accessories. Also on Helmcken.

S. Lampman
2126 W 41st near West Blvd
261-2750

Designer sportswear and accessories.
Custom-made dresswear.

Harry Rosen
Pacific Centre, upper level
683-6861
Ivy League designer fashions: Calvin
Klein, Armani, Hugo Boss and the
like. Sportswear and dress-for-success
clothes. Also in Oakridge.

See also Clothing for Men and
Women, above.
For children's clothing, see With
the Kids (Shopping).

Gifts and Souvenirs

It's always a challenge to find an unusual gift or a special memento. No
tacky souvenirs here.

Chachkas Design
1075 Robson near Thurlow
688-6417
Looking for a small gift that will
elicit a big response? Go to Chachkas
and check out the unique imports
and Canadian arts and crafts.

Chocolate Arts
2037 W 4th near Maple
739-0475
Top-quality chocolates with a B.C.
flavour: 3-D medallions of Haida
motifs designed by Robert Davidson
or chocolate-dipped B.C. organic
fruit leather. The former is almost
too lovely to eat. Many other delicious delights.

Lightheart & Co.
535 Howe near Dunsmuir
684-4711
Give a Lightheart gift basket to your
hostess, your lover, your friend. It'll
have the perfect combination of
treats to suit even the most difficult
gift-receiver. Also in Gastown.

Moule
1994 W 4th at Maple
732-4066

Nothing you really need here but lots you'd love to buy. Crystal wands, carousel cookie jars, glamourous candlesticks, fragile or funky jewellery and locally designed, flowing woven clothing. Also in Park Royal.

To purchase Native art or books, see also Museums/Art Galleries (Museum of Anthropology and Indian or Inuit (Eskimo) Galleries).

Home Furnishings

Yaletown is one of the prime areas for interior designers and furniture stores. Check out Mainland, Homer and Hamilton Streets from Davie to Smithe. Also, many of the well-known stores have outlets in specific areas of Richmond and Coquitlam.

Chintz and Company
950 Homer at Smithe
689-2022
A cornucopia of design ideas—a unique candelabrum, a batik cushion, some bizarre folk art—it's all here along with a vast selection of fabrics. There are also dishes, glassware, tables, sofas and other furnishings. Chintz and Company specializes in complete design services.

The Cloth Shop
4415 W 10th at Trimble
224-1325
Anything and everything you need for quilting. They run lots of workshops. Also in North Vancouver.

Country Furniture
3097 Granville at 15th
738-6411
If you like pine, it's here—rocking chairs and four-poster beds with country-look accessories. Good prices and excellent quality.

Form and Function
4357 W 10th near Trimble
222-1317

Contemporary furniture with a clean, uncluttered Shaker look: beds, tables, sideboards and cabinets, all made from solid wood. The store does custom design and also stocks glass tables and rattan pieces inspired by antiques.

Industrial Revolution
2306 Granville at 7th
734-4395
Great selection of designer products. Noted for their storage systems, patio furniture and halogen lighting fixtures. Furniture is modern and stylish.

Inform Interiors
97 Water St at Abbott
682-3868
The latest in ultramodern furniture design. Some of it is designed by the owner. Also home and office accessories and a good selection of imported light fixtures.

Jordans Interiors
1470 W Broadway near Granville
733-1174
The best store if you are looking for that "polished designer look" in fine furniture. Also office furnishings, flooring and interior design services. Several locations.

Kama Design
104–1926 W 4th near Cypress
739-4003
Hand-dyed, 100 per cent linen or cotton bedding in a rainbow of colours. Also custom-made slipcovers and gauzy curtains.

Metropolitan Home
450 W Hastings near Richards
681-2313
Specializes in midcentury modern furniture (1900–1960); also antiques and collectibles.

New Look Interiors
1275 W 6th near Hemlock
738-4414

Large showroom with modern sofas, carpets, lamps, console units and children's furniture at good prices. Lots of teak and rosewood.

Roche-Bobois
716 Hastings near Granville
669-5443
If you fantasize about glove leather and down-filled sofas, go to Roche-Bobois, one of a worldwide French chain of elegant, modern furniture stores. European and very expensive, but true quality.

Sofas à la Carte
909 W Broadway near Oak
731-9020
A fun concept in furniture buying: the large, well-organized showroom has a dozen styles of sofas and armchairs and thousands of large samples of price-coded fabric. You make your choice, and in a few weeks your locally made, custom-crafted sofa is ready.

Urban Barn
1992 W 4th at near Maple
731-9047
Neat furniture and accessories. Some rustic Mexican imports, locally made pine furnishings, sofas, unusual book shelves, lamps, glassware and other goodies. Also in City Square and Metrotown.

Yaletown Interiors
1004 Hamilton at Nelson
669-7544
Good service and a good selection of contemporary styles from North American and European manufacturers.

Jewellery

Bustopher Goldsmiths
110–1058 Mainland near Helmcken
683-8243
In this small Yaletown studio-workshop, Andrew Costen creates dazzling jewellery. He is famous for his Renaissance rings—elaborate bands of gold and platinum set with diamonds and precious stones.

Catbalue
1832 W 1st near Burrard
734-3259
Fine jewellery designed on the premises. Well worth a stop, but be forewarned: you will want to buy.

Martha Sturdy Originals
3039 Granville near 14th
737-0037
775 Burrard near Robson
685-7751
Bold and dramatic jewellery by this internationally recognized designer. A local success story.

Toni Cavelti
565 W Georgia near Richards
681-3481
A must-visit. Exquisite jewellery showcased in an exquisite store. Cavelti is an award-winning goldsmith and jeweller.

Kitchenware and China

Basic Stock Cookware
2294 W 4th near Vine
736-1412
Large kitchenware store with complete selection, including major sections devoted to table-top, baking and coffee paraphernalia, including the beans.

Casa
420 Howe near Pender
681-5884
Specializes in Majolica dinnerware, made and hand-painted in a small town in Italy. There's also glassware, stainless steel flatwear and linens—if you wish to grace your table with real French linen, you can find it here.

The Cookshop
3–555 W 12th, City Square Mall
873-5683
Jam-packed with everything from elaborate kitchen machines to gadgets. Cooking classes available.

Market Kitchen
1666 Johnston, Granville Island
681-7399
Small but very well-stocked kitchenware store across from the market.

Ming Wo
23 E Pender at Carrall
683-7268
A large old cookware store in Chinatown, jammed full of much more than woks and cleavers—you'll find tortilla presses, pasta machines, soufflé dishes, etc. Ten outlets, including two on 4th Ave.

Outdoors Equipment

Coast Mountain Sports
2201 W 4th at Yew
731-6181
Serious outdoors equipment and lots of outdoors clothes, all top of the line—the L. L. Bean of Vancouver. In general, more high end than their main competitor, Mountain Equipment Co-op. Second outlet in West Vancouver.

Helly Hansen
2025 W 4th near Maple
730-5576
Offers a full selection of the Norwegian sportswear. Includes rainwear as well as clothes for skiing, sailing and snowboarding.

Mountain Equipment Co-op
130 W Broadway at Columbia
872-7858
Huge, busy and rather chaotic. Sells equipment for wilderness-oriented recreation. This is a non-profit business owned and directed by its membership, meaning sub-stantially lower prices. Lifetime membership is only $5 and is necessary if you're making a purchase. Members get beefy spring and fall catalogues. Pay parking on the roof. Closed Sun.

Taiga
390 W 8th at Yukon
875-6644
Locally made, quality outdoor gear from clothing to tents.

Three Vets
2200 Yukon at 6th
872-5475
This shop has the best prices as it offers out-of-stock items as well as modern gear. Good selection of hiking boots.

Don't miss the small room crammed with Native art. Collected by one of the owners, there's everything from silver jewellery to carved masks and talking sticks. You may have to ask for the key.

See also Sports/Recreation.

Photo Supplies/ Film Processing

ABC Photocolour
1618 W 4th at Fir
736-7017
Best colour processing. Stores in Richmond and Surrey.

Kerrisdale Cameras
2170 W 41st near Yew
263-3221
Local chain, but the main store has the largest selection and is the most service oriented. New equipment, trade-ins and rentals, some darkroom supplies.

Lens and Shutter
2912 W Broadway at Bayswater
736-3461
Excellent sales staff in this huge store. Like most camera stores in

town, it will match competitors' prices.

London Drugs
540 Granville near Dunsmuir
685-0105
1187 Robson near Bute
669-8533
The camera department is the best for everyday low prices and sales. No darkroom supplies. One-hour photo finishing. Other locations.

You can also get film processed quickly at:

1 Hour Photo
Pacific Centre, lower level
681-2511

Recorded Music

A & B Sound
556 Seymour near Dunsmuir
687-5837
A high-volume chain with a more daring selection than others. Often has loss-leaders on the current hits. Great jazz and classical sections upstairs. Other locations.

Banyen Books & Sound
See Books and Magazines, this chapter.

Black Swan
3209 W Broadway near Trutch
734-2828
Specializes in jazz, blues, folk and some rock. Domestics and imports.

D & G Collectors Records
3580 E Hastings near Boundary
294-5737
Best place for vintage 45s, LPs, albums and CDs. Heavy on rock and country. Can special order, even golden oldies pre-'50s.

Highlife Records and Music
1317 Commercial near Charles
251-6964
Specializes in reggae, African, Caribbean and jazz, but you'll also

find folk, Latino, blues, pop and country. A discriminating though not large selection. New and used.

HMV
1160 Robson near Thurlow
685-9203
CDs and tapes from alternative to blues, jazz to classical. The best selection, though, is in the pop and rock sections. Other stores.

Magic Flute Record Shop
2203 W 4th at Yew
736-2727
A well-stocked store selling classical CDs as well as jazz and world music.

Sikora's Classical Records
432 W Hastings near Richards
685-0625
The classical music specialists; new and used records, tapes and CDs.

Virgin Megastore
788 Burrard at Robson
669-2289
The largest music store in Canada, with over 125,000 titles on CD and cassette. Also videos and laser discs, computer multimedia software (the best selection in town for both IBM and Mac) and books covering all aspects of music and entertainment. There are 140 individual listening stations where you can sample some 400 CDs. Pop into the in-store café for a java.

Zulu Records
1869 W 4th at Burrard
738-3232
Best independent rock record store in the city. Lots of imports and used records, CDs and tapes. Owned and operated by one of the friendliest guys around.

Shoes (Men's and Women's)

Look for shoe stores on Robson St and in Pacific Centre.

For shoe repairs while you wait, two city centre locations are:

Bentall Centre Shoe Repair
Lower level, Dunsmuir and Burrard
688-0538

Silvano's Shoe Renew
520 Robson near Richards
685-5413

Specialty Food Stores

Bakeries

La Baguette et L'Échalote
1680 Johnston, Granville Island
684-1351
This French bakery and gourmet take-out sells baguettes, croissants, fancy cakes and more. Very busy on weekends. Also a location at Lonsdale Quay.

Bombay Sweets
6556 Main near 50th
321-1414
A sleek shop that makes traditional Indian sweets from almonds, carrots, pistachios, coconut, and so on. The carrot halvah demands a return visit.

Bon Ton
874 Granville near Smithe
681-3058
This European-style pâtisserie and tearoom has been around since 1931 and is famed for the most decadent cakes in town.

Ecco Il Pane
See Restaurants (Bakery Cafés).

Elsie's Bakery
1555 Yew near Cornwall
731-7017
One of the best all-round neighbourhood bakeries. Handy to Kits Beach. Great care with ingredients and preparation puts Elsie's a step above. The coffee cake and bran muffins get our highest recommendation.

Keefer Chinese Bakery
251 E Georgia near Main
685-2117
Great varieties of buns, cakes, tarts—especially coconut buns—are delicious here. The three other Chinese bakeries in this same block are also good.

Don't miss a barbecued pork bun (slightly sweet buns with the meat mixture inside) from this bakery. One day we sampled them from each Chinatown bakery. The Keefer won.

Pâtisserie Bordeaux
3675 W 10th near Alma
731-6551
Excellent croissants, but it's really the gâteaux and tarts that win us over. They look fabulous and taste even better. Reasonably priced, open Sun. Haven't had a thing we didn't like. Very French.

Siegel's Bagels
1883 Cornwall at Cypress
737-8151
Apparently Vancouver did not know how real bagels tasted until Siegel's came along. Its tasty treats —14 varieties of bagels, some sweet—are often steaming hot from the brick oven. Also on Davie near Bute.

Terra Breads
See Restaurants (Bakery Cafés).

Uprising Breads
1697 Venables near Commercial
254-5635
A healthy, East End bakery run by a workers' co-operative. Super whole-grain breads, scones, cakes and muffins. Popular lunch stop.

Cheese

Dussa's Ham & Cheese
Granville Island Public Market
688-8881

Imagine 300 cheeses—everything from fine French goat cheeses to hearty Canadian Rat Trap cheddar.

Forster's Fine Cheeses
2104 W 41st, near West Blvd
261-5813
Small store with an enormous array of quality cheeses you won't find elsewhere, and you can count on freshness. Also cheese accompaniments like pâtés and lox.

Coffee and Tea

This city is caffeine crazy. Here are a few favourites.

Continental Coffee
1806 Commercial at 2nd
255-0712
A "Little Italy" coffee store where Anita will fix you up with a dark-roast Italian coffee. Cappuccino to go.

Murchie's Tea & Coffee
970 Robson near Burrard
669-0783
Murchie's boasts 40 blends of coffee and 50 varieties of tea. Other stores and a small museum in Yaletown.

Starbucks
See Restaurants (Espresso Bars).

T
2460 Heather near Broadway
874-8320
More than 170 teas to choose from, and everything you need to make it. The selection of pots and tea sets is not large but is so delightful that you'll find something you want for yourself or a friend.

Torrefazione Coloiera
2206 Commercial at 6th
254-3723
Even if you can't pronounce the name, visit this Spartan, East End Italian coffee store. Some of the best coffee around.

Delis and Gourmet Take-Out

La Baguette et L'Échalote
1680 Johnston, Granville Island
684-1351
You will find everything for an elegant picnic except the bottle of Nuits St-Georges. There are mousses, pâtés, quality cheeses, stuffed croissants and brioches, breads, pastries, cakes and chocolates.

Bread Garden
812 Bute at Robson
688-3213
A wide selection of healthy salads, entrées such as chicken pie, vegetable torte or frittata and desserts. Eat in or take out. Other locations. See Essential Information (Late Night Services).

Dussa Delicatessen
4125 Main near 25th
874-8610
Easily the best European-style deli in town; too bad it's not in a handier location. But you know it's worth the effort as soon as you walk through the door. Fine homemade salads, lots of sausages and cheeses at low prices, and some pastries.

Don't miss a chance to combine a browse with a picnic. Start at 20th to visit the funky second-hand furniture stores. Walk south and pick up lunch at Dussa, continue strolling up to 30th, and then walk west a couple of blocks to Queen Elizabeth Park for a picnic.

Lazy Gourmet
1505 W 5th at Fir
734-2507
Take-out that's a step above the usual fare. Wraps, sandwiches, salads, pizzas and hot dishes and wonderfully extravagant sweet treats. Great for catering parties.

Lesley Stowe Fine Foods
1780 W 3rd at Burrard
731-3663

This topnotch caterer's retail food store sells exquisitely prepared take-out dishes and specialty packaged foods.

Stock Market
Granville Island Public Market
687-2433

A brilliant concept carried out perfectly—soup stocks by the litre (beef, chicken, fish, vegetarian, Chinese, duck, etc.). Also wonderful sauces. Three different soups are prepared daily to be taken home or eaten there. *Everything* is produced out of a 28 m² (300-square-foot) stall at the market. The place is truly a wonder.

Don't miss breakfast at the Stock Market if you are a fan of hot cereal. It's seven-grain and comes topped with chunky homemade applesauce or maple syrup and surrounded by cream.

Ethnic Foods

For Asian foods, try the following;

South China Foods
212–2800 E 1st Ave at Renfrew
251-1333

This good-sized store sells Asian and some European foods. Excellent produce.

South China Seas Trading Company
Granville Island Public Market
681-5402

Excellent selection of seasonings, spices, sauces, cookbooks, fresh noodles and produce.

Yaohan Supermarket
3700 No. 3 Rd at Cambie, Richmond
276-8808

One of Asia's largest chain stores. The specialty here is Japanese food, but there is also everything else you could desire—geoduck, prepared ingredients for sushi, wasabe root—for an Asian cooking frenzy.

T & T Supermarket
179 Keefer Place near Abbott
899-8836

A humongous Chinese market. You could spend hours here among the tanks of live lobster, crab and fish. Also stores in Richmond and Metrotown.

Shop on Main from 48th to 51st Ave to find the makings for an East Indian meal:

All India Food
6517 Main near 49th
324-1686

The only place where you can get everything from produce to spices under one roof. Packed with merchandise; there are bulk foods (the air is redolent with the fragrance of spices) and fresh produce.

Don't miss All India Surat Sweets on the corner. Feast on the buffet. It's served on shiny tin divided plates just as it would be in India. The price is $5.95. It's served all day. You can also get samosas to go. Of course, there's a full selection of the very sweet Indian desserts.

For Filipino ingredients we suggest:

Philippine Tropical Express
116 W Broadway near Manitoba
879-8441

A tiny market but if you want Filipino sauces, noodles, canned fish or other products, stop by.

Look for Greek foods on W Broadway from Macdonald to Trutch. We recommend:

Parthenon Wholesale and Retail Food
3080 W Broadway near Bayswater St
733-4191

Greek treats to take-out or eat, or to buy for home cooking. Everything here is the real thing. The best place to buy freshly made filo pastry.

Granville Island Market Tips

- Shop weekdays instead of weekends.
- If you must shop on weekends, go between 9 and 10 AM or between 5 and 6 PM. Otherwise, grin and bear it.
- Once you are on the island, don't waste time looking for a parking spot close to the market—just take the first one you see. You will be at most a five-minute walk away.
- On weekends you can avoid the whole congestion problem by parking on 1st, 2nd or 3rd Ave, just east of Burrard. It's then a 10-minute walk.

A Sampling of Favourite Market Foods

- **Duso's** Sauce, a decadently rich cheese, cream and herb sauce for pasta.
- Freshly squeezed juice from the **Fraser Valley Juice & Salad Bar**: carrot, watermelon, hot apple-ginger, etc. Also the best salads.
- Fresh goat cheeses from **Dussa's Ham & Cheese**.

- Coffee roasted on the spot at the **Coffee Roaster**.
- A litre of freshly made fish stock from the **Stock Market**.
- The freshest Fraser Valley produce—whatever's in season, whether it's raspberries or tiny new potatoes.
- Marinated kabobs ready for the barbecue from **Armando's Meats**.
- A whole wall of chili sauces as well as fresh chilis from **South China Seas**.
- Smoked salmon packaged to travel from **Seafood City**.
- Golden mantle oysters from the **Salmon Shop**.
- 40 varieties of breads from **Stuart's**.
- Chocolate fudge from **Olde World Fudge**.
- The stunning display of pastries, breads, chocolates and take-out foods at **La Baguette**, just outside the market building.

For information about the rest of Granville Island, see Sightseeing.

Some shops on and around Commercial stock Italian goods:

A. Bosa & Co.
562 Victoria Dr near Turner
253-5578
Everything Italian you could wish to buy, including the equipment to cook it in. Great prices.

The First Ravioli Store
1900 Commercial Dr at 3rd Ave
255-8844
Don't think of cooking up an Italian feast without a visit here. There's also a super deli supply. Daily made fresh pastas and sauces.

La Grotta Del Formaggio
1791 Commercial Dr near 2nd Ave
255-3911
An Italian cheese selection to die for, and other goodies like the best extra-virgin olive oils and vinegars.

Try Powell from Jackson to Gore for Japanese items. Also try:

Fujiya
912 Clark Dr at Venables
251-3711
Great selection of Japanese foods and kitchenware. Fresh fish prepared for sushi, as well as sushi to take-out. Other locations.

Kobayashi Shoten Asian Grocery Store
1518 Robson near Nicola
683-1019
Lots of Asian merchandise, particularly Japanese; friendly service.

For Kosher foods try:

Kaplan's Deli
5775 Oak at 41st
263-2625
Get your lox and all things Kosher at this deli.

If Mexican food is your passion, indulge at these shops:

Que Pasa Mexican Foods
1647 W 5th near Fir
737-7659
The best tortillas in town (eight types). Also has molés and salsas by the pound, a complete Mexican cookbook reference shelf and a good variety of take-out dishes.

Salza Mexican Deli
4140 E Hastings near Gilmour
299-4690
Try a sun-dried tomato shell burrito and you'll be back to sample the guacamole, salsa and more made-on-the-premises treats.

North Vancouver has a few Middle Eastern shops. In particular, try:

Iransuper
3–987 Marine Dr near Lloyd
987-0987
The place to get spices for a luscious lamb stew or a hearty lentil soup. Imported canned goods, olive oils, rices and spices as well as kitchenware.

Fish/Shellfish

Lobster Man
1807 Mast Tower, Granville Island
687-4531

Longliner Sea Foods
Granville Island Public Market
681-9016

Salmon Shop
Granville Island Public Market
669-3474

Seven Seas
2344 W 4th near Vine
732-8608

Cheena
667 Howe near Georgia
1-800-663-1110

See also Fujiya under Ethnic Foods.

Fish can be packaged to travel.

Ice Cream

La Casa Gelato
1033 Venables at Glen Dr
251-3211
Every ice cream flavour you can imagine—Vince Misceo makes 150 flavours; 60 are here to taste—and some you can't imagine. Ginger, garlic, edible flowers, red bean, wasabi, and more, and you are encouraged to taste before you buy. The ice cream is *the* best—made with cream, eggs, freshly squeezed fruit and little sugar. There are sorbettos for the health-conscious.

Local Seafood

You've got your flatfish—sole or flounder, a delicate white fish served in thin fillets.

Ling cod, which comes in fillets or steaks, is available any time of the year but is best in the winter.

Lean firm halibut steaks are best from May to Sept.

Thick red snapper fillets are around all the time.

You've also got a choice of five kinds of salmon: sockeye (which usually ends up in a tin), pink, chum, or the prized chinook and coho. Big salmon harvests are in the summer and fall.

Pacific mackerel is an oily fish with a distinctive flavour.

Steelhead trout, similar in taste to salmon, is best in winter.

Clams harvested locally are either littleneck or butter.

Mussels are a delicacy that turns up on restaurant menus.

Dungeness crab, usually weighing only half a kilogram or so (a pound or two), stalk the local waters year-round.

Alaskan king crab, with legs 60 cm (2 feet) long, is brought in fresh, Aug to Nov, from the Queen Charlotte Islands on the northern B.C. coast.

Shrimp and prawns, 5 to 20 cm (2 to 8 inches) long, are in season year-round.

Sea scallops from the north coast are available all year, and tiny, delicate bay scallops are fresh in winter.

The large Pacific oyster, which was imported from Japan in 1912, is now the most popular commercial oyster. You'll be offered them raw, stewed, baked, barbecued, smoked, pan-fried and deep-fried.

With the Kids

At Maplewood Children's Farm the younger set can mingle with friendly goats. (Maplewood Children's Farm)

Many of these activities are not just for kids and so are described in more detail in other sections. Pick up *Westcoast Families,* an excellent publication available at McDonald's Restaurants as well as libraries and other places. Also check the What's On section of Thursday's *Vancouver Sun* under Families and under Children for the week's special events.

Kids and Animals

Maplewood Children's Farm
405 Seymour River Pl, North Van
929-5610
Maplewood is a 2 ha (5-acre) petting farm of barnyard animals run by the North Van Parks Department. The original farm dates back to the early 1900s. Complete with a barn, over 200 animals and birds, small pastures and a creek, it is an ideal getaway for city kids.

Visitors can pet a rabbit, feed guinea pigs and waterfowl, and check out horses, cows, donkeys and pigs. The favourite spot seems to be Goathill, where the younger set cavort with frisky goats that love to nibble shoelaces and other clothing. A milking display is held daily at 1:15.

Open Tues to Sun, 10–4. Closed Mon except on holidays. Call for admission prices.

Drive over the Second Narrows Bridge to North Van and take the Dollarton Hwy exit (#23B); turn left at Seymour River Place. Two B.C. Transit bus routes go right by the farm: #212 Deep Cove and #211 Seymour.

Richmond Nature Park
11851 Westminster Hwy, Richmond
273-7015
Richmond Nature Park is 40 ha (100 acres) of shrubbery and peat bog, with paths leading you on a nature expedition. The boardwalk around the pond—where you may spot ducks, turtles or crimson dragonflies, depending on the season—is accessible to strollers and wheelchairs. Longer trails introduce you to the community of plants and animals that thrive in forest or bog. This is an adventuresome walk where you may see owls, hawks, coyotes, butterflies and birds. The bog is a delicate wetland—wear boots if it's been wet and remember to stay on the trails.

The Nature House is full of games and displays on natural history, as well as live animals like snakes, frogs and salamanders. Check out the bee exhibit and the one on forest life. The Nature House is open daily, 9–5. Admission is by donation.

Drive south on Hwy 99 and take the Shell Rd exit; then go left onto Westminster Hwy. There is public transit to the park, but it is long and involved (call 521-0400).

George C. Reifel Migratory Bird Sanctuary

Some of the Canada geese, ducks and swans at the entrance to the refuge are quite tame—some were injured, have been rehabilitated and have decided to stick around—and are a particular delight to young children. Bird feed can be purchased in the shop. Children love hiding in the wooden shelters to peek out at waterfowl and climbing the four-storey observation tower. See Parks/Beaches/Gardens for more information.

Horse Shows

Southlands Riding Club (263-4817) at 7025 Macdonald off 53rd holds hunter/jumper and dressage shows from spring to fall. Call to find out about events.

Vancouver Aquarium

Children love the killer whale show, colourful tropical fish, rainstorm and close-up views of the octopus as well as everything else about this aquarium. If you are rushed for time, the beluga and harbour seal pools on the west side of the aquarium were built to be viewed from both outside and inside the complex, so there is no admission charge for this preview. See Parks/Beaches/Gardens for more information.

Stanley Park

For animals, visit the Children's Farmyard, where children can mingle with pigs, cattle, chickens and the like. Lost Lagoon and Beaver Lake have lots of ducks, geese and swans, but please don't feed them bread—it's very bad for them. Bring lettuce or buy bird seed at the Lost Lagoon concession. Also, brazen little squirrels all over the park are used to being fed by hand.

Day Trips

Granville Island

Take a bathtub-sized ferry from either the Aquatic Centre or the foot of Hornby for a five-minute trip to the island and visit the Kids Only Market, the impromptu performers around the public market, the water park, glass blowers (1440 Old Bridge), wooden boat builders (1247 Cartwright) and the adventure playground.

The Kids Only Market is in a refurbished two-storey building at the entrance to Granville Island. It is jam-packed with over 24 colourful, vibrant stores as well as a lunch spot geared to the younger set. Books, kites, puppets, arts and crafts, clothing and any toy or gizmo that a child would fancy are all found in the shops. There's a two-storey play area that features a fun slide, and many places to crawl around, one of them filled with balls. The Kids Only Market is chaotic on weekends. Every Sat in summer there are free events for the whole family—during special events, clowns, magicians and face painters wander the Market. Open daily year-round.

The water park and the adventure playground near the False Creek Community Centre are supervised daily, 10–6. The water park is a riot. It's a huge wading pool, at the centre of which are a revolving fire hydrant and hoses that kids can use to douse anyone in reach. The adventure playground has innumerable rope and log configurations and a water slide.

See Sightseeing (Granville Island) for other ideas.

Stanley Park

Besides the animals and aquarium listed above, there is a miniature train ride, pitch and putt golf, tennis courts, several playgrounds, picnic spots, totem poles, a traffic school for kids aged 5 to 8, bicycle paths (bicycle and stroller rentals are just outside the park), beaches and swimming pools.

Don't miss the water adventure playground across from Lumbermen's Arch on a warm day. Also, Second Beach Pool has waterslides and a lifeguard; there's a sandy beach beside it and an adventure playground that has an old fire engine to explore.

See Parks/Beaches/Gardens (Stanley Park); also Sports/Recreation (Swimming).

Chinatown

Older kids might enjoy a trip to Chinatown to shop for inexpensive gifts and souvenirs: paper kites, Chinese tops, chopsticks to try out at lunch. See also Sightseeing (Chinatown) and Restaurants (Chinese).

Kits Beach/Kits Pool

At the beach, the water's a bit chilly for real swimming, but it's fine for wading and a lifeguard is on duty all summer. There are grassy areas all around the beach, as well as swings and monkey bars and a concession stand.

The heated outdoor pool at Kits Beach sits right at the water's edge. An enormous pool with lanes marked off for serious swimmers, it also has a long and gradual slope at one side that is perfect for young children. The pool gets congested on sunny weekend afternoons, but mornings are fairly quiet. See also Sports/Recreation (Swimming).

Don't miss the Maritime Museum. It's an ideal combo excursion from Kits Beach with the kids. Walk the seawall to Vanier Park. The Pacific Space Centre takes longer to visit so save it for another day.

Royal Hudson

Ride a vintage steam locomotive up the coast. See Sightseeing (Train Trips).

Pedal Boats on Deer Lake
255-0087

Deer Lake is in Burnaby, a 30-minute drive from downtown. At the east end of the lake are boat rentals with pedal boats, canoes, rowboats and kayaks, as well as picnic tables, a sandy beach and a lifeguard. There's lots of waterfowl. The only access to the east side of the lake is via Canada Way, Burris or Buckingham St. Even though it is a small, urban lake, it is citified only at one end; most of the shoreline is wooded and good for exploring by water.

Don't miss visiting the Burnaby Village Museum and Carousel. See Museums/Art Galleries (Museums Outside the City).

Canoeing at Deep Cove
929-2268

Deep Cove is a small community on a deep inlet of the North Shore and is accessible from downtown by public transit. Deep Cove Canoe and Kayak Rentals will supply a canoe so that you can paddle to the nearby islands and parks. Since you're in this area, stop at Honey Doughnuts and Goodies at 4373 Gallant. The kids will love the luscious doughnuts, and the adults will savour the gourmet coffee. See Sports/Recreation (Canoeing/Kayaking/Rowing).

Grouse Mountain Skyride/Mount Seymour Chairlift

See Parks/Beaches/Gardens/(Grouse Mountain).

Seymour Demonstration Forest

See Sightseeing (Special Interest Tours).

Queen Elizabeth Park/Bloedel Conservatory

Things of interest at the park are the duck pond; the Bloedel Conservatory, with its tropical plants and birds under a geodesic dome; and the giant Henry Moore sculptures (great to climb on).

Cycling Barnston Island

You pedal quiet country roads on this small island in the Fraser River. After a short, free ferry ride, you can cycle a 10 km (6-mile) circle route where you encounter little traffic. Pack a picnic in your backpack and have lunch overlooking the Fraser at Robert Point Rest Area. This GVRD-run park, which has a washroom and tables, is the only public area on the island. Head east on Hwy 1 to 176th St and then go north; then go east on 104th Ave. There's parking, and the ferry runs continuously.

Berry Picking

The U-pick raspberry, blueberry and black currant season runs roughly from mid-June to late July, depending on the weather. Call Bissett Farms at 946-7139 for more information.

The farm is just before the entrance to the George C. Reifel Migratory Bird Sanctuary at 2170 Westham Island Rd. Take the Ladner exit from Hwy 99.

Cruises

Take the Starline Tours (272-9187) cruise to see sea lions. The kids will be thrilled. Another must for families is the Paddlewheeler River Adventures (525-4465) cruise to Fort Langley to experience a day in the 1850s. These trips run Thurs, Fri, Sat and Sun and include lunch. See Sightseeing (Touring Vancouver).

University of British Columbia/ Pacific Spirit Regional Park

Walk through the forest in the park, swim in the pool at the Aquatic Centre, or see the dinosaur skeleton and fabulous gems in the geology museum. Older children keen on science will enjoy the cyclotron at TRIUMF. See also Parks/Beaches/Gardens (Pacific Spirit Regional Park), Sports/Recreation (Swimming) and Sightseeing (Special Interest Tours).

West Van Playgrounds

Some of the best playgrounds in town are in West Vancouver, at Ambleside Park, off Marine Dr at 13th; John Lawson Park, at the foot of 16th St and Dundarave Park at the foot of 25th St. Ambleside has a spray park, John Lawson has a wading pool and all have playground equipment. All three of these parks are connected by the West Van seawall, so you can get your exercise and keep the kids happy.

Lynn Canyon Park

Visit the ecology centre, go hiking and picnicking, and walk across the suspension bridge 73 m (240 feet) above the rapids.

Lynn Canyon is accessible from downtown by public transit via the SeaBus and the #229 Phibbs Exchange/Westlynn bus. Everything in the park is free.

Lighthouse Park

A good place for kids to get a taste of the wilderness. They'll love exploring the wooded trails and scrambling on the boulders near the lighthouse. Take precautions; this is a wilderness park. See Parks/Beaches/ Gardens.

Newton Wave Pool

13730–72nd Ave near King George Hwy
501-5540

Body surfing in Vancouver?! Besides the wave pool with metre-high (3-foot) waves, there is a waterslide, a wading pool, ping pong, an exercise room, a whirlpool, a steam room, babysitting and a coffee shop. You can also rent inner tubes, air mattresses and kick boards. Well worth the drive. Phone for directions.

Splashdown Park
943-2251

Twisting waterslides—a mile of them—are the main attraction, but there are also hot tubs, patios for tanning, lawns for picnics, a snack bar, a video arcade, volleyball, basketball, mini golf, smaller slides for little kids and a toddlers' pool. The water is heated. (Even if the weather is marginal in town, it is always sunny in Tsawwassen.) Located near Hwy 17 (access off of 52nd St north) just before the Tsawwassen ferry terminal. Admission is $14.95 for 11 and older, with discounts for younger children and half-days.

Skiing

Preschool ski lessons are given at Grouse Mountain (downhill) and at Cypress (cross-country); you must register in advance. Drop-in ski lessons for juniors are held on Grouse weekends and holidays. Call the Grouse Mountain Ski School (980-9311) for particulars.

Other Fun Places

Ball Games and More

Combine a picnic in Queen Elizabeth Park with a Vancouver Canadians game at neighbouring Nat Bailey Stadium. Weekend games usually start at 1:30 and at 12:15 during the week. Watch for Autograph Day, when kids can go an hour before game time and meet their favourite players. There's also between-inning fun contests (children are chosen at random to take part). The $7.50–$9.50 tickets are reduced to $4.75 for kids 14 and under. Call 872-5232 for the schedule.

Softball City is a four-diamond facility in White Rock. As well as softball action there is volleyball, a playground, video games and a restaurant. Located at 2201–148 St (531-3220), it's not far to a beach, so make a day of it.

Cliffhanger Indoor Rock Climbing Centre
The Edge Climbing Centre

Both have special equipment for youngsters who love to climb. See Sports/Recreation (Hiking/ Mountaineering/Indoor Climbing Walls).

Ice Sports Centre
6501 Sprott, Burnaby
291-0626

The Canucks practice here and it's possible to watch. Call for their schedule. You may see other NHL teams as well.

Playland
Exhibition Park
E Hastings near Renfrew
253-2311

The rides and miniature golf are open weekends in the spring and every day in the summer. Each year there is a new feature ride. Kids Playce offers fun activities for the 10 and under group. Hours vary; call ahead. A ride pass is about $18 but it differs depending on the height of the child. After 1999, Playland will be in a new location, as will the Pacific National Exhibition.

Power Plant
750 Pacific Blvd, foot of Robson
682-8770

Make your own cassette recording! Sing along with pre-recorded music in small studios that hold up to 10 people. You can choose from top 40, classic rock or country. Cost is $25 for 30 minutes and includes the cassette. During summer there are group rates for children.

Richmond Go-Kart Track
6631 Sidaway, Richmond
278-6184
An 800 m (½-mile) asphalt track
with lots of curves. Cost is $10 for 15
minutes. To ride solo, children must
be 10 years of age or over 137 cm (4
foot, 6 inches); others must ride with
an adult. Open every day from noon
to dusk, but closed if wet.

Drive south on Hwy 99, take the
No. 4 Rd exit, go east on West-
minster Hwy, and turn right on
Sidaway.

VanDusen Garden
Kids may not be interested in flowers, but this garden has an Elizabethan hedge maze that they will
love to wind their way through. It's
just over 1.5 m (5 feet) high, and
steps are placed throughout so that
younger children can get their bear-
ings. Parents can keep track of
progress from the grassy hill beside
the maze.

Museums

Science World is Vancouver's only
museum expressly for children. The
Omnimax Theatre is a winner with
the whole family. Kids also love
walking on board the *St Roch* (a restored two-masted schooner) and the
tugboat wheelhouse, both in the
Maritime Museum.

The **Museum of Anthropology** at
UBC sometimes has family events
scheduled on Sundays. Another
favourite is the **B.C. Sports Hall of
Fame and Museum**; kids love the
action in the Participation Gallery.
Take the youngsters to the H.R.
MacMillan Planetarium at the
Pacific Space Centre, where they
can "experience" a full-motion
spacecraft ride and much more. And
don't forget the special events at the
Burnaby Village Museum. For more

*There are many hands-on experiences at
Science World. (Science World)*

details about these and other museums, see Museums/Art Galleries.

Babysitting

See Essential Information
(Babysitting).

Entertainment

CN Imax Theatre
Canada Place
682-4629 (info)
280-4444 (tickets)
A huge, five-storey screen shows
edge-of-your-seat films: ride the
Colorado River through the Grand
Canyon, or explore the mysteries of
flight, speed, space or some such delight. Reserved seats.

Metropolis at Metrotown in Burnaby
has everything from stadium-style
theatres to interactive entertainment. There's virtual reality, wall
climbing, you name it. Parents can

The Maritime Museum is a favourite with children. "Steering" a ship is one of many hands-on activities. (Maritime Museum)

relax in some of the many restaurants or shop in the attached mall, B.C.'s largest. See Shopping (Shopping Centres).

Restaurants

Chinese restaurants cater to families, and so mess and noise are not usually a problem. Bite-sized *dim sum* is served in small portions. See Restaurants (Chinese).

Isadora's
See Restaurants (Breakfast/Brunch).

Old Spaghetti Factory
53 Water near Abbott, Gastown
684-1288
Old-time paraphernalia, a vintage streetcar and silent movies. Children's portions available.

Simpatico Ristorante
See Restaurants (Greek).

Sophie's Cosmic Café
See Restaurants (Breakfast/Brunch).

Tomahawk Barbecue
See Restaurants (Breakfast/Brunch).

Topanga Café
See Restaurants (Mexican).

Shopping

Books

Vancouver Kidsbooks
3083 W Broadway at Balaclava
738-5335
Run by a former librarian and mom. The best assortment of children's books, as well as an excellent selection of board books for babies. Also carries CDs and tapes. Good selection of French titles.

Clothing and Shoes

Absolutely Diapers
2050 W 4th near Arbutus
737-0603
A cute little store with parenting products and, yes, a variety of cloth

Vancouver Children's Festival

The premier event for children each year is the Vancouver Children's Festival, held in May at Vanier Park. Top-notch local and international actors, mimes, musicians, clowns, storytellers, jugglers and puppeteers gather solely to entertain young people.

Huge, colourful tents are set up at Vanier Park on the shores of Burrard Inlet, and events are staged for a whole week. About 200 entertainers come from all over B.C. and as far away as New York, Europe and Asia. An excellent detailed program, available at ticket outlets, describes the performances and the ages they appeal to.

Outside the performance tents, there is free entertainment— strolling musicians, mimes, jugglers and the clowns who delight in painting small faces. Activity tents are set up for storytelling, games, kite-making, dance and toddlers'

activities, and one holds a Goliath-size sandbox.

Although the festival is well attended, some tickets are available the week of the festival. Tickets go on sale in March at Ticketmaster outlets. Once the festival starts, tickets are available on site.

If you can't get tickets for the event you have your heart set on, go anyway as the on-site entertainment and activities are delightful. Entrance fee is $5. For more information, call 708-5655.

In 1998 the producers of this popular event launched "X-SITE," an arts festival for young people from 14 to 19. Cutting-edge theatre, poetry readings and artwork are some of the features of the week-long event held at the Vancouver East Cultural Centre. This will also be an annual event. For information: 708-5655.

diapers. There are also toys, books, stuffed animals and other paraphernalia for infants.

Angels on Bellevue
1463 Bellevue near 15th, West Van
926-8737
Down the block from Bears Toy Store. Angels carries mostly European designers' lines. Sizes from one year to eight.

Bratz
2828 Granville near W 12th
734-4344
Designer clothes for kids. The European clothing is lovely and incredibly expensive. Also shoes and gifts. Sizes are for newborn to junior adult. Kids' hair salon in the store.

Isola Bella
5692 Yew near 41st
266-8808
All clothing and shoes sold here are made in Europe. For 3 months to 16 years.

Kiddie Kobbler Children's Shoes
Park Royal South, West Van
926-1616
Good selection of quality children's shoes. Knowledgeable staff makes sure you get the right fit.

Peppermintree Children's Wear
4243 Dunbar near 27th
228-9815
One of the best kids' stores in Vancouver. Fashionable, quality clothes, shoes and accessories in the

medium price range, mainly Canadian labels. Sizes are from newborn to 16. The friendly staff are experienced moms with helpful suggestions. Kids' play area. Open every day.

Please Mum
2041 W 41st near Arbutus
264-0366
Clothing for newborns to 10 years; most are of 100 per cent cotton, all Vancouver designed and manufactured.

Toys

B.C. Playthings
1065 Marine near Lloyd, North Van
986-4111
Definitely warrants a detour. Educational and creative toys at good prices, including art supplies, preschool supplies, construction sets, puppets, puzzles, games and an excellent selection of CDs and tapes. Wonderful wagons and face-colouring crayons. Catalogue available. Call the above number or 1-800-663-4477 to order.

Bears Toy Store
1459 Bellevue and 15th, West Van
926-2327
Teddy bear buffs should bring their

wallets. This is the home of more than 1000 teddy bears. There are other toys too, many European, and a good selection of imported dolls. All the toys on display are meant to be touched. Open daily.

3-H Craftworks Society
2112 W 4th at Arbutus
736-2113
All the toys here are handmade, often by the homebound and the disabled. There are items like colourful felt storytelling aids and puppets. Their Raggedy Ann and Andy dolls are magical.

The Toybox
3002 W Broadway at Carnarvon
738-4322
Excellent range of toys for newborns up to 10-year-olds. Good selection of board books and cassettes.

The Zoo Wildlife Boutique
Metrotown
434-4338
A great place to buy children's gifts. There is some clothing but mostly stuffed toys and all sorts of fun paraphernalia. Also in several malls.

See also Day Trips (Granville Island) earlier in this chapter for Kids Only Market.

Excursions from Vancouver

Gulf Islands

Islands offer the opportunity to escape, to experience life in the slow lane and to commune with nature. Close to Vancouver are the southern Gulf Islands—a cluster of tree-shrouded retreats between the mainland and the south end of Vancouver Island. Galiano and Mayne are close enough for a day-trip, although you will definitely want to stay longer; Saturna, North and South Pender, and Salt Spring are just as appealing but a bit more of a ferry ride.

Because the easiest public access is by ferry, the islands are fairly undeveloped. In the '50s and '60s they were a community of artists, writers, retired people and others looking for an alternative style of living. Now, with increased ferry and air service, there are many weekend cottagers.

The climate of the islands is lauded as being Canada's best—it is sunnier and drier than Vancouver's.

Note that if you are calling the Gulf Islands from the mainland or ferry, the area code is 250.

Getting There

B.C. Ferries travel to all the Gulf Islands. The ferry ride to Galiano and Mayne takes 50 to 90 minutes. Ferry service runs from Tsawwassen and times vary depending on the season. There are more sailings on weekends and during the summer. Because these ferries are small and traffic is heavy, you must make a car reservation. Phone **B.C. Ferries** in Vancouver at 277-0277 for the schedule and 1-888-223-3779 for reservations. See also Getting Around (Ferries).

The Gulf Islands are serviced regularly by air from Vancouver with **Pacific Spirit Air** (1-800-665-2359), **Harbour Air** (1-800-665-0212) and **Seair Services** (1-800-447-3247).

Services

There are no banks or bank machines on Galiano or Mayne, but each has a few restaurants, post office, gas station, liquor store, bakery, and deli and small grocery stores. Salt Spring is much more developed—in the town of Ganges you'll find a small shopping centre and two banks.

Accommodation

Canadian Gulf Islands Reservation Service
250-539-2930 or 1-888-539-2930
Accommodation on the islands is limited; don't count on finding a place to stay without a reservation, particularly on summer and holiday weekends. The best way to book accommodation on any of the Gulf

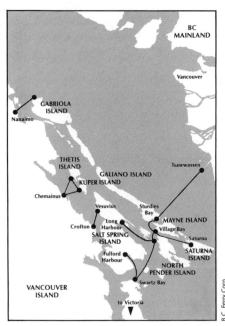

B.C. Ferries' routes in the Gulf Islands.

Islands is through Canadian Gulf Islands Reservation Service. Using this booking service opens up a variety of choices; should the selected B&B be booked, the Hennessys, who run the service, will do your shopping for you. All the accommodation has been checked out. Many B&Bs and inns will pick you up from the ferry if you are coming without a car. Request this when making your reservation.

The choice of accommodation includes rooms in private homes, bed and breakfast in large Victorian houses that cater to several guests, rustic cabins and elegant inns. There are also privately owned cottages available for extended stays.

Prices for high season average $65–$200 for B&B accommodation and $85–$150 for cabins. Inns—some extremely elegant—range from $95 to $295. Privately owned cottages (some are homes) average $100–$125 nightly. See Where to Stay listings for each island.

Island Hopping

Whether it's a case of the grass being greener or packing as much as possible into your holiday, you will probably want to visit other islands. You can take inter-island hops with B.C. Ferries. Enthusiastic cyclists enjoy exploring different islands. (Cost for the bike on an island-hop is $.75.)

Galiano Island

Galiano, a skinny island that is 26 km (16 miles) long, is the first ferry stop. Year-round residents number about 900, most of whom live at the south end. The logging giant Mac-Millan Bloedel owns about half of the island.

From the ferry arrival dock, Sturdies Bay Rd eventually leads you on to Porlier Pass Rd, the island's main artery. Half a block from the ferry dock you will find a post office at the market and a gas station (250-539-5500). There is also a real estate and insurance office, gallery and gift shop. A little further uphill is the excellent Trincomali Bakery and Deli (250-539-2004) and at the corner of Sturdies Bay and Georgeson Bay Rd is the Corner Store (250-539-2986). As well as stocking groceries, the Corner Store has camping gear and fishing tackle, and the liquor store is housed here.

Tourist Information

A tourist booth, at Sturdies Bay just up from the ferry dock, keeps irregular hours but is generally open in the summer when the ferry lands. Maps of the island are available here as well as on the ferry. Throughout the year you can write to the **Galiano Island Travel Infocentre Association**, Box 73, Galiano, BC V0N 1P0. Or phone 250-539-2233.

Getting Around the Island

Go Galiano! (250-539-0202), a bus shuttle/taxi service, will pick you up from the ferry. This company also does some sightseeing tours. The Hummingbird Pub operates a cheery red-and-white bus from Montague Harbour (for campers and boaters) to the Pub. It runs during summer months only and departs Montague Harbour on the hour 6 PM–11 PM.

Where to Stay

Woodstone Country Inn
743 Georgeson Bay Rd
250-539-2022
Driving up to the Woodstone Inn is like driving into a pastoral postcard scene. The large, two-storey inn on 3 ha (7½ acres) overlooks farm land.

Galiano's Bellhouse Inn combines ocean views with a comfortable country stay. (Judi Lees)

The 12 guest rooms are furnished with antiques, Persian carpets and exude a country elegance. All have bathrooms, half have patios and all but one have a fireplace. Request a room with a valley view.

The living room has a huge stone fireplace and chintz-covered wing-backed chairs. Newly added is a library with inviting loveseats. A meeting room is available. The somewhat formal dining room has fixed-price, three-course dinners. Breakfasts are hearty—Belgian waffles with berries and cream—and there is also afternoon tea. Both are included with your room.

A stroll away from the inn is a marsh teeming with bird life. The inn provides gum boots, binoculars and bird books. The Woodstone is a non-smoking, adult-oriented establishment. Doubles $99–$185. Closed in Jan.

The Bellhouse Inn
250-539-5667 or 1-800-970-7464

A stay at The Bellhouse Inn combines country living with harbour views. A turn-of-the-century farmhouse faces Bellhouse Bay and backs onto lawns, fruit trees and fields where sheep, horse and donkey graze. Three homey bedrooms—bed quilts are filled with wool from Bellhouse's own sheep—

all have balconies and private baths. Cosy down in front of the fireplace or enjoy private time on the spacious deck. This is a step back to yesteryear as you play croquet, cycle quiet roads or check Active Pass for killer whales. Sherry is in all the rooms and sumptuous breakfasts include delights like David's Eggs Galiano (casserole of eggs, cheese and herbs). The protected bay is good for swimming in summer. Located close to ferry terminal. Open year-round. Non-smoking. Adults only. $95–$175.

Down the beach there are two 2-bedroom cabins; each have full kitchen, patios and are ideal for families. $125 per night (two-night minimum) or $700 per week.

Moonshadows Guest House
771 Georgeson Bay Rd
250-539-5544
1-888-666-6742

Set on two wooded acres, Moonshadows is typically West Coast with large rooms, skylights, warm cedar and generous decks. There are many treats. Snuggle in front of the vast stone fireplace, take a book to the small, stairway-landing library, or relax in the bubbling hot tub that overlooks the duck pond.

There are two lovely guest rooms upstairs complete with robes, lots of books and rural views. Downstairs is an elaborate suite—a Jacuzzi, private, covered deck, fancy exercise bike and a shower you could hold a party in.

Breakfasts have fresh fruit and enticing baking to complement main courses of free-range eggs, frittatas, pancakes or souffles. Moonshadows is a short walk away from the Woodstone, which serves dinners, as well as a short cycle or long walk to the Hummingbird Pub. Non-smoking, adults and children over 12. Open year-round. $90–$135.

Sutil Lodge Heritage Guest House
Southwind Dr, Montague Harbour
250-539-2930
Built as a fishing lodge in 1928, Sutil
Lodge is tucked down a hidden drive-
way and set at the end of picturesque
Montague Harbour. Rooms are cosy
and charming (brass beds and original fir panelling) but tiny. You will do
your lounging in the old-fashioned
sitting room complete with fireplace,
view and old photographs of the
lodge. You'll find your gregarious
hosts, Tom and Ann Hennessy, chat-
ting about Galiano's history or orga-
nizing water activities such as the
daily picnic supper cruise or a kayaking trip on their catamaran (see
Sports and Recreation, below).
Canoes are available for a peaceful
paddle. Breakfast is a hot entrée with
baked goods and fresh jam. Sutil has
seven rooms: three have queen-size
beds and water views; two have double beds and orchard views; all share
bathrooms. Good for a family stay.
No smoking. Open March to Oct.
$75–$85.

Driftwood Village Resort
Bluff Rd
250-539-5457
These 11 cottages are set on a lightly
treed lot about five minutes from the
beach. There are small studio units
plus one- and two-bedrooms. Some
are woodsy, others have pretty sitting areas. All are well equipped with
kitchens, electric heat, TVs and private patios. All have fireplaces or
wood-burning stoves. The cottages
are built around a lovely naturally
landscaped garden that has a badminton net, barbecue pit, picnic tables and fruit trees. Some cabins now
have skylights and Jacuzzis; there's
an outdoor hot tub. Pets and families
are welcome but it's also ideal for
couples as all the cabins are very private. Easily accessible for cyclists and

small groups on a retreat. Doubles
$80–160.

Bodega Lodge Resort
120 Monastie at Cook Rd
250-539-2677
The resort is located on 50 acres at
the north end of the island. The six
log cabins each have three bedrooms, two bathrooms, three decks,
a kitchen and a fireplace. The main
lodge has two small bedrooms, a
suite, a lounge and a meeting room.
A dining room has been added and is
open during summer only. A big attraction at Bodega is the horses—this
is the only place on the island to go
on guided trail rides. There are 40
km (25 miles) of trails for horses or
hikers. Open year-round. Lodge
rooms plus breakfast, $60; cabins,
$80, plus $15 for additional people.

Other Lodging

Other B&Bs to consider: **High Bluffs**
(250-539-5779), secluded forest setting, good for families; **Cain Beach
Cottage** (250-539-5465), 3 bedrooms, close to ferry; and **Tide
Winds** (250-539-2478), oceanfront,
close to ferry.

Restaurants

La Berengerie $$
Montague Harbour Rd
250-539-5392
La Berengerie has a cozy country-
style dining room. The fixed-price,
four-course menu varies but leans to-
wards continental. You'll generally
find regional specialties such as
salmon and local produce. Arrive
early for an apéritif on the porch.
Frequent live dinner music such as
classical guitar. Must book in ad-
vance.

Woodstone Country Inn $$
Georgeson Bay Rd
250-539-2022

The Woodstone's dining room is the island's most formal and it is open to nonguests for dinner. Request a table by the window looking out on a lovely pastoral scene. The fixed-price, four-course menu with several entrée choices changes daily. This is award-winning cuisine served in the glow of candlelight. Entrée choices may be a roasted breast of pheasant served with succulent vegetables and peppercorn sauce or a vegetarian spinach and ricotta pie with eggplant and tomato ragout. Roast of lamb is always a favourite dish here. Reservations a must. (See Where to Stay, above.)

Hummingbird Inn   **$**
Sturdies Bay Rd at Porlier Pass Rd
250-539-5472
Go to the Hummingbird, generally known as the Pub, to mingle with the locals. The Hummingbird serves a wide variety of simple food: burgers, chowder, fish and chips, seafood, salads. Often crowded in the evenings. Open every day for lunch and dinner. Occasional live entertainment.

Bodega Lodge Resort   **$**
120 Monastie at Cook Rd
250-539-2677
This popular lodge now serves dinners during July and Aug. Nonguests are welcome. Book ahead as it seats only about 25. There are several choices of hearty, fresh fare, including vegetarian.

Other Eating Spots

Montague Marina Coffee Bar (250-539-5733), **Daystar Market Café** (250-539-2800), **Trincomali Bakery & Deli** (250-539-2004) and **Max & Moritz Spicy Island Food House** (250-539-5888), small take-out at ferry terminal.

Sports and Recreation

Cycle Galiano if you want a workout. The island is long and hilly, and you may find yourself walking up some hills. The narrow winding roads have no paved shoulders; you *must* ride single file. Rent bikes at **Galiano Bicycle** (250-539-9906).

No experience is necessary for year-round guided kayak trips, offered by **Gulf Island Kayaking** (250-539-2442). Trips range from three hours to five days, and longer ones combine kayaking with camping or stays at bed and breakfasts. They also offer kayak and canoe rentals. Other rentals and guided trips are available from **Galiano Island Sea Kayaking** (250-539-5390 or 1-888-539-2930). Daily during the summer, Tom Hennessy of **Canadian Gulf Island Catamaran Cruises** (250-539-2930) sets sail on his 14 m (46-foot) catamaran for a four-hour cruise. Catamarans are fast and smooth and have plenty of flat deck space, so they are safe for children. You will sail to Seal Rocks, a bird sanctuary, and stop at a sandy beach on Salt Spring Island for a picnic supper. Cost is a reasonable $39.

Two campgrounds with a total of 39 sites are located in **Montague Harbour Provincial Park**. You must hike to one of them; the other is accessible by car. It is first come, first served, and finding a spot can be difficult during the summer or on long weekends. There are no RV hookups on the island. In Canada the beach below the high tide line is public property. Because tides are much lower in the summer, it is possible to camp on the beach. Summertime campfires are prohibited.

Fishing gear and bait are available at **Sturdies Bay Gas and Groceries** (250-539-5500). For fishing charters try **Mel-N-I Charters** (250-539-3171) and **Montague Harbour Marina** (250-590-5465).

The pretty nine-hole **Galiano Golf Course** (250-539-5533) was established in 1975 and has a licensed clubhouse that serves lunch and dinner.

Bodega Resort (250-539-2677) offers guided trail rides on 40 km (25 miles) of scenic trails with 360° views.

The Gulf Islands are probably the most popular diving destination in southwestern B.C. Air is available at **Madrona Lodge** (250-539-2926), at the north end of the island, near excellent diving spots at Virago Point and Alcala Point. **Galiano Dive Services** (250-539-3109) also provides air, instruction and charters.

If you want to swim, keep in mind that water on the east side of the island is warmer than on the west. Beaches with public access are at Coon Bay in **Dionisio Point Provincial Park** at the north end of the island. There are shell and pebble beaches on both sides of the peninsula at Montague Harbour Park.

There is one tennis court at **Galiano Golf and Country Club**.

Scenic Spots

By Galiano standards it's a long drive to the northern tip of the island at **Coon Bay**, but the beaches here are perhaps the best on the island: sand or smoothly sloped sandstone rock.

Montague Harbour Provincial Park is the site of 3000-year-old Aboriginal middens that are still visible in the cliffs by the shore. An island/peninsula juts out of the park into the harbour; at low tide you can walk around on the beach, and at high tide you can take the path up above.

Galiano Bluffs Park was be-

queathed to the people of Galiano. You can drive via Burrill Rd and Bluff Rd to the top of the bluffs through stands of old-growth fir and cedar and arrive at views of Victoria and the American San Juan Islands. There are also hiking trails in the park.

Bellhouse Park, also a legacy to islanders, is a good picnic spot, with tables and views of Active Pass and the Mayne Island lighthouse. Access is by Burrill Rd and Jack Rd.

Special Events

An island-wide fire sale is held at the fire-hall on the Victoria Day weekend. On the July 1 long weekend the Jamboree, a family event, is held at North End Hall. The Fiesta, on the Aug 1 long weekend, includes a parade, salmon barbecue, homemade pies, pony rides and games of chance. A Wine Festival happens mid-Aug. In Oct there is a Poetry Festival and Oktoberfest. A craft sale takes place American Thanksgiving weekend. Dances are held at the community hall near the Pub on Saturday nights of long weekends.

The Arts

The **Dandelion Gallery** (250-539-5622) in Sturdies Bay exhibits local painting, sculpture, glass, jewellery and photographs and sells books written by Galiano Islanders. Open every day in the summer and every weekend the rest of the year. **The Thistledown** (250-539-2592), just across the street, has crafts, carvings and jewellery, and some unique gift ideas. **Ixchel Craft Shop** (250-539-3038) located next to the Corner Store and at the Marina has an eclectic assortment of crafts, local and imported. Readers can browse and buy at **Galiano Island Books** (250-539-3340).

Oceanwood Country Inn on Mayne is renowned for its deluxe accommodation and great cuisine. (Oceanwood)

Check at the Travel Infocentre for amateur theatre productions. Most summer weekends there are special events, from art shows to readings by visiting novelists.

Mayne Island

Compared to long, narrow Galiano, Mayne, the second ferry stop, is small and compact—you can drive anywhere in about 10 minutes. Mayne is a pastoral place with a population of about 850. Choice of restaurants and accommodation is limited; its charm lies in the landscape, wildlife and the slower pace of life. The closest thing to a village is the cluster of buildings around Miners Bay.

Tourist Information

Pick up the indispensable map produced by the islanders, which is available free on the ferry and at any store on Mayne. Not only will it help you get around but it also lists all the services and attractions on the island. In high season, tourist information is available at the museum in Miners Bay. During the year write to **Mayne Island Community Chamber of Commerce**, Box 160, Mayne Island, BC V0N 2J0.

Services

Tru Value Market has excellent produce and deli products. In this same small mall on Village Bay Rd just near Miners Bay is **Manna Bakery Café**, which has a great variety of goodies plus a cappuccino bar. **Miners Bay Trading Post** (250-539-2214), in the same area, is a grocery/liquor store, as well as a service station, and you can buy fishing tackle here. At Fernhill Centre, **Mayne Open Market** (250-539-5024), known as MOM's, has fresh and natural foods, snack food, housewares, gifts, stationery; the post office is here along with fax service. There is no bank or bank machine on Mayne.

Where to Stay

Oceanwood Country Inn
Dinner Bay Rd
250-539-5074
Eleven of the 12 deluxe rooms at the Oceanwood have a view of Navy Channel, which separates Mayne from North Pender. All have bathrooms, and most have whirlpools or soaking tubs, French doors, fireplaces and decks. Each room is decorated differently, with Canadiana pine, Victorian mahogany and romantic chintzes. The inn sits on 4 ha (10 acres) of wooded waterfront property. You can soak in a hot tub, bicycles are available or you may arrange to rent a kayak; there is croquet on the lawn, a library and a games room with bridge tables. Afternoon tea, served in the Garden Room, is a daily treat. Oceanwood has a small conference room. Breakfast and afternoon tea are included. No children, no pets. Closed Dec, Jan and Feb. Doubles $130–$295. See also Restaurants, below.

Bayview Bed & Breakfast
764 Stewart Dr
250-539-2924 or 1-800-376-2115
The Bayview B&B sits on a bluff facing Horton Bay and Curlew Island. There are three guest rooms each with a private bath, deck and entrance. Two have queen-size beds; one has twin beds. Rooms are equipped with coffeemaker, kettle and the makings for tea and coffee. You awaken to birdsong and enjoy the first cup of coffee on the deck that faces the peaceful inlet. After a hearty country-style breakfast it's time to simply enjoy. Cycling, peaceful walks or snoozing on the deck are all options. There is a barbeque and picnic tables and a 42-foot serviced dock if guests wish to arrive by boat. You can beachcomb or swim, or on a cool day, curl up in front of the fireplace and let the world go by. There is a resident dog and two cats; should you wish to bring pets or children, please check ahead. Open May to Oct. Doubles $80–$90.

Blue Vista Resort
563 Arbutus Rd
250-539-2463
Close to a safe beach, a parklike setting—the Blue Vista is a good bet for a family vacation. There are eight one- and two-bedroom, fully equipped cabins, which are more modern than rustic. Some have fireplaces and all have decks. Barbecues and bicycles are available. Located close to Bennett Bay, Blue Vista is popular with kayakers. Pets welcome in off season. Closed mid-Jan to mid-Feb. Doubles $50–$70.

Root Seller Inn
Miners Bay
250-539-2621
This warm and friendly country-style bed and breakfast has four guestrooms and two bathrooms. The location is popular with hikers and

The shoreline of much of the Gulf Islands is either steep cliffs or this smooth sandstone. Odd formations have been sculpted by thousands of years of hammering by the sea. (Dick Tipple)

cyclists because it is in the heart of activity at Miners Bay—within walking distance of stores and the pub. This is a casual, make-yourself-at-home stay—food is left out and you fix your breakfast as you like it. Joan Drummond has been hosting guests for over 15 years and everyone is treated like family. Doubles $65–$75.

Other Lodging

A few other B&Bs to consider: **Fernhill Lodge** (250-539-2544), **Tinkerers B&B** (250-539-2280). For a romantic stay, try **A Coachhouse on Oyster Bay B&B** (250-539-3368) or **Argonauta** on Mayne (250-539-3374). Built during the 1890s, **Springwater Lodge** (250-539-5521) is reasonably priced.

Restaurants

Fernhill Lodge $$
Fernhill Rd
250-539-2544
Fernhill Lodge has built its reputation on historical dinners. One night's dinner may be inspired by Chaucer; the next, by Cleopatra or

Mayne Island's Springwater Lodge is B.C.'s oldest hotel. (Chris Potter)

the Romans. These themed meals are now available on request, but usually the menu consists of a choice of two four-course dinners. This lodge has three guest rooms, a charming, book-filled sitting room, sun room with a piano and the dining room, which seats 20. Reservations a must.

Oceanwood Country Inn   **$$$**
Dinner Bay Rd
250-539-5074

The Oceanwood is open to non-guests for dinner, a fixed-price meal that is seasonal and focusses on herbs and vegetables from the inn's garden. The pretty dining room takes advantage of the lovely ocean-front setting. Entrées include mouth-watering offerings like pan-seared Fraser Valley duck breast with glazed sweet potatoes, apple cider jus or oven-roasted Sooke rainbow trout. All wines are from the West Coast. Book in advance. Closed Dec, Jan and Feb.

Springwater Lodge   **$**
Miners Bay
250-539-5521

Strictly pub food—burgers, sandwiches, and fish and chips—but it's well done, and when you eat in the sun on the deck overlooking Miners Bay, it's even better.

Sports and Recreation

Although Mayne is not flat, it is one of the easier islands to bicycle around. Rentals are available at **Tinkerer's Retreat** (250-539-2280) and **Bayview Bike Rentals** (250-539-2924).

Fishing bait and licences are available at **Active Pass Auto Marine** (250-539-5411) in Miners Bay. The best spot for summer fishing around the islands is in Active Pass, the body of water separating Mayne and Galiano.

Island Charters (250-539-5040) will arrange charters on a Saturna 33 sailboat for a half day, a day or overnight. The company will pick you up or drop you off at one of the other Gulf Islands.

Mayne Island Kayak and Canoe Rentals (250-539-2667), located on Seal Beach, has 40 kayaks and rents by the hour or by the day. They will pick up at the ferry and have a variety of put-in areas around Mayne. They also have a campground with hot tub and showers. You can camp and do kayak day trips—a touch of outdoor heaven.

The best swimming beaches are the long, wide, sandy beach at Bennett Bay and the protected Campbell Bay beach, known for its warm waters. Dinner Bay Community Park with beach, barbecues, playground and playing fields is ideal for families. Piggott Bay is also a good beach, popular with windsurfers.

A public tennis court is located behind the fire-hall on Felix Jack Rd off Fernhill Rd.

There are two private campgrounds on Mayne—**Fern Hollow Campground** (250-539-5253) and **Journey's End Farm** (250-539-2411).

Scenic Spots

If you are with locals who know the access into **Helen Point**, this is a treasure of a walk. This area was designated an Indian Reserve in 1877; today it is a patch of wilderness that encompasses the best of the Gulf Islands. A forested trail occasionally opens to deserted bays where you may see seals, waterfowl, eagles overhead or a ferry going by.

Mount Parke is a 63 ha (158-acre) wilderness park (much of the land has been generously donated by locals) and the highest point on the island. Access is off Fernhill Rd via Montrose Rd, and you can drive to the start of a trail. There is hiking here for all levels of ability; views of Vancouver, Active Pass and Vancouver Island are almost 360°. The unmanned satellite radar station on the mountain top monitors ship traffic in Active Pass.

St Mary Magdalene Church, built in 1898, is one of many fine Victorian buildings on Mayne. Stately old houses of the same era are in Miners Bay and on Georgina Point Rd. You can glean a little of the history of the island from the old cemetery beside the church. Across the street a stairway leads down to the beach.

The lovely point where you'll find **Active Pass Lighthouse** has been designated a public park, Georgian Point Heritage Park. The lighthouse was built in 1885 and is open to the public, but the hours vary depending on the season. There are picnic tables and public washrooms. This is a good bird-watching spot, particularly in winter, and there are many tidal pools along the sandstone shore.

The beach at **Bennett Bay** is the warmest for swimming.

Special Events

The Fall Fair is held on the third weekend in August, the same time as the Springwater Salmon Derby. The

Mayne's Island Cottage is a delightful place to gift shop. (Judi Lees)

Salmon Bake is on the Sunday before Labour Day. The third week in November is a Christmas Craft sale.

The Arts

Several artists and craftspeople open their studios to the public daily in the summer and on weekends during the rest of the year. Check the map published by the islanders for locations and times.

There are a number of places to browse for crafts. Two not to be missed are **Island Cottage** (250-539-2099) in Miners Bay (gifts for everyone, from clothing to made-on-the-island crafts) and **Rabbits Haven** (250-539-2401) on Georgina Point Rd (stuffed rabbits, garden stones, quilts, etc.).

Mayne Island Little Theatre stages amateur productions in spring and fall; watch for posters.

Salt Spring Island

If you have visited other Gulf Islands, you will notice how different Salt Spring is. It has the same wonderful greenery as the others, but it is the largest, most populous

(10,000 residents) and most developed island. Ganges is a real town, with a small shopping centre and a few busy streets hugging the harbour. Amenities include the Bank of Montreal and Canadian Imperial Bank of Commerce, (both have ATMs) and a credit union; a large grocery store and several smaller markets; and a variety of services—post office, liquor store—as well as retail outlets and galleries. Art lovers are in for a treat on this island as there are more than 30 galleries. There are two sleepy, little communities around Fulford Harbour and Vesuvius.

Salt Spring also has over 100 B&Bs and more real estate agents than you'd care to see in one place. Other features are the several small lakes, which provide warm swimming spots, and the 14 briny springs (they are on private land so can't be visited) at the north end of the island that gave the island its name.

The island started and developed as an agricultural community and is now famous for its Salt Spring Island lamb and its hospitality—during summer it can be packed with tourists.

Ferries from Vancouver's Tsawwassen terminal arrive at Long Harbour. (Ferries from Vancouver Island arrive at Fulford Harbour and Vesuvius Bay.) There are regularly scheduled float-plane flights from Vancouver Harbour and Vancouver Airport to Ganges Harbour by Harbour Air (1-800-665-0212), Pacific Spirit Air (250-537-9359 or 1-800-665-2359) and Seair Services (1-800-447-3247).

It would be difficult to visit Salt Spring without a car, but some B&B hosts will pick you up at the ferry terminal or from Ganges Harbour. Check when making a reservation. Silver Shadow Taxi (250-537-5696) provides transportation. Azure Transport (250-537-4737) does sightseeing tours. At Fulford Harbour there is Heritage Car & Truck Rentals (250-537-4225). This company will also pick up and drop off at the ferry or from a float-plane arrival.

Tourist Information

Tourist information is available year-round at the Travel Infocentre (250-537-5252) at 121 Lower Ganges Rd in Ganges: July and Aug, 9 AM–6 PM; Dec, Jan, Feb, 11 AM–3 PM; rest of the year, 10 AM–4 PM. You can write to the **Salt Spring Island Chamber of Commerce**, 121 Lower Ganges Rd, Ganges, BC V8K 2T1. Email: <chambers@saltspring.com>.

Where to Stay

Hastings House
160 Upper Ganges Rd
250-537-2362 or 1-800-661-9255
Hastings House is the most deluxe and expensive lodging on the island, an elegant and gracious 12 ha (30-acre) estate. Five beautifully restored buildings house 11 guest accommodations. Most have wood-burning fireplace or freestanding stove, some have features like antiques, Laura Ashley fabrics, hand-painted florals, soaking tubs; all are exquisitely furnished. Doubles $365–$495.

Of the many B&Bs on Salt Spring, here is a sampling:

The Old Farmhouse
1077 North End Rd
250-537-4113
Step back in time with a stay at this 1890 farmhouse. Gerti and Karl Fuss have enhanced the charm of this heritage house by adding space and amenities without losing the wonderful hominess. The four guest rooms are cozy with floral wallpapering, comfy furnishings and private baths. The two downstairs rooms have pri-

Mallard's Mill Bed & Breakfast is unusual on Salt Spring Island. (Jan Macpherson)

vate patios, and the upstairs ones have small balconies that overlook the grounds—it's not unusual to see deer wandering by. There are fluffy robes, fresh flowers and sherry in your room. Television and telephones are brought out only on request. Guests prefer to wander the grounds, which are spangled with flower beds that in summer explode with colour—there are over 2,000 sunflowers alone in bloom. You can walk the orchard, relax in the shade of the gazebo or curl up in a hammock.

Guests are truly pampered. Morning coffee or tea arrives magically outside your door. Then it's into the country-elegant dining room for Gerti's freshly baked cinnamon buns, croissants and muffins along with fresh fruit that often includes raspberries from the garden. Gerti will even supply a doggie bag so you can take her warm-from-the-oven treats for later. Doubles $150.

Mallard's Mill Bed & Breakfast
521 Beddis Rd
250-537-1011

For the unusual blended with comfort, stay at Mallard's Mill. Should you choose the Otter Tail Honeymoon Cottage, your gourmet breakfast is delivered on the small-gauge train that circles the property. Jack Vandort and Jan Macpherson have put a lot of thought into their bed and breakfast—the reconstructed 1890s water wheel runs from spring water and feeds into a peaceful pond that, yes, is often inhabited by mallards. There is a hot tub, outdoor decks and brilliantly hued flowers everywhere. Jack takes guests for a short rail trip just for the fun of it. Mallard's Mill has three rooms in the main house. All have king- or queen-size beds, handmade quilts, private baths and fireplaces. The cottage has a king-size bed, fireplace, and a jetted indoor tub fit for two, under a skylight.

Jack serves a three-course breakfast that includes homemade breads and entrées like his famous "berry french toast." This home has the feel of a well-appointed lodge—rustic wood blends with antiques and wicker. There is an abundance of books and fresh flowers. Return guests are treated to champagne in their room! Closed Dec/Jan. Double $115–$159.

Weston Lake Inn
813 Beaver Point Rd
250-653-4311
One guest called it "an excellent place to recharge your batteries." Set on 10 acres, high on a hill, where wind whispers through the Douglas fir, the Weston Lake Inn has decks, a hot tub and exquisite gardens overlooking Weston Lake. Indeed, a walk through Susan Evans's ornamental garden with Cass, the Evans's friendly English sheepdog, is good for the soul. There are three guest rooms beautifully furnished, complete with original art. All have private baths; one has a queen-size and twin bed. It's adult oriented but children over 14 are welcome. Robes are provided so that you can wander down to the hot tub. There are two spacious lounges for guest use.

Susan makes her own granola. Special offerings, like three-cheese scones, are favourites with repeat guests. Susan's also a whiz with low-fat sauces. Ted offers sailing charters on the 10 m (36-foot) sloop *Malaika*. Doubles $110–$125.

Gardens on the Lake Bed and Breakfast
126 Natalie Lane
250-537-0092 or 1-888-428-4233
Very new, very West Coast and very welcoming, Gardens on the Lake is tucked down a lane facing Cusheon Lake. The post-and-beam (with abundant glass) home has a ground-level floor ideal for families or two couples. There are two guest rooms with ensuite bathrooms and queen-size beds; one is spacious enough to have a roll-away bed added. Guests have the use of a large sitting room

with fireplace and entertainment centre (lots of videos). Furnishings are tasteful and comfortable. Rooms face the lake, open to private decks and have their own entrance. Complimentary canoe, paddle boat and windsurfer are on hand. Doubles $115.

The Cottage Resort
175 Suffolk Rd
250-537-2214
Go to sleep to the symphony of frogs and awaken to paddle the peaceful waters of St. Mary Lake. There are eight cottages here in a variety of sizes. Five have wood-burning fireplaces (wood is provided), two are duplexes, all have decks, full kitchens and outdoor eating table. This is the perfect place for a family vacation. The gently-sloping lawn spreads to the lakeshore, there is a playground, complimentary canoes and rowboats; badminton, horseshoes and fishing are options. Should you desire it, there is a television complete with movie channel in each cabin. Regulars rave about this place. Doubles $85–$95; for four $135–$140; three-bedroom unit $165.

Other Lodging

A few other recommended B&Bs are **Beddis House** (250-537-1028), **Partridge House** (250-537-2822), **Anne's Oceanfront Hideaway** (250-537-0851), **Cranberry Ridge B&B** (250-537-4854) and **Water's Edge** (250-537-5807). Besides the two mentioned that take children, also check with **Applecroft Family Farm** (250-537-5605), **Bullock Lake Farm** (250-537-4895), **The Eagles Nest** (250-537-2129) and **Anchorage Cove B&B** (250-537-5337 or 1-888-537-5360).

Cabins can be rented on the sea or by a lake. **Lakeside Cottage** (250-

537-2571 or 1-888-529-2567) is a 3-bedroom cabin, ideal for families as there's kayaking, canoeing, fishing, swimming and use of sauna. Lakeside's owners also run youth wilderness camps. Also **Salty Spring Seaside Resort** (250-537-4111), **Spindrift Resort** (250-537-5311) and **Cusheon Lake Resort** (250-537-9629). **Salt Spring Island Hostel**, a member of Hostelling International, has dorm accommodation as well as some camping spots (250-537-4149).

One way to tour Salt Spring Island is via horse and carriage. (Island Rose Carriages)

Restaurants

Hastings House (250-537-5362) has a formal dining room and serves five-course dinners with a choice of entrée. It also has The Snug, a smaller, more casual dining room. The dining rooms are open to the public but reservations are a must.

The best restaurants in the village of Ganges are **House Piccolo** (250-537-1844), European cuisine served in a charming little house; **Moby's Marine Pub** (250-537-5559), pub fare at its best, jazz on Sunday nights; and **Bouzouki Greek Café** (250-537-4181), owned by Steve and Georgia Asproloupos, authentic Greek dishes and super desserts. The **Vesuvius Inn** (250-537-2312) serves pub food and showcases spectacular sunsets from its outside deck at Vesuvius Bay. Other restaurants are **Tides Inn** (250-537-1097) and **Sea Court** (250-537-4611). There are two good bakeries in Ganges, **Embe Bakery** (250-537-5611) and **Sweet Arts Patisserie & Cafe** (250-537-4205). The latter serves super breakfasts.

Sports and Recreation

Bicycles can be rented at **Salt Spring Kayaking** (250-653-4222) or **Salt Spring Marine Rental** (250-537-9100). Rent canoes, kayaks and small power boats at the **Salt Spring Marine Rental** (250-537-9100). They also have a full-service scuba shop and will arrange fishing and sailing charters. Purchase fishing licences here or at **Mouat's Hardware** (250-537-5551). There is an excellent sport-fishing brochure at the Chamber of Commerce.

Sail with the Bee's (250-537-9988 or 1-800-360-6194) does 2–8 hour skippered day cruises; children are welcome.

Salt Spring is a mecca for kayakers. **Island Escapades** (250-537-2537, 1-888-KAYAK67) offers kayaking, sailing, hiking and climbing day trips and instruction as well as longer expeditions. This company also offers summer wilderness-camp youth programs. Kayaks can be rented from **Salt Spring Kayaking** (250-653-4222) and **Sea Otter Kayaking** (250-537-5678). These companies both give lessons and guided trips. A full-moon paddle is a favourite.

Arrange horseback riding through **Salt Spring Guided Rides** (250-537-5761). For a guided tour via horse and carriage, try **Island Rose Carriages** (250-653-9444).

Four public tennis courts are located on Vesuvius Bay Rd near North End Rd, next door to the outdoor pool. Book these by calling 250-537-4243.

On a clear day Salt Spring's Ganges Harbour is perfect for sailing. (Helen Tara)

There are two nine-hole golf courses, **Salt Spring Island Golf and Country Club** (250-537-2121) and **Blackburn Meadows** (250-537-1707). Both are open to visitors all year.

Scenic Spots

Ruckle Provincial Park is both a wilderness area and a historic site. The Ruckles were one of Salt Spring's first farming families; their farmhouse and outbuildings still stand in the park and are identified by plaques. The park's **Beaver Point** is a great picnic spot; smooth rocks slope into the water, arbutus trees grow on the point and small pebble coves offer beachcombing opportunities. Follow the **Beach Trail**—spectacular water views, lots of waterfowl, seals and lovely forested pathway—and then circle back to the parking lot.

Don't miss Everlasting Summer (250-653-9418), a lovely herb and flower garden open daily March to Dec. There is a gift shop. It's on the way to Ruckle Provincial Park.

Mount Maxwell is not the highest point on the island, but it has a viewpoint that you can drive to and a network of easy trails. It's a great place to view a sunset.

Beddis Beach at the end of Beddis Rd is wide and sandy (at low tide) and is good for sun-bathing, bird-watching and beachcombing. Other beaches are at Beachside Dr on Long Harbour, **Booth Bay** (access is via Baker Rd) and **Drummond Park** at Fulford Harbour.

The Arts

During the summer (usually from June into Sept) more than 250 artists and artisans from the Gulf Islands sell their work daily at **Artcraft** in Mahon Hall in Ganges. The **Salt Spring Festival of the Arts** offers music, theatre and dance in July. Watch for posters or inquire at the Travel Infocentre.

Volume II (250-537-9223) is a small but first-rate bookstore in Mouat's Mall in Ganges. (While you are in the mall, stop at fragrant **Salt Spring Soapworks**; all the soaps are handmade using natural products.) Also at the mall is the **Pegasus Gallery of Canadian Art** (250-537-2421) which, among other works, has some wonderful native masks and art. Many galleries and artists' studios are tucked away down shady lanes overlooking the water. At the Travel Infocentre there is a map of artists' studios, and you can do a self-guided tour every Sun from Apr to Oct.

Don't miss the Tufted Puffin Gallery (250-653-9139) to see David Jackson's world-famous decoys and bird carvings. Also a collection of

English ceramics—unusual and expensive.

For island crafts visit the **Waterfront Gallery** (250-537-4525). Also, check out **Turtle Craft & Co.** (250-653-2002), where you can have dinnerware custom-designed.

Special Events

There is a Saturday market in the centre of Ganges from Apr to Oct that features everything grown or crafted on the island.

The Wine Festival, in July, is often accompanied by a concert. Mid-July there is a House Tour; you get to oggle some extravagant homes. The fall fair—a real country fair with animals, games and midway—is held the third weekend in Sept.

Whistler

Whistler Resort is a phenomenal success story. It is a mistake to visit Vancouver and not take a few days at the mountain resort if you have the time. Consistently ranked North America's number-one ski resort by several ski magazines, Whistler now attracts visitors year-round. In summer the streets of the village take on a party atmosphere with daily entertainment, from musicians to magic shows; cafés and bistros spill out onto the sidewalks, and festivals abound—most are musical, celebrating jazz, classical, rock, and rhythm and blues. Golf, hiking, fishing, mountain biking, rafting, horseback riding, tennis and even summer skiing make Whistler an outdoor mecca. In winter, the village is festive in a dressing of snow and lights. The two mountains provide more than 200 runs for skiers and snowboarders, and visitors can cross-country ski, snowshoe, snowmobile or hang out in the village.

Although Whistler has a permanent population of under 8,000, it does not have a small-town feel. It exudes an international-resort ambience—all the glamour and glitz associated with Aspen and other "name resorts" is evident here. Classy shops, trendy restaurants and high-tech attractions are all part of the Whistler scene. The resort can be confusing for a first-time visitor, since it's made up of several villages with sprawling residential neighbourhoods stretching along the road and up the mountainsides.

Approaching from Vancouver, you first come to Whistler Creek, where the original development began in the '60s. Today there is a gondola to Whistler Mountain as well as a ski and rental shop, small retail mall, and several pubs and delis popular with the locals. There are plans for a major development of Whistler Creekside.

Driving another 3 km (2 miles) brings you to Whistler Village, the hub of the resort. Its award-winning compact layout is a pedestrian area with everything—from a grocery store and a pharmacy to classy restaurants—no more than a five-minute walk away, including ski runs.

A 10-minute walk or short drive uphill is the Upper Village, which has several large hotels and condominium complexes, shops, restaurants and mountain access. The heart of the Upper Village is Chateau Whistler. In summer, in particular, many people enjoy this area for a quieter stay and the posh surroundings of the Chateau. In winter, lift lines are less crowded here and there are several good pubs for après-ski—one with a large outdoor deck that's popular on sunny spring days.

From the lower Whistler Village, a footbridge over Village Gate Blvd links to the most recently developed area, Town Plaza. Similar to the

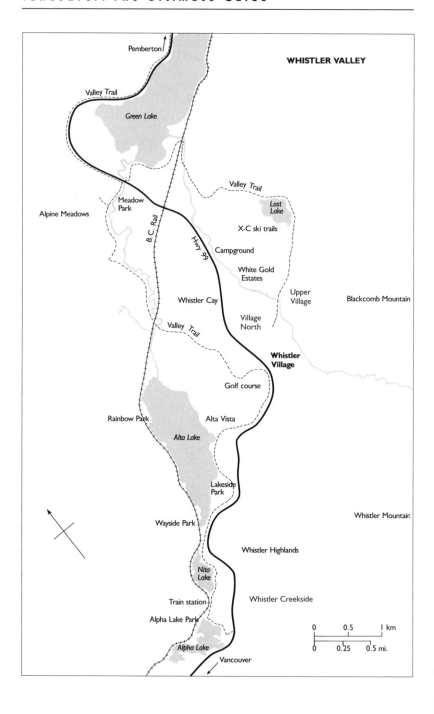

Pemberton

WHISTLER VALLEY

Valley Trail

Green Lake

Valley *Trail*

Lost Lake

Meadow Park

Alpine Meadows

X-C ski trails

B.C. Rail

Hwy 99

Campground

White Gold Estates

Upper Village

Blackcomb Mountain

Whistler Cay

Village North

Valley *Trail*

Whistler Village

Golf course

Rainbow Park

Alta Vista

Alta Lake

Lakeside Park

Whistler Mountain

Wayside Park

Whistler Highlands

Nita Lake

Train station

Whistler Creekside

Alpha Lake Park

Alpha Lake

Vancouver

0	0.5	1 km
0	0.25	0.5 mi.

village, it has pedestrian walkways and a plaza, a condominium complex above retail and restaurant space and underground parking. There is also the Marketplace, which is primarily retail space and has some amenities for locals, such as an insurance office, real estate offices, dry cleaners and a bank. If you are visiting for the day, free parking is available on the east side of Blackcomb Way behind the Village. Drive to the end of Village Gate Blvd and turn left.

Getting There

Whistler is 120 km (75 miles) north of Vancouver on Hwy 99, a 90-minute drive. This winding "Sea to Sky" highway is scenically spectacular but is not an easy drive in bad winter weather. Snow tires are mandatory and chains are sometimes necessary. Call the **Department of Highways** (1-900-451-4997) for road conditions. Car rentals are available at Whistler through **Budget** (932-1236) and **Thrifty** (938-0302).

Throughout the year you can travel by train from Vancouver to Whistler (**B.C. Rail**, 984-5246 or 1-800-663-8238). It's a relaxing way to travel, but there is only one train daily. The station is closest to Whistler Creekside; a free shuttle bus transports train passengers to the village.

There are over half a dozen bus and coach services; **Maverick Coach Lines** (662-8051) departs from Vancouver Bus Depot and drops off at Whistler Creekside, Whistler Village and Whistler North, and **Perimeter Transportation** (261-2299) runs daily trips between Whistler and Vancouver International Airport.

There is no scheduled air service to Whistler. Charter service is available with **North Vancouver Airlines** (278-1608 or 1-800-228-6608), **Helijet Airways** (273-1414) and **Whistler Air** (932-6615 or 1-888-806-2299). Flights land at Pemberton, 35 km (22 miles) north of Whistler. There is a shuttle service to Whistler, usually included in the price of your air ticket. Whistler Air also provides float-plane service from Vancouver Harbour to Green Lake 3 km (2 miles) north of the Village.

Tourist Information

A tourist information booth (932-5528) is on the highway at Lake Placid Road, 3 km (2 miles) south of Whistler Village. Another booth is at the front door of the Conference Centre in the village. You can also call the **Whistler Resort Association**. To book accommodation call 932-4222 in Whistler, 664-5625 in Vancouver or toll free in the U.S. and Canada (except Vancouver) at 1-800-944-7853. For other information, call the association's activity line at 932-2394.

Where to Stay

Accommodation at Whistler falls roughly into the following categories: high-priced luxury hotels, new condominiums with a variety of rates, older midrange condominium hotels, pensions, and a few hostels and B&Bs. Off-season rates generally apply Nov, Dec and Apr (also Jan at some places). During high season, minimum stays of three nights are required when you make a reservation. The Whistler Resort Association (see above) will book accommodation for you.

The best hotels, the **Chateau Whistler** (938-8000 or 1-800-606-8244), the **Delta Whistler Resort** (932-1982 or 1-800-268-1133) and the Radisson's **Le Chamois** (932-

Whistler Village hums with activity in summer as well as winter. (Leanna Rathkelly)

2882), are costly (always check on packages). The **Hyatt Regency Whistler Resort**, due to open in the autumn of 2000, will join this five-star category. Wherever you stay, visit the Chateau. Nothing has been spared in this Canadian Pacific hotel. The lobby is fabulous: huge fireplaces, stone pillars, overstuffed wingbacked sofas, handmade Mennonite rugs, antique pine furniture and Canadiana folk art. Stop for a drink in the Mallard Bar and visit the shops. An expansion completed in 1997 saw the addition of 221 hotel rooms, a large ballroom and additional conference facilities complete with a rooftop terrace. The new wing includes the exquisite Entree Gold floor, cp's most elaborate rooms (fireplaces and Jacuzzis) plus amenities like the Entree Gold lounge, complimentary continental breakfast and a concierge. The Chateau, which has a health club, tennis courts and golf course, now has a full spa with 14 treatment rooms. Open to others besides hotel guests, The Spa at Chateau Whistler (938-2086) is yet another reason to visit. For a luxurious stay, the Chateau cannot be beat. In high season, room price range is $199–$409 for doubles.

Wherever you look, a new condominium complex or multi-unit resort has popped up. Some, like the **Pan Pacific Lodge** (905-2999 or 1-888-905-9995), which has 121 units (studio, one- and two-bedroom), all with kitchens and fireplaces, offer five-star amenities. Prices during high season start at $350.

Many of the midrange hotels were built in the late '70s and have been refurbished. A good example is the **Whistler Village Inn & Suites** (932-4004 or 1-800-663-6418). These units were made for skiers—all have kitchen facilities, fireplaces, sleep at least four people (many have queen-size Murphy beds) and include indoor parking. The complimentary continental breakfast makes for a quick morning departure to the slopes. All the units can accommodate two couples (or three friendly ones) or a family. It might be a bit of a tight squeeze (there are ski lockers) but it is a way to keep the cost down. High season rates begin at $190.

Another accommodation group, the pensions, are chalet style and are often run by Austrian, German or Swiss Canadians. They are in large houses with half a dozen guest rooms and private family quarters. Most pensions are in residential areas rather than in the village, though many are only a 15-minute walk away. If you are coming without a car, the innkeepers will drive you to and from the ski lifts. In the evening you could walk or take a cab to a restaurant. Hearty breakfasts are included, and many rooms have private baths. Pension rates are about $130 for two in high season and $95 during the rest of the year.

Pensions are a great deal because, along with comfortable accommodation, you get affable and informative hosts and interesting breakfast companions, perhaps from Boston or Berlin. The pensions are **Edelweiss** (932-3641), **Lorimer Ridge** (938-9722), **Chalet Luise** (932-4187), **Durlacher Hof** (932-1924), **Alta Vista** (932-4900) and **Cedar Springs B&B Lodge** (938-8007).

There are 15 small lodges and B&Bs, which cost about $110 a night—for example, **Stancliff House** (932-2393), **Idylwood B&B** (932-4582) and **Belle Neige Bed & Breakfast** (938-9225 or 1-800-611-4869). Book through Whistler Resort Association.

In the budget category, there are four dormitory-style hostels (some have private rooms as well) with rates in the $20 a night range. **Whistler Hostel** (932-5492) is a

Whistler Resort is among the top ski destinations in North America. (Whistler Resort Association)

member of Hostelling International and has a beautiful setting on the shore of Alta Lake.

Restaurants

There are many expensive restaurants in Whistler. For fine dining on a weekend during ski season, make a reservation a few weeks in advance.

Vancouver pasta guru Umberto Menghi operates two Italian restaurants here: **Il Caminetto** (932-4442) and **Trattoria di Umberto** (932-5858). Another favourite for pasta, and its wine list, is **Araxi Ristorante** (932-4540) in the centre of the village. Highly lauded for its continental cuisine is **La Rua** (932-5011), in Le Chamois Hotel. **Quattro at Pinnacle** (905-4844) also serves continental and pleases those happy to spend the extra. For pasta without breaking the bank, and a fun atmosphere, there's **Caramba** (938-1879) in the Town Plaza. **Hy's Steak House** (905-5555), famous for years in Vancouver, has now joined the Whistler restaurant roster.

The **Rim Rock Café & Oyster Bar** (932-5565) at Whistler Creekside has a big reputation for seafood. **Val d'Isère** (932-4666) serves classic French food and is in the village.

Both restaurants in the Chateau Whistler are excellent. The **Wildflower** (938-2033) is charmingly decorated with a display of old wooden birdhouses. It offers lavish buffets for breakfast, lunch and dinner or a menu featuring foods of the Pacific Northwest. There is also healthy spa cuisine noted on each menu. It's one of Whistler's best. **Portobello** (938-2040) new at the Chateau, is a restaurant with a difference. There's a deli-style section that includes a bakery—great food for families, and it has a "to go" window on the Wizard walkway—and there's also a bar featuring B.C. microbrewery beers and vQA wines, plus a retail shop with Portobello products.

There are two popular Japanese restaurants, **Sushi Village** (932-3330) in the village and **Sushi-Ya** (905-0155) in Village North. For Thai cuisine, there's **Thai One On** (932-4822) in the Upper Village.

If all you want is a decent burger, try **Spliz Grill** (938-9300) or **Monk's Grill Steak House** (932-9677) or go to **Cinnamon Bear Bar** (932-7346) in the Delta. **Citta** (932-4177) offers pub fare and is a popular hangout for young people. Families should try Portobello (above), **Old Spaghetti Factory** (938-1081) or **Moe's Deli** (905-7772) in Village North. If you like Greek, **Zeuski's Taverna** (932-6009) is a bargain. Another bargain for take-outs (there are a few seats) is **Ingrid's Village Café** (932-7000).

Pubs are popular hangouts—for après ski there's **Merlin's Bar** (932-3141) at the Blackcomb base, **Longhorn Pub** (932-5999) in Whistler Village or **Dusty's Bar** (905-2171) at Whistler Mountain base. **Brewhouse** (905-2739) at the far end of Village North is humongous and includes brew pub, restaurant, lounge and patio.

Shopping

If you would rather shop than ski or hike, you won't be bored at Whistler. For a resort, there is an excellent variety of retailers. There are clothing, cigar and children's shops, and wonderful places to find an unusual gift—check out the many craft shops, such as **Skitch Knicknacks & Paddywacks**. For body products there are **The Body Shop** or **Escents Aromatherapy of Whistler**. Victoria's famous (and decadent) **Rogers' Chocolates** is in Village North. To take home a photographic work of art, visit **Mountain Moments Photography** in Whistler Village. There are more than half a dozen galleries; **The Northwest Connection Art Gallery** (938-4646) and **Whistler Inuit Gallery** in the Whistler Chateau (938-3366) specialize in Native and Inuit art.

Sports and Recreation

For specific information, call the **Whistler Resort Association** activity line at 932-2394 or go to the **Whistler Activity and Information Centre** in the Conference Centre. If you want more detailed information about summer activities like hiking, mountain biking or canoe routes, you may want to purchase a copy of *The Whistler Outdoors Guide*, which is available from bookstores in Vancouver and Whistler.

For skiing in winter, see Sports/

Recreation (Skiing and Snow-boarding). There are many other winter activities. You can try snow-mobiling, which gets you into the back country; call **Blackcomb Snowmobile** (932-8484), **Whistler Snowmobile Guided Tours** (932-4086) or **Canadian Snowmobile Adventures** (938-1616). The latter has an evening trip up the mountain to a log cabin for a candlelit fondue dinner. There's ice skating at **Meadow Park Sports Centre** (938-3133) and snowshoeing with **Outdoor Adventure at Whistler** (932-0647). Backcountry ski touring and ice climbing is available with **Whistler Alpine Guides** (932-4040). For sleigh rides, contact **Blackcomb Sleigh Rides** (932-7631).

Winter or summer, visit the **Whistler Museum & Archives** (932-2019) in Village North. Next door is the **Whistler Library** (932-5564); visitors can pay $5 to take out three books. You can tour **Whistler Brewery** (932-6185). In both sea-sons, the very adventuresome can experience paragliding; call **Parawest Paragliding** (932-7052).

Summertime can be action-packed. **Whistler Summer Adventures** (932-8484) is located on the lower level of Chateau Whistler and can book a va-riety of activities.

You can rent mountain bikes and either set off on your own or join a group. Novices can enjoy the paved Valley Trail network, a 42 km (26-mile) route that winds past golf courses, lakes and gives spectacular views. Intermediates and experts will be challenged by the variety of sin-gle-track trails such as A River Runs Through It and Bart's Dark Trail.

Bike-rental companies include **Mountain Riders** (932-3659), **Whistler Backroads** (932-3111), **Evolution** (932-2967) and **Trax & Trails** (938-2017).

Whistler's wooded paths and mountain trails make it ideal for mountain biking. (Leanna Rathkelly)

Another option is to join a bike tour. Itineraries are geared to dif-ferent levels of ability. A popular guided ride is the Descent; you take your bike up Blackcomb or Whistler Mountain on the gondola or chair and ride back down. Call **Whistler Backroads** (932-3111). This com-pany also has a heli-biking trip, in which you are transported to some remote destination with mountain bikes and a guide.

In-line skating rentals are available from **Whistler Blades** (932-9669) and **Wild Willies** (938-8036) among oth-ers. There is a freestyle skate park at the base of Blackcomb (lots of room to

Snowmobiling offers quick access to backcountry in the Whistler area. (Eric Sinclair)

practice for beginners) and the Valley Trail, also used by cyclists and walkers, is excellent for in-line skating.

Five lakes are within 5 km (3 miles) of the village. **Whistler Sailing & Water Sports** (932-7245) can equip you to sail, windsurf, canoe or kayak; **Whistler Windsurfing** (932-3589) or **Whistler Kids Windsurfing** (932-3898) has boards and lessons; **Wild Willies** (938-8036) rents kayaks and **Canadian Voyageur Canoe** (932-2070) looks after canoeists. **Whistler Outdoor Experience** (932-3389) rents canoes, windsurfing boards and Laser sailboats at Edgewater Outdoor Centre on Green Lake. The company also offers windsurfing lessons and short canoe trips. For a four-hour pedal-paddle trip, you are provided with a bicycle to pedal to Green Lake. There you can paddle the canoe that's waiting for you and then cycle back.

Whistler is near the edge of **Garibaldi Provincial Park** (898-3678) and a few kilometres north of **Brandywine Falls Provincial Park**; both have campgrounds.

Fishing attracted people here for decades before anyone thought of skiing. The five lakes and many rivers and streams surrounding Whistler still provide great trout fishing. Go to **Whistler Fishing Guides** (932-4267) for tackle, licences and guided trips. There is catch and release fly-fishing available.

Golf is available May to Oct. The area boasts four courses. Arnold Palmer designed the **Whistler Golf Course** (932-4544 or 1-800-376-1777), an 18-hole championship course (6100 yards, par 72) adjacent to the village. The **Chateau Whistler Golf Course** (6635 yards, par 72; 938-2092) was designed by Robert Trent Jones. There is also the **Nicklaus North Course** (938-9898) with 6925 yards (par 71) and, in Pemberton, 35 km (22 miles) north, there is **Big Sky Golf & Country**

Club (894-6106 or 1-800-668-7900). Between Whistler and Vancouver, just south of Squamish is **Furry Creek Golf Club** (896-2224).

You can take a lift up Blackcomb or Whistler, where there are many trails for hiking on your own. Or join a group for a free guided mountain-top hike. Call **Whistler Mountain** or **Blackcomb Mountain** (932-3434). The Valley Trail, which leads in several directions from the village out to the five lakes, is good for a family stroll.

Don't miss the challenging trek to Singing Pass and Russett Lake (about eight hours return trip); it's hard work, but the reward is lovely alpine meadows. Try to get a ride to the trail head. Trail maps and other information are available at the Whistler Activity & Information Centre. For organized group trips, call **Whistler Nature Guides** (932-4595) or **Outdoor Adventure at Whistler** (932-0647).

For the extraordinary experience of heli-hiking call **Tyax Heli-Skiing** (932-2070) or **Whistler Heli-Skiing** (932-4105); they will organize heli-hiking upon request.

Flightseeing trips take in the area's phenomenal glaciers. Call **Alpine Adventure Tours** (932-2705), **Blackcomb Helicopters** (938-1700) or **Whistler Air** (932-6615).

Horseback riding is available (also in winter); call **Pemberton Stables** (894-6615).

Climbing specialists at **Whistler Alpine Guides** (932-4040) or **The Escape Route** (938-3338) will arrange equipment rental, instruction or guided trips if you wish to learn about rock climbing and mountaineering techniques.

The area offers both scenic rafting and whitewater trips, which vary from two hours to full days. Wet suits are included in the whitewater excursions—a perfect thing to do if it's raining. Call **Whistler River Adventures** (932-3532) or **Wedge Rafting** (932-7171).

Summer glacier skiing on Blackcomb (932-3141) usually lasts until mid-Aug. There is also a selection of ski clinics and camps. If you are an experienced skier, you could try a day of heli-skiing: four glacier runs on fresh powder—3660 vertical meters (12,000 feet). Call **Tyax Heli-Skiing** (932-2070) or **Whistler Heli-Skiing** (932-4105).

Four outdoor tennis courts are available at **Myrtle Philip Elementary School** at the village. Courts are also located at **Alpha Lake Park**, **Meadow Lake Park** and **Emerald Park**. If you're serious about the game, **Chateau Whistler** has excellent tennis clinics. The Chateau, as well as the **Delta Whistler Resort** and **Tantalus Lodge**, have pay-as-you-play courts. The **Whistler Racquet and Golf Resort** (932-1991) has 10 courts; 3 are covered for year-round use. The new **Hyatt Regency Whistler** will have both indoor and outdoor courts.

For some unusual and exciting entertainment year-round, visit **Mountain World Whistler** (932-5000), where virtual reality will have you racing down a ski hill, fighting aliens or racing cars. Kids and adults love this huge entertainment mecca on the lower level of the Conference Centre. Not all the adventures are wild; for example, you can take a peaceful soar on a hang glider. There are also pool tables, a climbing wall where attention is paid to children, and a restaurant. The young, friendly staff are helpful; perfect when the weather plays havoc with other activities.

Index